MRS. KENNEDY AND ME

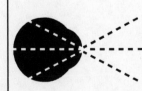

This Large Print Book carries the
Seal of Approval of N.A.V.H.

Mrs. Kennedy and Me

Clint Hill
with Lisa McCubbin

THORNDIKE PRESS
A part of Gale, Cengage Learning

GALE
CENGAGE Learning·

Detroit • New York • San Francisco • New Haven, Conn • Waterville, Maine • London

GALE
CENGAGE Learning®

LIBRARY OF CONGRESS CATALOGING-IN-PUBLICATION DATA

Hill, Clint.
   Mrs. Kennedy and me / by Clint Hill and Lisa McCubbin.
     p. cm. — (Thorndike Press large print biography)
   Originally published: New York : Gallery Books, 2012.
   ISBN 978-1-4104-5139-2 (hardcover) — ISBN 1-4104-5139-9 (hardcover)
   1. Hill, Clint. 2. Onassis, Jacqueline Kennedy, 1929–1994—Friends and
associates. 3. Presidents' spouses—Protection—United States. 4. United
States. Secret Service—Officials and employees—Biography. I. McCubbin,
Lisa. II. Title.
   E843.K4H47 2012b
   973.922092—dc23
   [B]   2012019206

Published in 2012 by arrangement with Gallery Books, a division of
Simon & Schuster, Inc.

This book is dedicated to the men and women of the U.S. Secret Service, both past and present, who have continued to steadfastly provide protection for the leadership of this great country as well as its financial interests. Your unwavering and selfless dedication to duty set an example for all to follow. I am proud but humble to have served among your ranks.

And to Caroline Kennedy, known as "Lyric" to the agents and "Buttons" to your father. I sincerely hope that many of the stories in this book bring back fond memories of your years in the White House. Your father adored you and John, and as you well know, your mother was extraordinary — a lady in every sense of the word.

CONTENTS

7

PART ONE:
1960

1
MEETING MRS. KENNEDY

It was with great trepidation that I approached 3307 N Street in Georgetown on November 11, 1960. I was about to meet the wife of the newly elected president of the United States, who I had just been assigned to protect, and I wasn't looking forward to it at all. Being on the First Lady's Secret Service detail was the last place I wanted to be. Looking back, I'm quite sure that Jacqueline Bouvier Kennedy was filled with even more anxiety about our meeting than I was. Neither of us had much choice in the matter. She could refuse to accept me — as she had done with the first agent assigned to her — but if I rejected the assignment, it would be the end of my career.

Just twenty-four hours earlier, I had been with outgoing President Dwight D. Eisenhower, as he played a post-election round of golf at Augusta National Golf Course. The fact that the Republicans had lost the election was still sinking in, and while the entire administration was about to change, one of the few things that would remain the same was the Secret Service. It had been a great honor for me to be on President Eisenhower's Secret Service detail, and, while it would be bittersweet to see him leave office, I was excited for the challenge and experience of protecting the new president. It never entered my mind that my job might not be as secure as I thought it was.

There were just forty of us on the White House Secret Service detail — the elite team whose sole mission was to protect the president around the clock. We were not affiliated with any party or political group, and we were a tight group of men. The transition would require the Secret Service to adapt to the new president's style, and even though I hadn't yet met President-elect John F. Kennedy, it was obvious that protecting him was going to be a whole different ball game than it had been with Ike. We were going from a seventy-year-old former general who ran the White House with military precision, to an energetic forty-three-year-old Irish Catholic Democrat from Massachusetts with a lot of new ideas to take America into the 1960s.

I had been working the golf course with two other agents, and as soon as the president's foursome finished the round, Jim Rowley, the Special Agent in Charge (SAIC) of the White House Detail, sent word that he needed to speak to the three of us. I had a feeling that this was probably my last game of golf with President Eisenhower and fully expected that Rowley was about to reassign the three of us to President-elect Kennedy.

When we walked into the office, Rowley explained that he had to shuffle the personnel in order to cover President Eisenhower, along with President-elect Kennedy, until the Inauguration in January.

First he addressed the other two agents, Jerry Blaine and Bill Skiles.

"Jerry and Bill, you'll be on the president-elect detail. Mr. Kennedy is going to spend the next month and the holidays at his father's estate in Palm Beach, Florida, so you guys need to get on a flight down there this evening."

He warned that they would likely remain in Florida until the Inauguration, meaning they'd be away from their own families for Christmas and New Year's, and suggested they have their wives arrange to get some warm-weather clothing to them. As I was listening to Rowley give Blaine and Skiles their new assignment, an uneasy feeling started to come over me.

Finally, Rowley turned to me and said, "Clint, Defense Secretary Tom Gates is here briefing the president and is returning to Washington shortly. I want you to fly back with him, then go to Secret Service headquarters and talk to Chief Baughman. The chief is expecting you."

"Yes, sir," I said with a nod. *Why does Baughman want to speak with me? Why am I not going to Palm Beach with Skiles and Blaine?* I had a dozen questions, but I would

14

never question Rowley's authority or decision: he was our leader. Still, I had a foreboding feeling that whatever lay ahead for me could not be good.

Secret Service headquarters was located in the U.S. Treasury Building, right next to the White House on Pennsylvania Avenue. I had never been in the chief's office before, and in fact, had never personally met Chief U. E. Baughman, who had been head of the Secret Service since 1948. I was more than a little apprehensive when I checked in with his secretary, but I tried to sound as confident as possible.

"I'm Special Agent Clint Hill. Here to meet with Chief Baughman."

"Yes, Mr. Hill, the chief is expecting you," she said. "You may go on in."

As I walked through the doorway into the chief's spacious office, the first thing I saw was a plaque hanging on the wall that said: *You ain't learning nothing when you're talking.* Sound advice, I thought.

Then, as I looked around the room, and saw not just Chief Baughman but his deputy chief and an assistant chief as well as two inspectors, a feeling of dread suddenly came over me. The entire top echelon of the Secret Service was standing there, appar-

15

ently awaiting my arrival.

"Come on in, Clint," Baughman said as he moved toward me and shook my hand. "Have a seat and make yourself comfortable."

His cordial manner seemed to be an attempt to help me relax, but I still had an uneasy feeling about why I had been summoned. After introducing me to the other men in the room, Baughman asked casually, "Clint, how long have you been in the Secret Service?"

"I started in the Denver Field Office on September 22, 1958, sir."

"And when were you transferred to the White House Detail?" Baughman asked.

"Just over one year ago. On November 1, 1959."

This is strange, I thought. *Surely all of this information is in my file.*

Baughman asked a couple of more innocuous questions, and then each of the other men began asking me things, all sorts of things about my past, both personal and professional, as well as my attitude about protective activities.

What did you do prior to becoming an agent? Where did you grow up? Where did you go to college? Are you married or single? Do you have any children? Do you swim? Do

16

you know how to play tennis? Have you ever ridden horses? I answered the barrage of inquiries as honestly and candidly as possible, but each new question increased my anxiety, as I still had no idea what this was all about. My mind was spinning as I replayed the events of the last couple of weeks, trying to figure out what I could have done wrong, and though my stomach was in knots, I did my best to stay calm and composed.

At times, the men would go off into a corner of the room and confer, just out of earshot, so I couldn't hear what was being discussed. I was thoroughly convinced that I was about to be fired. Why else wouldn't I have been sent to Palm Beach?

The interrogation went on for nearly one and a half hours. One and a half hours in which I'd done all the talking, and just like it said on Baughman's plaque, I hadn't learned a damn thing.

Finally, Baughman said, "Clint, we have made a decision. You are being assigned to protect Mrs. John F. Kennedy. Jim Jeffries is the leader of the First Lady's Detail and you'll be his assistant."

I was too stunned to speak. *The First Lady's Detail? Me? But why?*

"Yes, sir," I said. There was nothing more

17

to say. I was relieved that I wasn't being fired, but I was deeply disappointed that I wasn't going to be with the new president.

Baughman told me to report to 3307 N Street Northwest, to the Kennedy home in Georgetown. Mrs. Kennedy would soon be arriving from Hyannis Port, Massachusetts.

My mind was spinning as I left the chief's office. Why was I selected for this assignment? What actions or experience in my background caused them to make this decision? It felt as though I had been demoted from the starting lineup to the bench. From grade school to college, in all my years playing football, basketball, and baseball, I'd always been a star player, and now, in the most important game of my life, I'd just been kicked off the first team. I was devastated.

The more I thought about it, the more upset I became. I had been on the White House Detail for just over a year and had traveled with President Eisenhower on several unprecedented trips that took us throughout Europe, Asia, and South America. At the time, I was twenty-seven years old and had never flown in a jet aircraft. Having grown up in the high plains of North Dakota, I could never have imagined I would accompany the President of the United States to ancient cities I'd only read about in history books: Rome, Ankara, Karachi, Kabul, New Delhi, Tehran, Athens, Tunis, Toulon, Paris, Lisbon, and Casablanca. To top things off, I was issued a diplomatic passport, which allowed for preferential treatment, as if I were a dignitary myself. I felt so privileged and I thrived on the constant activity.

One of the things I most enjoyed was the camaraderie among all the agents as we worked together as a team. Now all that excitement was over, and I could just envision what lay ahead. While my buddies on the President's Detail would be right in the middle of all the action, I knew where I was going to end up: fashion shows, afternoon tea parties, and the ballet. I felt as if my career had come to a screeching halt.

I pulled my Secret Service commission book out of my suit coat pocket and held it in my hands. The impressive midnight blue grosgrain leather case was engraved on the front cover with the gold five-point Secret Service star. Within the star it read: UNITED STATES SECRET SERVICE.

As I went over and over in my mind what had just transpired, the only conclusion I could come to as to why I'd been chosen for this assignment was that Mrs. Kennedy and I were fairly close in age — I was now twenty-eight and she was thirty-one — and that I had a child nearly the same age as her three-year-old daughter Caroline. I couldn't come up with any other reason.

I finally realized I had no recourse. I was a Secret Service agent on the White House Detail, and the first lady required protection. Somebody had to do it. So I pulled myself up, grabbed the keys to one of the Secret Service sedans, and headed to the historic streets of Georgetown.

The three-story redbrick townhouse at 3307 N Street stood so close to the street that the front door was just two steps up from the sidewalk. The house was not very big — just three windows across on the upper two floors and two windows next to the front door on the ground floor.

The Secret Service agent posted in front of the house had been alerted to my arrival and allowed me inside without difficulty. Agent Jim Jeffries was waiting inside and came to the door to greet me.

Agent Jeffries was about five foot ten, the same height as me, with a medium build, and was about thirty-two or thirty-three years old. He had light, reddish hair, and a ruddy complexion, which I imagined would burn to a crisp if he spent more than a few minutes in the sun. As he approached me, he had a serious, almost stern look on his face that didn't do much to calm the apprehension I was already feeling.

"Come on in, Clint," he said, in a clipped voice. "I'm Jim Jeffries. Glad to have you aboard. Let me go find Mrs. Kennedy and introduce you."

"Great. I'm looking forward to meeting her," I said, with as much sincerity as I could muster.

As Jeffries walked out, I looked around the living room to try to get a feel for Mrs. Kennedy's tastes and what kinds of things she liked. The room was elegantly decorated, but it had a feeling of warmth to it as well. Dark wood antiques were mixed with light-colored upholstered pieces and the furniture seemed as if it were arranged in such a way to invite guests to stay for long, lingering evenings by the fireplace. Built-in bookshelves were filled with a mixture of books and decorative ornaments that had a distinctly European feel. Everything seemed to be placed just so, and I got the feeling that should an object be moved ever so slightly, it would be noticed immediately. It was a home for tea parties and ladies' luncheons. Just thinking about it made the

21

feelings of disgust and disappointment wash over me again in a sudden wave.

After a few minutes, Jacqueline Bouvier Kennedy walked into the room, with Agent Jeffries a few steps behind.

I'd seen newspaper photographs of her, of course, but in person she was much more striking than I had imagined. She was tall — about five foot seven inches — but it was the way she carried herself, almost gliding into the room with a dancer's erect posture, that exuded an air of quiet confidence. Her chin-length, dark brown hair was perfectly coiffed, and she wore just a touch of makeup, enough to accentuate her dark brown eyes and full lips but still look natural. She was very attractive, very gracious, and very pregnant.

"Mrs. Kennedy," Jeffries said matter-of-factly, "this is Clint Hill. He will be the second agent for your personal protection."

Mrs. Kennedy approached me and smiled warmly as she offered her hand.

"It's a pleasure to meet you, Mr. Hill," she said in a soft, breathy voice.

"It's very nice to meet you, too, Mrs. Kennedy," I said with a smile, as I shook her hand and looked directly into her eyes. She returned my gaze for an instant, then blinked and looked away, giving me the impression that, while she wanted to appear confident, on the inside she was rather shy.

The three of us sat down in the living room, as Agent Jeffries took the lead in explaining our duties, and how we would need to work with Mrs. Kennedy and her staff.

"There will be various agents assigned to handle the perimeter security of your residence — whether that's here, the White House, Palm Beach, or Hyannis Port — at all times. Either Mr. Hill or I will be with you whenever you leave the residence, and if you travel outside of Washington, both of us will accompany you."

The smile had worn off Mrs. Kennedy's face as she resigned herself to the fact that, from now on, she would never be alone.

Calmly, in a measured tone, her voice almost whisper-like, she said, "Well, you don't have to worry about me traveling in the next few weeks. My baby is due in a month and I plan to stay here in Washington. My biggest concern, really, is maintaining as much privacy as possible — not only for me, but for Caroline and the new baby, as well. I don't want us to feel like animals in a zoo, and I certainly don't want someone following me around like a puppy dog."

Her gaze transferred between Jeffries and

me, making sure that both of us understood her wishes.

"I also know that as soon as the baby is born, the press will be overbearing. They can be so intrusive." She pressed her lips together, turning her mouth into a sly smile, and looking directly at me, she added, "I used to be one of them, you know, and I'm well aware of how they operate."

In that instant, I realized that Mrs. Kennedy was a lot more intuitive and in control than her public image at the time suggested.

"Yes, Mrs. Kennedy," I replied. "Part of our job will be to protect you from the press, and to make sure that you and your children can live as normal a life as possible. Believe me, we don't like the press any more than you do."

Her smile widened for an instant, and then she stood up and said, "It's been lovely meeting you, gentlemen. Now I have some things to attend to."

Jeffries and I stood up as Mrs. Kennedy walked out of the room. She had decided the meeting was over.

It was clear that she wasn't excited about having two Secret Service agents around, and I realized that, if I was going to be able to do my job effectively, I would have to earn her trust.

"Let's go outside and discuss how we'll handle the schedule," Jeffries said. "With just two of us on her protection, we're going to be working a lot of overtime."

Agents temporarily assigned from field offices would handle the perimeter security of her residence, no matter her location. One of us had to be available whenever Mrs. Kennedy was awake, and be prepared to perform whatever task was required to provide a secure environment in which Mrs. Kennedy could function in her capacity as wife of the President of the United States. Whether it was work or play, it was our job to make sure she could do the things she wanted or needed to do, safely. That included each and every location she visited. In order for either of us to have a day off, it required the other agent to work a full day, with no relief. When Mrs. Kennedy traveled outside the Washington, D.C., area, we both would have to work a full day in order to provide adequate coverage. A full day meant we worked during the periods Mrs. Kennedy was up, awake, and active. When she slept, we slept.

Thus began my new assignment.

I hadn't been briefed on Mrs. Kennedy at all, so I had very limited knowledge of her background, her likes and dislikes, or what activities were of interest to her. I didn't like this feeling of being unprepared and I knew it was going to require a great deal of research to become knowledgeable about my new protectee. In those first few days, I collected newspaper and magazine articles to find out as much about Mrs. Kennedy as I possibly could. The more I read, the more I realized that her background and mine were about as different as they could possibly be.

Jacqueline Lee Bouvier had grown up on the East Coast in a sophisticated environment, learning social graces and developing an appreciation for art and literature from a young age. She was born on July 28, 1929, in Southampton, Long Island, to Jack and Janet Bouvier, and while her father instilled in her a love of horses and horseback riding, her mother developed her interest in painting, reading, and foreign languages. She had a sister named Lee, who was four years younger, and when the two were around eleven and seven years old, their parents divorced. Two years later, Janet Bouvier remarried a very wealthy man named Hugh Auchincloss.

The young Jacqueline Bouvier attended Miss Porter's School, an exclusive boarding school in Farmington, Connecticut, where she was a straight-A student. Upon graduation from Miss Porter's, she enrolled in Vassar College, in Poughkeepsie, New York, and in 1948 she was named "Debutante of the Year." Summers were spent at her stepfather's estate — a twenty-eight-room oceanfront "cottage" in Newport, Rhode Island, called Hammersmith Farm.

She became fluent in French when she spent her junior year of college in France, studying at the Sorbonne in Paris and the University of Grenoble. Upon her return from Europe, Jackie enrolled for her senior year at George Washington University in Washington, D.C., where she graduated, in 1951, with a bachelor of arts degree in French literature.

Two years later she married John Fitzgerald Kennedy, a junior senator from Massachusetts, in a highly publicized wedding in Newport that was deemed the "social event of the year." Twelve hundred guests attended the lavish reception, which was held at Hammersmith Farm.

I, on the other hand, grew up in North Dakota in a very small town called Washburn. It was a farming community, with a large Norwegian population, and my father, Chris Hill, was the county auditor. My mother, Jennie, was a homemaker, and was devoted to my older sister, Janice, and me. My mother was hearing impaired and we, as family, made adjustments to cope with that situation. We spoke louder and always spoke in front of her so she could see that we were talking to her. She handled this difficult problem very well, but from a young age, I learned to anticipate her needs and was always protective of her.

My mother had long, dark brown hair that hung straight down her back — so different from my jet-black hair that grew in tight curls — but I never thought anything about it, until, when I was about six years old, the girl who lived across the street told me I was adopted.

I didn't know what "adopted" meant, so I ran inside the house to ask my mother. She tried to explain it in six-year-old terms — how she and my father had driven 240 miles to Fargo in our 1929 DeSoto to the North Dakota Children's Home for Adoption to choose me from all the other babies, how my aqua blue eyes beckoned to them — but it certainly wasn't the way she had planned on me finding out. It turned out my sister was also adopted, and my mother was fearful that we wouldn't feel as loved as if we had been her natural children. The truth

Clint, Jennie, Janice, and Chris Hill, circa 1943

was, I was lucky to have been raised in such a loving, stable home.

It wasn't until many years later — after the world crashed in around me and I was searching for something to cling to — that I returned to North Dakota to meet my birth mother, and learned, as she lay on her deathbed, how I happened to become available for adoption.

I was the sixth child of Alma Peterson, born January 4, 1932, in Larimore, North Dakota. Seventeen days after my birth, on a cold, snowy day, which happened to also be Alma's thirty-ninth birthday, she had me baptized in a Lutheran church in Fargo, and then turned me over to the Children's Home.

By the time I met her, she had suffered a stroke, and the details of the story were told to me by one of my half sisters. It wasn't clear who my father was, she said, but she remembered Alma sending her to a French Canadian man named Vassau, who was the proprietor of the hotel where Alma was a maid, to collect some money for my birth.

Growing up in Washburn, though, I didn't know any of this, and it didn't really matter. I had a great childhood. Even though I never had my own room — I shared the porch with my grandfather and kept my belongings in one drawer of a dresser that was jammed next to the piano — I never went hungry, and was always supported by my family. My adoptive parents were very conservative — they didn't smoke or drink alcohol — and were quite religious. Our whole family was active in the Evangelical Lutheran Church, where my sister played piano and I was an altar boy.

I attended the public schools in Washburn and was involved in many school activities: I played trumpet in the high school band, sang in the glee club, acted in plays, and played football and basketball and ran on the high school track team. I also played

30

Clint Hill family home, Washburn, North Dakota

baseball for the Washburn American Legion team and, in my junior year of high school, had the great honor of being selected to attend the Boys State leadership program as the representative from Washburn. In 1950, I graduated from high school and when I left Washburn that fall to attend Concordia College, in Moorhead, Minnesota, the sign at the edge of the city read: WASHBURN POP. 912.

Now, ten years later, I was responsible for protecting the wife of the president-elect of the United States. I realized I had nothing to complain about, and I might just as well get used to it. Little did I know that life with Mrs. Kennedy was going to be anything but dull.

2
THE FAMILY

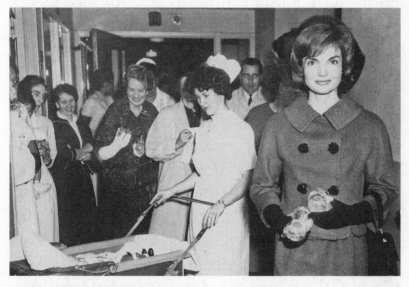

Clint Hill with Mrs. Kennedy and John, Jr. leaving Georgetown Hospital

With every presidential transition, it is not only the first family that changes, but the entire political and personal staff as well. There is a period of adjustment between the Secret Service agents and the incoming administration, which sets the tone for the next four years. It was evident from the beginning that the Kennedy administration would be much less rigid and far more unpredictable than the Eisenhower administration, and even though this was my first experience with a changeover in power, I quickly realized that there were certain people in the Kennedys' inner circle who could either make my job a whole lot easier or be a constant headache. It was important to get these relationships started on the right foot.

The first staff member I met was Providencia Paredes, whom Mrs. Kennedy introduced as her "personal assistant." Everybody called her "Provi," and her duties included doing Mrs. Kennedy's personal laundry, ironing, packing and unpacking for trips, and everyday errands. Whatever Mrs. Kennedy needed, Provi was there to assist. Originally from the Dominican Republic, Provi appeared to be about my age, and spoke broken English with a heavy Spanish accent. She had a delightful, cheery disposition and we quickly became friends.

One big adjustment for the Secret Service was that there were going to be young children in the White House. Caroline was not quite three years old, yet she too would have her own Secret Service agents. Initially two agents were assigned to the "Kiddie Detail" to protect Caroline, and since she was frequently with her mother, Agent Jeffries and I worked closely with them.

Like her mother, Caroline had been a tremendous asset to Jack Kennedy in his campaign for president, but she was oblivious to the fact that she was now world famous. My son, Chris, was just sixteen months older than the president-elect's daughter, and even though I was not technically on Caroline's detail, I was instinctively protective of her. She was a beautiful little girl with sandy brown hair that curled naturally just below her ears, and big, blue eyes that matched her father's. She was very active and very inquisitive, but perhaps the thing that impressed me most was that even at this young age, she had wonderful manners. This was something that was critically important to her mother.

"Caroline will address you as Mr. Hill," Mrs. Kennedy told me from the outset. "And she is to be respectful at all times. If there are any issues, I want to know about them immediately."

Despite her public role and growing responsibilities, Mrs. Kennedy was adamant that there would always be time each day with her daughter. She was a very attentive mother, and her eyes had a special sparkle when she was with Caroline — almost as if she were constantly in awe of her child's view of the world. Watching the two of them interact, I saw a playful and spontaneous side of Jacqueline Kennedy that, thus far, only came out when she was with her daughter. But most of the time Mrs. Kennedy spent with Caroline was activity-related. When it came to the day-to-day caring for her child — the dressing, bathing, feeding, and playground dates — she relied heavily on the family's nanny, Maud Shaw.

Originally from Great Britain, Miss Shaw was quite the contrast to Provi, but yet another wonderful ally for me. She was in her mid-fifties and spoke with a proper British accent, in a sort of singsong voice. Her hair was a light reddish color, streaked with tinges of gray, and it always seemed to be just a bit mussed, as if she had begun to brush it, then got interrupted, and never could be bothered to have another look in the mirror.

Standing about five foot two with her shoes on, Miss Shaw wasn't a big person by any means, but with her matronly, methodical manner, she exuded an air of gentle authority, and in many ways seemed more like a grandmother than a nanny. Her standard uniform was a crisply ironed dress that hung just below her knees, paired with sensible shoes that allowed her to romp with Caroline. She had been in the employ of the Kennedy family since Caroline was a newborn, but it was clear to me that Miss Shaw understood her position as an employee and not a substitute mother. She and Mrs. Kennedy were cordial, but there was no question that Mrs. Kennedy was in charge.

As the wife of the president-elect, Mrs. Kennedy had a sudden onslaught of responsibilities, the first and most important of which was preparing for the Inauguration. Even though, at eight months pregnant, she would often become physically tired, she seemed to have an endless amount of mental energy. From the planning of the pre-inaugural gala to the formal balls and the finalization of the guest lists and the invitations, she was intent on putting her touch on everything, and she was well aware that the eyes of the world would be on her.

I was somewhat surprised by the level of attention the media was already paying to the new first family — especially to Mrs. Kennedy. The press had rarely covered anything President Eisenhower's wife,

Mamie, did, but suddenly the American public seemed to have an insatiable appetite for any news at all about Jacqueline Kennedy. At thirty-one years old, she was the youngest first lady in seventy-five years to occupy the White House, and American women, in particular, were fascinated by what she wore, where she shopped, and what her interests were.

This intense interest by the public was also one of the biggest problems Agent Jeffries and I had to contend with in terms of protection. Whenever we took her anywhere, she'd immediately be recognized, and before we knew it there would be a swarm of people gawking, and often approaching her to shake her hand. She would smile graciously and offer a polite greeting, but as soon as we were alone, she'd quip, "You'd think I was somebody important, for heaven's sake."

She didn't enjoy being the center of attention in these situations, and I quickly realized that one of the best ways for me to protect her, and to gain her confidence in me, was to come up with creative ways for her to do the things she wanted, with as much privacy as possible.

Getting exercise in some form — preferably outdoors — was something that was important to Mrs. Kennedy. She really enjoyed, and seemed to need, a certain amount of physical activity each day. She didn't have a set schedule, but she would take walks in the various parks, and through the streets of Georgetown. I knew she had previously had one miscarriage and had also delivered a stillborn child, and it was obvious that she was cautious to not overexert herself. In those first days I tried to remain close, but unobtrusive, rarely initiating conversation, but allowing her to take the lead. I wasn't there to be a friend — my job was to protect her.

One day we walked down Thirty-fourth Street toward the Potomac River, just a couple of blocks from the Kennedys' home, to the Chesapeake & Ohio Canal towpath. This gravel trail was situated down a steep set of stairs built into the bank alongside the canal, which parallels the Potomac. Heavily wooded and very secluded, the path was quiet and peaceful — a slice of nature hidden from the noise and bustle of the city — and it soon became our route of choice. Usually it would be just the two of us, unless Caroline and Maud Shaw came along, and it was on these walks that both of us began to let our guards down with each other.

She set the pace and, although she was pregnant, she had excellent posture. She walked very erect, with a brisk yet cautious stride.

"Mr. Hill," she explained, "I have to take it somewhat easy because of my pregnancy, as my doctor has advised me. But I need to get as much exercise as possible to maintain my strength, and I do think that being in the fresh air is so good for one's well-being."

Most of the time the path was wide enough for us to walk side by side, but at times it would narrow and I would allow her to walk ahead, while I walked behind, constantly scanning our surroundings. This allowed me to see what was happening in front of us yet also be in a position to protect her from behind.

I never initiated conversation, but waited for her to take the lead. Sometimes we would walk for a while in silence and then she'd suddenly say something like, "My, the river is really flowing today. Isn't that a lovely sound?"

She was very aware of her surroundings and appreciative of nature — the sound of the birds, the changing colors of the leaves, the rush of the river. I, too, enjoyed being outdoors, but she made me more aware of the aesthetics of our surroundings. It was as if she were walking in a living painting, conscious of how the colors and textures worked together.

She was also very curious as to how the Secret Service operated and how it would impact her life. She had endless questions about protocol and what kinds of things needed to be cleared by the Secret Service. This was all new to her and I got the feeling that, while she didn't like the fact that she could no longer go anywhere alone, if she had to be with someone, I was acceptable company.

There was a continuous flow of people in and out of the residence as decisions were made regarding the selection of the new White House staff. We as agents had to learn who these people were and for what position they were being considered. This was the first change of administration I had witnessed, and I found it very interesting to watch how various people jockeyed for the prime positions.

The first two weeks went by quite rapidly as I settled into somewhat of a routine with my new assignment. The more time Mrs. Kennedy and I spent together, the more comfortable our relationship became. I sensed that she was slowly beginning to trust me and I was beginning to realize that she was not going to be a first lady who was going to merely stand in the shadows of her husband.

The day after the election, President-elect Kennedy had flown directly to Palm Beach, Florida, where his father had an oceanfront estate, to focus on the transition and selection of his cabinet and staff. Meanwhile, Mrs. Kennedy, despite being eight months pregnant, was handling a myriad of decisions and new responsibilities, with the world watching, and she appeared to be fearless. I was impressed not only with her capabilities, but also the fact that she was dealing with all of this completely on her own.

On Wednesday, November 23, the president-elect returned to Washington to spend Thanksgiving with his wife and daughter, and I met John F. Kennedy for the first time.

"Jack," Mrs. Kennedy said to her husband, "this is Mr. Hill."

He was slightly taller than me, but had a thin, somewhat lanky frame. He had clearly spent time in the sun, as his face was tanned. But the thing you noticed most were his eyes and his smile. He had captivating blue eyes, blue as the ocean, and when he looked at you, it was like he scooped you into his universe, paying attention to you and you alone in that moment. He immediately reached out his hand and gave me a firm, vigorous handshake.

"I've heard a lot about you, Clint," he said as an infectious grin spread across his cheeks. "Jackie tells me you are a devoted walker and that she has been well taken care of these past couple of weeks. I do appreciate it."

He spoke with enthusiasm and sincerity, his words rolling out in that unmistakable Boston accent so quickly that you really had to pay attention.

"It's a pleasure to meet you, Mr. President-elect," I said.

Caroline would turn three years old on November 27 and he had brought some wrapped gifts, along with a rather unique present for his daughter, for an early birthday celebration. The nine-year-old daughter of a West Palm Beach city councilman had given him a cage containing two live white ducks to present to Caroline for her birthday, and he had brought them back to Washington, eager as could be to see his daughter's reaction. Those ducks were just the beginning of what would be a never-ending flow of animals into the Kennedy household.

Even in that brief meeting, I got a sense of John F. Kennedy, and it was easy to see how he had been able to connect with the voters. He was energetic, friendly, a people person. And charming as hell. But I also saw a man who really cared about his family as well as the people around them. I liked him, and I knew from that first meeting that this was going to be a very interesting administration to work with and observe.

The next day, the family had their Thanksgiving dinner early in the afternoon. In addition to a traditional Thanksgiving menu of turkey, bread stuffing, creamed onions, string beans, and both apple and pumpkin pies for dessert, Pearl Nelson, the Kennedys' cook, made homemade clam chowder, a family favorite. The smells coming from the kitchen made my stomach growl, but as an agent, that is something you get used to. You might dress up in a tuxedo to attend a black-tie dinner with the president, but you are there to do a job, not partake in the wining, dining, and socializing.

I remained on the residence perimeter, along with the agents on the president-elect detail, guaranteeing a safe environment in which the Kennedy family could enjoy the Thanksgiving holiday in peace.

I had thought the president-elect would

stay in Washington to meet with various people about the transition, as well as be there for Mrs. Kennedy in her last few weeks before the birth of their child, so I was surprised to learn that he was actually returning to Palm Beach for another week or so. The plan was that he would come back in mid-December prior to Mrs. Kennedy's due date, for which there was a planned Caesarean section. It seemed an odd arrangement, since most of the people he was interviewing for cabinet and staff positions were based in Washington. It wasn't my business, but I felt empathy for Mrs. Kennedy.

At 8:25 P.M. Thanksgiving evening, the president left to return to Florida on the Kennedys' family plane, the *Caroline*. The *Caroline* was a twin-engine Convair 240 that had originally been used as a commercial plane with seating for about forty-four passengers. Bought by Ambassador Joseph Kennedy in 1959, it had been customized so that it had living-room style seating, along with an actual bed, and could still accommodate fifteen to twenty passengers. The *Caroline* was the first private plane to ever be used by a candidate in a presidential election, and it had allowed Jack Kennedy great freedom to effectively campaign all around the country. It wasn't nearly as fast as a jet aircraft, but the plane was a comfortable and convenient way for Kennedy to commute between Washington and Palm Beach.

Once the president-elect had departed, Mrs. Kennedy advised me she was not planning to leave the house. With the field agents posted outside the residence, I went home to my two-bedroom apartment in Arlington, hoping my wife might have left me some turkey, stuffing, and gravy in the refrigerator.

A couple of hours later, I had just got into bed when the phone rang.

It was Jeffries. "Clint, Mrs. Kennedy was having labor pains and has been rushed to Georgetown Hospital in an ambulance. Get over there as fast as you can."

Oh God.

The baby wasn't due until December 15. The president was en route to Florida. Mrs. Kennedy had already lost two babies. I jumped in my car and raced to the hospital.

When I arrived, Jeffries informed me that Mrs. Kennedy had been taken to a fourth-floor surgical room, where her personal obstetrician, Dr. John Walsh, was performing the Caesarean section — nearly three weeks early.

"The president-elect is on his way back," Jeffries said. "We got the word to him just as he landed in Palm Beach and it was decided he should come back on the press plane to get here faster."

The press had chartered a four-engine DC-6 to follow Kennedy to Palm Beach, and it could make the return trip at least thirty minutes quicker than the *Caroline.*

While Jeffries made phone calls and helped coordinate the logistics for the president-elect's arrival, I waited outside the door of the operating room as the procedure went on, pacing as if I were the father to be, anxious for the outcome.

I had missed the birth of my firstborn son, Chris, because when I took my wife, Gwen, to the hospital when she went into labor, I was told it would be a number of hours yet before the baby would arrive. As it turned out, I got a call in the middle of the night that my wife had delivered a baby boy, and there were complications, requiring him to have a blood transfusion. I knew the anxiety President-elect Kennedy must have been feeling on that long flight back to Washington. Knowing the difficulty Mrs. Kennedy had had with her earlier pregnancies, I was concerned, and hoped to God that both she and the baby would be all right.

I hadn't been there too long when the door opened, and a nurse walked out.

"Sir, I'm supervisory nurse Mrs. Robinson. I'm pleased to tell you that the delivery was successful. At 12:22 A.M., Mrs. Kennedy delivered a six-pound three-ounce baby boy and both mother and child are doing fine. Since he is premature, however, the baby is being placed in an incubator as a precautionary measure."

I breathed a sigh of relief, just as Agent Jeffries walked toward us.

"It's a boy," I said with a smile. "Nurse Robinson says that Mrs. Kennedy and the baby are both doing fine."

Just then another nurse came out of the operating room holding the baby, swaddled in a blanket.

The nurse said, "I'm taking him to the incubator now."

As Agent Jeffries went with the nurse and the baby, I caught a glimpse of the new member of the Kennedy family, his perfectly shaped face, his eyes closed, completely oblivious that he was the son of the future president of the United States.

Then the realization hit me: we had a new person to protect and to worry about. More responsibility, the need for more people. The baby was the first child to ever be born to a president-elect. Another new challenge for the Secret Service and me — an infant in the White House.

President-elect Kennedy arrived about 4:30 in the morning. He first went in to see his wife, who was sleeping and still under sedation, and then to see his son for the first time. He was ecstatic — a father again, but this time of a son, born just two days before Caroline's third birthday.

The early birth announcement spread like wildfire as newspapers across the country rushed to post the news in the morning editions.

IT'S A BABY BOY FOR THE JOHN
KENNEDYS!
STORK BEATS KENNEDY'S
PLANE;
NEW SON ARRIVES

Over the next few days, Agent Jeffries and I rotated shifts outside Mrs. Kennedy's room, carefully screening guests and inspecting the countless bouquets of flowers that arrived for Mrs. Kennedy. Most of the flowers were fairly modest and equal in size so when a particularly large one arrived, I was especially curious. Not only was the arrangement larger and more elaborate than the others, but the container was unique as well. The flowers sprung out of two receptacles on either side of the back of a ceramic donkey, being carried like cargo in baskets. The donkey itself was about the size of a full-grown cocker spaniel and was very authentic looking. The significance, of course, was that the donkey was the symbol of the Democratic Party. A card was attached and when I read whom it was from, I couldn't have been more surprised. The arrangement had been sent by Frank Sinatra.

The baby boy was named John Fitzgerald Kennedy Jr. and despite being premature, he was thriving. The president-elect would visit Mrs. Kennedy and their newborn son each day, in between the never-ending meetings with staff and advisors in preparation for the start of his administration. Each time he came to the hospital, he was extremely cordial and always called me by name.

"How are you doing today, Clint?" he'd ask.

"I'm fine, Mr. President-elect. Thank you."

"And how did Mrs. Kennedy fare through the night?"

I'd tell him whether she had slept well or

had called for the nurses on occasion. He wanted to have as much information as possible before striding into her room. It was obvious he was sincerely concerned, and despite the endless decisions that needed to be made as he prepared for the presidency, the well-being of his wife and son was uppermost in his mind. The more I got to know him, the more I liked him, which made the fact that I was not on his protective detail all the more disappointing.

A week after his son's birth, on December 2, the president-elect flew back to Palm Beach, taking young Caroline and the nanny, Maud Shaw, with him, while Mrs. Kennedy and young John remained as patients in the hospital. Both Mrs. Kennedy and the baby were recovering well, but there wasn't much activity other than the comings and goings of visitors. Mrs. Kennedy was largely confined to the bed in her room, and spent most of her time poring over reference materials about the White House. Frequently she would ask for me to come in to the room because she had some questions. Since Agent Jeffries had not worked on the White House Detail prior to this assignment, he had little knowledge of the type of information she wanted. So, she asked for me.

I'd go into her room and she'd be sitting in bed, propped up with pillows. Dressed in her bedclothes, with no makeup on, she looked younger and more fragile than she had prior to John's birth, and I could tell she was physically drained. Still, her thick eyebrows and eyelashes framed her big brown eyes against the pallor of her skin, and even in the drab hospital room, she exuded a natural, timeless beauty. With me, she had no need to impress. She had already become accustomed to my constant presence and realized I would see her at her best and her worst.

She was focused on learning as much as possible about the White House — its history, its décor, and how everything worked on a daily basis. Who did the grocery shopping? Who handled the housekeeping? Where would the family eat their private meals? Was there any privacy? What about functions and dinner parties? What were the various rooms — the Red Room, the Green Room, the Blue Room — used for?

She would have a list of questions written out on a lined, yellow legal pad, and as I answered her, she would listen intently, taking voracious notes and interposing questions as they occurred to her. She was savvy and smart, and it was clear that she was eager to make a good impression and wanted to have as much information going into her new role as possible, to avoid making any blunders. I sensed her vulnerability and tried to be as detailed and informative as possible. Our conversations were relaxed and comfortable, and while I enjoyed spending time with Mrs. Kennedy, I missed the camaraderie with the other agents. During those long days at the hospital, I really envied my colleagues who were constantly on the go with the president-elect.

One afternoon she called me in and asked, "Mr. Hill, do you ride horses?"

"I have in the past, as a youngster," I replied. "One of our neighbors in Washburn, North Dakota, had a Shetland pony."

She smiled slightly, as if trying to determine whether I was kidding or being serious.

Quickly I added, "Some of my friends had horses on a ranch near my home and I was allowed to ride every so often. A local rodeo cowboy used to give me lessons."

There was a pause, and then she said, "The reason I ask is that we have arranged to have a place in Middleburg to spend weekends away from Washington, and I'll have horses there. I love to ride."

I wondered why they would need a place

53

in Middleburg, Virginia, when the Kennedys would have the use of Camp David — a magnificent property specifically retained as a weekend retreat for the sitting president and his family. I had been there many times with President Eisenhower.

It certainly wasn't my place to advise the future first lady, but the knowledge that the Kennedys had obtained their own weekend retreat was a surprise to me, and I was quite certain that no one else in the Secret Service knew about it, either. I thought I had better try to get as much information as possible so I could pass it along to my supervisors.

"Middleburg is beautiful," I answered. "How did you come across this place?"

"Our dear friend Bill Walton found it for us. It's called Glen Ora, and I haven't actually seen it myself — just photographs, but I trust Bill's judgment and it seems perfect for us. It's a colonial home with a swimming pool, pool-house, and stables on four hundred acres in the hunt country. Four hundred acres of privacy where the children and I can have a very normal life and the president can get to very easily."

"It sounds very nice," I said.

"Well, the grounds are lovely, but the interior of the house needs to be entirely redone. Fortunately, the owner, Mrs. Raymond Tartiere, has kindly allowed me to make some changes so it suits our needs."

The news of the rented house in Middleburg created a variety of concerns for me. First, how would we adequately protect her while she was riding, yet still give her the privacy she desired? I knew she was an accomplished equestrienne and I was quite certain that my childhood riding experiences would not be enough to keep up with her. In addition, we would have to make sure there was adequate space for helicopter takeoffs and landings, and additional personnel would be required to maintain security at all times.

On December 8, President-elect Kennedy returned to Washington for the christening. Mrs. Kennedy and the baby were still patients in the hospital, so the service took place in the chapel at Georgetown University Hospital. It was clear that Mrs. Kennedy didn't have much energy, but she was determined to stand for a few minutes during the service. The press was eager to snap photos of the Kennedys holding their newborn son in his traditional flowing white christening gown, but Mrs. Kennedy, especially, was very concerned about the privacy of her children. The few members of the press who had been invited were very restricted, and although they were only allowed a brief amount of time to photograph and speak with the family, I could tell that even this slight bit of activity was wearing on Mrs. Kennedy.

First Lady Mamie Eisenhower had invited her to come to the White House the following day, December 9, at noon, for a tour of the mansion, including the private living quarters on the second and third floors. Dr. Walsh had agreed to release Mrs. Kennedy and John from the hospital, but everyone was concerned about her ability to go through with the White House tour, since she had struggled to stand during the brief christening ceremony. Mrs. Kennedy herself seemed apprehensive about her physical ability, but she was desperate to see her new home so that she could determine what changes she might want to make once they moved in on January 20, following the Inauguration.

"How about if I call J. B. West, the chief usher of the White House, and ask him to have a wheelchair for you, Mrs. Kennedy?" I asked her. "I know Mr. West well, and I am sure he will want you to be as comfortable as possible during the visit."

She had been looking rather forlorn, but

with this new option, suddenly her eyes lit up.

"That's a wonderful idea, Mr. Hill," Mrs. Kennedy said. She smiled and added, "Then I won't have to worry about fainting and making the headlines."

"Fine, then. I'll phone Mr. West and make the arrangements."

The chief usher holds a prominent position within the administrative staff, as he is responsible for the management of the White House. He must coordinate with the Secret Service and the presidential staff to ensure the effective and efficient day-to-day operation of the residential portion of the White House, known as the executive mansion, as well as the public and historical rooms. Mr. West had held the position of chief usher since 1957, but since the position is a presidential appointment, it hadn't yet been determined whether he would be retained with the new administration.

The next day, Mrs. Kennedy and John were released from the hospital and we took them to their home in Georgetown. Mrs. Kennedy barely had time to change clothes and freshen up before it was time to depart for the White House.

I pulled the Kennedy's three-year-old blue station wagon up to the front of the house and got out to help Mrs. Kennedy into the car.

When I went to open the back door, she asked, "Is anyone else coming with us?"

"No, it's just you and me, I'm afraid," I answered.

"I'll sit in the front seat then," she said.

"Certainly, Mrs. Kennedy," I said as I closed the back door and opened the front passenger door for her. I held her elbow as she timidly stepped into the car. She smoothed her dress as she sat down and looked up at me with a smile.

"Thank you, Mr. Hill."

When we arrived at the White House, J. B. West was there to greet us. He escorted us into the Diplomatic Reception Room, and I watched as Mrs. Kennedy's eyes took in the details of the décor — the walls, the rug, the flowers, and furnishings — all without saying a word.

We stopped at the elevator that led to the second floor, the private quarters, and Mr. West said, "Mrs. Eisenhower is waiting upstairs." He looked at me and added, "The first lady would like to take Mrs. Kennedy on the tour in private."

I nodded and Mrs. Kennedy stepped into the elevator with Mr. West.

I went to the chief usher's office to stand

by, knowing I would be fully aware of Mrs. Kennedy's activities from this location and not wanting to impinge on the tour of the two first ladies. A few minutes later, Mr. West joined me in his office and we caught up on all that had happened since I'd left President Eisenhower's detail.

Ninety minutes later, at exactly 1:30 P.M., the buzzer in the office sounded twice. Mr. West jumped up from his chair and walked quickly to the elevator. The buzzer system in the White House was set up to keep the usher's office, the uniformed White House police, and the Secret Service informed as to the first family's movements. Two buzzes indicated the first lady was moving.

I followed the chief usher and was waiting when Mrs. Kennedy and Mrs. Eisenhower appeared in the elevator. Mrs. Kennedy was extremely pale and looked like she was about to faint. I looked her straight in the eyes and raised my eyebrows as if to say, *Are you okay?* She returned my gaze and gave a slight nod.

The two women walked to the south entrance, as Mr. West and I followed several steps behind. The White House photographer took a photograph of the outgoing first lady and her successor smiling and saying good-byes, but I sensed that Mrs. Kennedy was simply being outwardly gracious. Something had happened upstairs.

I helped her into the front passenger seat and took my place behind the wheel of the station wagon, and headed toward the southwest gate. As soon as we turned onto State Place and proceeded to E Street Northwest, Mrs. Kennedy turned to me and asked, "Mr. Hill, did you call Mr. West and request a wheelchair?"

I turned to her and said, "Yes, I called him this morning and he said it would be no problem at all. He said it would be waiting for you. I assumed they had it upstairs for you."

"Well, when I got out of the elevator on the second floor, there was just Mrs. Eisenhower and no wheelchair in sight. She never mentioned it, so I assumed it simply hadn't been arranged."

I didn't know what to say. I didn't want to make excuses, but I had indeed spoken to J. B. West that morning.

"I'm terribly sorry, Mrs. Kennedy. I don't know what happened." I felt awful, imagining that somehow I'd done something that had caused her difficulty.

I later found out from J. B. West, whom President Kennedy did indeed retain as chief usher, that the wheelchair had been

ordered. The problem was that Mrs. Eisenhower didn't want anyone to accompany
her and Mrs. Kennedy, and she certainly
wasn't going to push the new first lady —
her political rival — through the executive
mansion. She had told West that the wheelchair would be available, but hidden, and
brought out only if Mrs. Kennedy requested
it.

Mrs. Kennedy didn't blame me at all for
the mishap. She was intuitive with people
and had figured that Mrs. Eisenhower had

simply ignored her request. She was far more concerned with the state of the White House.

"So what did you think of your new home, Mrs. Kennedy?" I asked.

"It's going to need far more work than I'd even imagined," she said in her soft, breathy voice. "We are going to be busy, Mr. Hill." After all our earlier conversations about the history and importance of the president's residence, I could see her mind already working as to how she intended to put her stamp on the White House.

The hour-and-a-half tour had depleted Mrs. Kennedy's energy and I could tell she needed a rest. Unfortunately, it had previously been decided that she and the president-elect would fly with their newborn son to Palm Beach immediately following the White House visit, so there was no time for her to relax, just yet.

The schedule had been set with little room for delay, so we returned to 3307 N Street to pick up President-elect Kennedy; baby John; Provi; Elsie Phillips, a new nurse and friend of Maud Shaw's who had been employed to help with John Jr.; Louella Hennessey, the longtime nurse of the Kennedy family, who had come to help Mrs. Kennedy with her recuperation; a mound of luggage for the first lady; and a suitcase each for Jeffries and myself, and headed to Andrews Air Force Base, where the *Caroline* was waiting for our departure.

The wind was blowing and the air was frigid as I followed Mrs. Kennedy up the steps to the plane. When we got on board, the president-elect helped her take off her coat and said, "The weather in Palm Beach has been beautiful. Some time in the warm weather and sunshine will do wonders for your recovery, Jackie."

"Yes, I'm looking forward to it," Mrs. Kennedy said as she sat down gingerly on the sofa-like lounge. She was pale and clearly exhausted from the day's outing.

I had never been on a private plane before, and as I settled into a seat next to a window, it struck me that the lifestyle that was normal for the Kennedys was beyond anything I'd ever imagined, let alone experienced. This trip on the *Caroline* was the first of countless flights I took with Mrs. Kennedy on the family plane. It soon became normal for me, too.

3
A PALM BEACH CHRISTMAS

Agent Jeffries, Pam Turnure, and Mrs. Kennedy with the Caroline *in background*

There was a great deal of turbulence on the flight from Washington to Palm Beach. Howard Baird, the captain of the *Caroline,* was a superb pilot, but the altitude limitations of the Convair 240 meant that the plane could not get above certain storm areas. The bumpiness made it impossible for Mrs. Kennedy to rest, and while she never complained, I could see that she was exhausted and physically drained from her tour of the White House.

It was evening by the time we landed, but the temperature was in the mid-70s — nearly 40 degrees higher than what we'd left in Washington, D.C. There was a crowd of people waiting at the Palm Beach Airport as well as some press photographers and as soon as Mrs. Kennedy saw them, she turned to her husband and said, "I am not talking to the press. And I don't want any photographs of the baby. I was hoping we would have more privacy down here."

The president-elect nodded in understanding. Members of the President-elect Secret Service detail had secured the area and had cars waiting for us. President-elect Kennedy stepped out of the plane and as he walked down the steps, he smiled and waved to the small but enthusiastic crowd. He walked over and shook some hands as a couple of Secret Service agents stayed close.

As soon as Mrs. Kennedy appeared in the doorway of the plane, at the top of the portable stairs, several people yelled, "Jackie! Jackie! Look over here!"

She looked at the crowd and smiled, but held tightly to the railing as she walked down the stairs and headed straight for the car. Unfortunately, the privacy Mrs. Kennedy sought would be elusive for the rest of her life. People were fascinated by her, and there would be few places she could escape. Palm Beach was certainly not one of them.

The town of Palm Beach is actually a long, narrow barrier island off the southeast coast of Florida, and it was like nowhere I had ever been before. The Intracoastal Waterway separates the island from the ordinary mainland cities of West Palm Beach and Lake Worth, like a moat, and when you cross one of the few bridges into Palm Beach, it is like you are crossing into a world imbued with privilege and power. Sixteen miles of pristine white sand beaches on the Atlantic Ocean form the east side of the island, along which is a string of mansions. From the interior roads, the homes are secluded by tall, natural barriers of hedge, bougainvillea, and palm trees. It is only when you fly overhead or sail along the coast that you can see the grandeur of these magnificent estates, which are used mainly as winter getaways by the ultrarich. The resort-like town offered an elite escape where the men would golf and socialize at the exclusive Palm Beach Country Club, while the women loved to shop in the glamorous shops of Worth Avenue.

Ambassador Joseph Kennedy bought the home at 1095 North Ocean Boulevard in 1933 as a place for his large family to congregate during the winter holidays when it was too cold on the Cape. The six-bedroom, 8,500-square-foot Mediterranean-style house sat on two acres of well-manicured lawns and gardens, and had a stunning view of the Atlantic Ocean. President-elect Kennedy had informed the Secret Service that this would be his "winter White House" and that in the weeks leading up to the Inauguration, this is where he would spend most of his time. Because this would be a regularly used residence for the first family, the Secret Service had to establish security on a semipermanent basis. This meant checking everything from the basic construction of the building to access from any and all directions. Secret Service agents would be posted at strategic points on the property, but because of the limited resources and personnel in the Secret Service, the security operations would have to be a joint effort on the part of the entire law enforcement community. Fortunately, the Palm Beach Police Department and the state and county

Ambassador Kennedy residence, Palm Beach

officials were all very cooperative, freely sharing information and personnel to ensure the safety of the Kennedy family.

As soon as our small motorcade arrived at the residence, Mrs. Kennedy immediately went to her bedroom to rest, and rarely emerged for the next week.

Prior to our arrival, one of the supervising agents on the president-elect detail had arranged accommodations for the Secret Service agents in nearby — and not so posh

— West Palm Beach, at a place called Woody's Motel. Woody's was a one-story, U-shaped building with a small rectangular swimming pool situated in the middle. It had been around for a while and was rather run-down, but it offered two key advantages: the rooms were air-conditioned and the price was right. The negotiated rate for our extended stay fit into our limited per diem allowance of twelve dollars, out of which we had to pay for hotel, meals, dry cleaning, laundry, and miscellaneous expenses while traveling. My annual $6,995 salary didn't stretch very far, and like the rest of the agents, I was very frugal and careful with expenditures.

Each morning I would report to 1095 North Ocean Boulevard, usually by 8:00 A.M. in order to be there prior to the time Mrs. Kennedy awakened. There was a garage attached to the front wall of the Kennedy's property, adjacent to the entry gate, which had been set up as the Secret Service Palm Beach Command Post. A telephone was installed with a direct line to the house so that if the president-elect or Mrs. Kennedy needed us for any reason, we could respond immediately. There was a coffeemaker, a small table, and a couple of chairs, but basically it was a corner of the garage.

Mrs. Kennedy was recuperating well, and slowly gaining strength, but she was hesitant to leave the privacy of the residence, especially after seeing the crowds that had greeted her at the airport upon her arrival.

We had been there just a few days when Mrs. Kennedy called me at the command post.

"Mr. Hill?" she asked in her soft, whisper-like voice.

"Yes, Mrs. Kennedy. What can I do for you?"

"I need some things from Elizabeth Arden, but I just know if I go to Worth Avenue, I'll be mobbed. I was wondering if you would call over there and arrange for someone to bring me some clothes and beauty supplies. I have a list all ready for you."

I had never heard of Elizabeth Arden, and arranging for home shopping wasn't something I'd ever done for President Eisenhower, but I did as Mrs. Kennedy desired, and arranged for one of the salespeople from Elizabeth Arden to come to the residence.

In addition to worrying about her wardrobe and makeup, the move to the White House — and how to make it a home rather than a museum — was uppermost on Mrs. Kennedy's mind at this time. She wanted the White House to be a place in which her children could grow up as normal as possible even with maids and butlers, doormen and ushers, and uniformed officers and Secret Service agents all over the place.

On another occasion, I was waiting in the Secret Service office when she called for me.

"Mr. Hill?" she said. "Will you please join me outside by the pool? I need to talk to you."

It was a beautiful afternoon and the sun felt warm on my face, as I walked across the lawn past the back of the house, toward the rectangular swimming pool. Two of my colleagues on the president-elect detail were standing post at the corners of the property bordering the beach, and I gave them each a quick wave. In Palm Beach the Secret Service agents shed our standard uniform of a dark suit and shined dress shoes for more casual clothing, with the intent of melding into the local populace to appear as inconspicuous as possible. The two agents in their cotton-knit shirts and cotton trousers looked like they could have just walked off the golf course. In the distance, a Coast Guard boat patrolled the waters along the coast.

Next to the swimming pool, Mrs. Kennedy was sitting on a chaise lounge, in a revealing bathing suit, with a stack of books by her side and a yellow legal pad in her lap. Caroline played and splashed in the pool while one of the agents who had been assigned to her protection stood watch nearby, ready to render assistance if needed.

"Yes, Mrs. Kennedy?" I asked as I approached her.

She looked up at me, her eyes hidden by a pair of large round sunglasses, and said, "Come sit down, Mr. Hill," as she gestured to the lounge chair beside her.

Dressed in my normal attire for working in Palm Beach — a pair of khaki slacks and a short-sleeved shirt worn outside my waistband to conceal the .38-caliber handgun strapped to my hip — I felt somewhat awkward sitting next to her in her bathing suit, but sat down as instructed.

After seeing how the Secret Service operated with her husband, Mrs. Kennedy was concerned about what their family life would be like in the White House.

"I'm worried, Mr. Hill," she said, as her brow furrowed slightly, "about losing all semblance of privacy."

She turned toward the two agents posted at the beach. "Are these Secret Service men and other agents going to be around us constantly? Even in the White House?"

Although she was used to having maids and cooks in the house, I could tell that having the Secret Service around all the time was troubling her, so I attempted to explain our role and tried to put her at ease.

"The second floor of the executive mansion is considered off-limits pretty much for all employees, including the Secret Service. This is the private area for use as a home by the first family, and you may restrict access to whomever you desire. The Secret Service agents will only come up there if called, or if there is an emergency. And the household staff is very professional — most of them have been around for years and are able to do their jobs unobstrusively."

"Well, that is good to know," she said, as her facial expression relaxed. "I'm just so worried about Caroline and John growing up in such a restricted environment. I want them to have as normal a childhood as possible."

As she said this, I thought to myself, *after January 20, Caroline and John will forever be the children of the president of the United States. They will be saddled with that title for the rest of their lives. A "normal" childhood will be impossible.*

"The goal of the Secret Service is to allow

73

you and your family to do the things you want to do, while maintaining your safety and security at all times," I said aloud. "The key is communication. If you can give us as much advance notice as possible about your plans, then we can make the appropriate arrangements. And if there's ever anything that bothers you, just let us know."

My answer seemed to appease her fears about privacy, so she moved to the next item on her legal pad.

"It seems that I am not receiving my mail in a timely manner. What is happening with our mail?" she asked.

"As a matter of security, all incoming mail to this address is redirected back to the White House mailroom from the Palm Beach Post Office for sorting, examination, inspection, and distribution. Unfortunately, this process causes a delay."

She tilted her head and looked at me quizzically. "All the mail has to be inspected?"

I didn't want to scare her, but I thought she should know exactly why we took this precaution.

"We need to ensure that there is no hidden explosive material or poisons prior to delivering letters and packages to you and the president-elect. And, of course, we screen for any mail that is threatening in nature."

What I didn't tell her was that we also weeded out the "hate" mail, of which there was plenty. The fact that President-elect Kennedy would be the first Catholic president did not sit well with many Americans. There was a fear that, as president, Kennedy's decisions would be based on his religion and dictated by the pope. Additionally, Kennedy's support for civil rights was unpopular in many parts of the country, and the violent nature of his opponents was of great concern to the Secret Service. Nothing was left to chance.

"But what about personal letters from my friends and family?" she asked. "Obviously those letters are safe, and it's important that I receive them in a timely manner."

We discussed a few options but none of them made me feel completely comfortable. Finally, I came up with an idea that I thought might work.

"How about if you have your friends and family put my name, 'Clint Hill,' along with your name as the addressee? This way, you can control who has this special access, and the post office can easily separate those letters and packages."

She seemed delighted with this idea. "It will be so clandestine. My friends will find it amusing, so secretive!"

Rather than the postal workers and me having to learn the names of all her friends, I thought this would be the easiest and quickest way to solve the problem. It also meant that every morning, my first stop of the day was the Palm Beach Post Office to go over incoming mail for the Kennedys and pick out those with my name on them. I would then hand carry them to Mrs. Kennedy. It became a regular routine and worked very well. I soon learned that Mrs. Kennedy had a large number of family and friends — I had never received so much mail in my life.

Meanwhile, some threatening letters had been intercepted by the Secret Service in Washington, which had everybody on high alert.

The first Sunday after our arrival in Palm Beach, the president-elect had decided to attend Mass at St. Edward Church, a Catholic parish in Palm Beach. Mrs. Kennedy was still recuperating, and while she didn't plan to join her husband, she and Caroline walked with him to the front gate of the estate, where some well-wishers had gathered outside, hoping to catch a glimpse of the family. Mrs. Kennedy waved to the onlookers before retreating into the privacy of the grounds, as Secret Service agents escorted the president-elect to the church, just a short drive away.

Four days later, a seventy-three-year-old man named Richard Pavlick was arrested by Palm Beach police following an intensive search based on letters Pavlick had written threatening to turn himself into a "human bomb" to kill President-elect Kennedy. Pavlick believed Kennedy's father had bought the election and Pavlick thought he'd be seen as a hero for killing John F. Kennedy before he was inaugurated. Police found dynamite, detonating caps, and battery wiring in Pavlick's car and at his West Palm Beach motel room. The mentally unstable man stated he had planned to set off the bomb outside the Kennedy residence as the president-elect was leaving for church the previous Sunday. He had parked his car on a nearby side street with the intention of ramming it into Kennedy's car, but the sight of Mrs. Kennedy with young Caroline made him reconsider his plan. He had no intention of harming the president-elect's family, so he decided to wait for another opportunity when Kennedy was alone.

President-elect Kennedy was informed of the incident, and it was left up to him to decide whether it was something he should share with his wife. I never discussed it with Mrs. Kennedy, but the knowledge that we had come so close to an assassination attempt prior to the Inauguration gave each of us a reason to be more vigilant and determined to ensure the maximum security possible even in this relaxed environment. Nothing could be left to chance.

Mrs. Kennedy gradually began to gain strength and her activities increased. One day she decided to accompany the president-elect to the Palm Beach Country Club to get some exercise walking the fairways, while he played a round of golf. This was not only good for her but for me as well. Inactivity was not my forte. She would watch intently as her husband hit the ball, but didn't intrude on her husband's conversations with the other members of the foursome as they discussed cabinet posts and other transition issues.

During this time in Palm Beach, there were people constantly coming and going. The president-elect's mother and father, Rose and Ambassador Joe Kennedy, were staying in the residence, while his younger brother Robert, known as "Bobby," was staying in a nearby home with his wife, Ethel, and their seven children. Both President-elect and

Mrs. Kennedy were choosing the people they would have as their staff and advisors, and it was important for the Secret Service agents to be able to recognize and get to know everyone who would have access to the president and his family, as a matter of respect as well as security. Some of their choices surprised me.

For the important position of attorney general, President Kennedy announced that he was appointing his brother Bobby. Thirty-five-year-old Bobby had been the campaign manager for Jack's presidential campaign, but his only government experience was as counsel of the Senate Rackets Committee. It was the first time in U.S. history that a president or president-elect had chosen a brother for his cabinet. While it was not illegal, the decision certainly raised eyebrows throughout the political arena. JFK would later confront the controversy head-on, in his inimitable way — while speaking to a Washington social and political organization, he quipped about his choice of Bobby as attorney general.

Looking down for an instant, as if the thought had just come to him, he said, "I don't see what is wrong about giving him a little legal experience before he goes out and practices law."

He broke into a big grin, the crowd roared with laughter, and the critics had no comeback.

Meanwhile, Mrs. Kennedy announced that twenty-three-year-old Pamela Turnure, one of her husband's former secretaries, would become her press secretary. She didn't have much experience and I thought she was an odd choice. But at the time Mrs. Kennedy still didn't grasp the interest the public had in her. "I can't imagine why I will even need a press secretary," she said at one point.

For her social secretary, Mrs. Kennedy chose her longtime friend and former classmate Letitia Baldridge, who turned out to be well-suited for the job. "Tish," as she was known by her friends, had attended both Miss Porter's School and Vassar, two years ahead of Mrs. Kennedy, and she came with a wealth of experience. She had been the social secretary to the wife of U.S. Ambassador David K. E. Bruce in Paris, as well as the social secretary to U.S. Ambassador Clare Boothe Luce in Rome, and was fluent in French and Italian. Standing six feet tall, Tish was a striking woman with a strong, confident personality. I liked her, and found that she would be another close ally.

As Christmas drew near, the realization that I would not be home for the holidays started to hit me. Caroline was eagerly awaiting the arrival of Santa Claus, and knowing I would not be able to share the excitement of Christmas morning with my four-year-old son, Chris, was difficult. Fortunately, I was able to use the White House switchboard at the Palm Beach Command Post to call home occasionally because there was no way I could afford to pay for long-distance telephone calls from a pay phone or from the motel. But hearing Chris's little voice on the phone really tugged at my heart.

All of the agents staying at Woody's Motel that Christmas were missing their families, so we tried to make the best of it together. We all took our jobs seriously and felt privileged to be on the White House Secret Service detail. Missing holidays with our families was just part of the job. With Christmas and New Year's behind us, the one thing we all had to look forward to was the Inauguration. The transition of power from one president to the next, in a free and peaceful manner, has always been a great symbol of American democracy. Not only would we be back in Washington with our families, but we'd also be participating in history.

For me, it would be my first presidential transition, and even though I would be protecting the first lady, rather than the president, I was filled with anticipation for the activities of January 20, 1961.

A few days before we were to depart for Washington, Jerry Behn, the acting Special Agent in Charge (SAIC) of the president-elect detail, took me aside in the Palm Beach Command Post.

"Clint," he said, "the president-elect and Mrs. Kennedy have decided that they won't bring Caroline and John back to Washington for the Inauguration. The children will be staying here with Miss Shaw, so we have decided to have you remain here in Palm Beach to supervise their security."

As the words came out of his mouth, I felt like I was being punched in the gut.

"Yes, sir," I said. "Whatever you need me to do."

"Jeffries will work Mrs. Kennedy alone during the inaugural activities."

I was surprised my supervisors only felt the need for one agent to be with Mrs. Kennedy during the very active period of January 18, 19, 20, and 21, but they were the ones in charge. I was just the worker. Once again I felt the sense that I was back on the second team. While my colleagues were being a part of history, I would be Chief Babysitter of the Diaper Detail.

On January 18, I escorted Mrs. Kennedy and Agent Jeffries from the Palm Beach residence to the local airport, where the *Caroline* was waiting to take her to Washington for the Inauguration. Word had leaked out that she was departing, and an enthusiastic crowd had gathered at the small airport.

Mrs. Kennedy waved graciously but stayed well away from the people. I stayed close to her as I scanned the crowd looking carefully at the eyes and the hands from behind my dark sunglasses. You look at the eyes for an unusually intense gaze, and at the hands for a flash of a knife or gun, or a sudden movement into a pocket or purse. Even though Mrs. Kennedy was very popular, the hate mail directed toward her husband was often vicious. No matter how positive and cheerful a crowd might be, you had to continually be on the lookout for that one lone lunatic who wanted to make a name for himself. Or herself. There was just as much a chance that a woman might try to harm Mrs. Kennedy as a man.

As we got to the bottom of the stairs leading up to the *Caroline,* Mrs. Kennedy turned to me and said, "Thank you for staying with the children, Mr. Hill. I know they'll be in good hands."

"Certainly, Mrs. Kennedy. Enjoy the festivities and I'll see you in Washington after the Inauguration."

As the *Caroline* taxied away I stood on the tarmac, alone and dejected, wishing I were making the trip.

On Inauguration Day, I joined Miss Shaw and Caroline inside Ambassador Kennedy's residence to watch the live coverage on television. Being from Great Britain, Miss Shaw was not familiar with the inaugural process, so I sat down with Caroline to try to explain what was happening.

"See your daddy, Caroline?" I pointed to the television as her father stood to take the oath of office.

She looked at the television and watched for a brief moment, her legs dangling from the sofa, as her father placed his left hand on the Bible and raised his right hand.

I John Fitzgerald Kennedy do solemnly swear . . .

"Where's mommy?" she asked.

That I will faithfully execute the Office of President of the United States.

"Mommy's there, too. I'm sure they'll

84

show her on the television in a minute."

And will to the best of my ability, preserve, protect, and defend the Constitution of the United States.

"I want to finish my finger painting," she said as she jumped down from the chair.

So help me God.

"Your daddy has just become the thirty-fifth president of the United States, Caroline," I said gently. I patted the chair and said, "Now he's going to make a very important speech. Come sit back down and let's watch."

Begrudgingly, she climbed back up on the sofa.

Eight inches of snow had fallen in Washington, D.C., the night before, blanketing the city with a mix of ice and snow. The U.S. Army Corps of Engineers and a thousand District of Columbia employees had worked overnight to clear the streets and remove hundreds of abandoned cars so the inaugural parade could proceed as planned. By noon on Inauguration Day, the snow had stopped and the sun emerged against a brilliant blue sky. The temperature did not climb above 22 degrees, however, and the hundreds of thousands who had come to witness this historic event were bundled up with heavy coats, gloves, hats, and mufflers in an effort to stay warm. As President Kennedy stood before the American people to give his Inaugural Address, you could see his breath hanging in the frigid air.

"I want to finger-paint some more," Caroline said, once again jumping off of the sofa.

I realized that, at three years old, Caroline could not possibly understand the importance of this moment, nor was it likely she would remember her father's historic speech.

"Okay, Caroline, go on outside with Miss Shaw and paint a nice picture for your mommy and daddy."

I turned back to the television and watched the rest of President Kennedy's speech. I could see U. E. Baughman, the chief of the Secret Service, seated just behind the president on one side, and SAIC Jim Rowley on the other side. Mrs. Kennedy was seated to the left of the podium, dressed in an ivory coat and matching hat, beaming proudly as her husband addressed the nation and requested citizens to ask not what the country could do for them but what they could do for the country.

As the president stepped away from the podium, the audience rose to its feet and burst into thunderous applause. The torch had been passed.

It was a powerful speech and you couldn't help but be moved by it. For me it had an even greater impact because I had also had the privilege of seeing him as an ordinary man. I'd seen his elation at the birth of his son, heard his laughter while playing with Caroline in the pool at Palm Beach, and witnessed the light in his eyes when he greeted his wife after they'd been apart. It hit me then that perhaps I had been looking at my assignment all wrong. I *was* serving the president, and the country, with an important task. I was responsible for protecting the things that were most important to him, personally — his wife and his children.

I had assumed that we would be taking Caroline and John back to Washington as soon as the Inauguration festivities were over, but Mrs. Kennedy wanted the children's rooms in the White House to be ready prior to their arrival, and that would be at least two more weeks. I got daily updates from Agent Jeffries about what was happening, about all the changes Mrs. Kennedy was making and how he was having a tough time getting used to her impulsive nature and lack of a schedule.

The funny thing was I realized that her spur-of-the-moment ideas and impromptu activities were what I missed most about not having her around.

I anticipated there would be new challenges with the first lady, and I looked forward to settling into a process of never knowing what was going to happen next, because that was the way Mrs. Kennedy preferred to operate. Spontaneity was what she thrived on. Everyone had to be on their toes. As time went on, I could anticipate what she might do or request, but she never failed to surprise me.

It has taken me many years to be able to remember the good times of that first winter in Palm Beach. It used to be — and it still happens occasionally — that the mere mention of Palm Beach would send my mind back to the day when the pain was too much for me to bear, when I couldn't face her anymore, when the laughter and hope had been washed away, like waves over a child's sand castle. But in December 1960, none of us could have imagined the way our lives would change.

■ ■ ■ ■

Part Two:
1961

■ ■ ■ ■

4
GLEN ORA

*Saturday, February 4, 1961, President Kennedy and
family enter White House for first time together*

In a repeat of the snowstorm that im-
mobilized Washington, D.C., for the Inauguration, a massive weather system had en-
gulfed the East Coast from New York to
Virginia the day before we were scheduled
to return to Washington with Caroline and

John. Eight inches of snow had fallen, but by the afternoon of Saturday, February 4, the runways in Washington had been cleared and pilot Howard Baird assured me we could depart Palm Beach as scheduled. Two-month-old John slept soundly, while Caroline was understandably excited to be reunited with her parents and to see her new home.

As the *Caroline* descended into the nation's capital, the crisp blue sky contrasted with the white snow that blanketed everything below. On the ground, a slough of reporters and photographers had joined President and Mrs. Kennedy at National Airport to greet their children. Mrs. Kennedy eagerly took baby John, who was bundled in a white blanket, from Maud Shaw's arms, as President Kennedy scooped up Caroline, smothering her with kisses.

It had stopped snowing, but the strong wind sent the banks of snow drifting in every direction. Mrs. Kennedy pulled John close to her to shield his face from the biting cold, and I quickly moved into a position to try to block the wind from hitting them.

"Welcome back, Mr. Hill," she said, as we strode toward the limousine.

"Thank you, Mrs. Kennedy. It's good to

be back."

She looked up at me with a glimmer in her eye and said, "Really? I was just thinking you'd probably rather be back in the warm weather and sunshine in Palm Beach!"

I laughed and said, "Well, I have to admit, I did get used to the weather down there. It sure beats this."

Agent Jeffries was waiting with the back door open and as soon as Mrs. Kennedy was settled, I joined the contingent of Secret Service agents in the follow-up car, and we sped away to 1600 Pennsylvania Avenue.

When we arrived at the White House, there was a big surprise waiting for Caroline. The head gardener had built a life-size snowman that stood at the edge of the driveway, its arms stretched out as if in a welcoming embrace to the new young members of the household. Caroline was delighted with her new "friend," who was adorned with coal buttons, a carrot nose, a Panama hat, and a bow tie made of red ribbons. She jumped out of the car and gingerly walked up to the smiling snowman that was more than twice her size, and as she reached out to touch him, White House photographer Abbie Rowe captured the precious scene.

After a brief meeting with Agent Jeffries about the schedule for the upcoming week, I drove the six miles to my two-bedroom apartment in Alexandria, Virginia, for my own reunion with my wife and son. This was the longest I'd been away from home, and the transition was not easy. My wife's perspective was that I had been on vacation in Palm Beach for two months, while she had been handling everything — paying the bills, maintaining the house, taking care of our very active four-year-old son — completely on her own. I knew it was rough on her, as it was on all the agents' wives, and I did my best to empathize, but also explain that this was just part of the job. Unfortunately my suntanned face and arms didn't help my case. I tried to reassure her that now that the Kennedys had moved into the White House, we would get into a routine, and presumably, I would be home more. What I didn't realize was that Mrs. Kennedy was already planning to be away from Washington as much as possible. And where Mrs. Kennedy went, I went.

Six days later, I was en route to Middleburg, Virginia.

Middleburg is only about forty-two miles from Washington, and typically an easy

drive, but the consistently bad weather had
left the country roads nearly impassable
because of the six- to eight-foot banks of
snow along the plowed roadways. Thus it
was decided that Mrs. Kennedy's first trip
to Glen Ora should be by helicopter. As
Agent Jeffries was the lead agent on Mrs.
Kennedy's detail, he rode in the chopper
with Mrs. Kennedy and Caroline, while I
drove a Secret Service Mercury to be there

waiting when they arrived.

The entrance to Glen Ora was marked by two simple stone pillars on either side of the driveway that looked like they'd been there since the Revolutionary War. The left pillar had a stone block engraved R. F. TARTIERE and the right, GLEN ORA FARM. You couldn't see the house or any other buildings from the main road, and if it weren't for the brand-new guard shack that had been erected at the entrance, you wouldn't take a second glance at the place.

The three-quarter-mile dirt driveway had been cleared for our arrival, but like the rest of the roads, the snow was piled so high on both sides that the approach to the residence felt like you were driving through a tunnel.

The unpretentious eighteenth-century stucco and brick main house was painted a golden yellow with creamy white shutters and trim, and had numerous chimneys sticking out of the gray slate roof. Even though the residence contained six bedrooms, five bathrooms, a kitchen, dining room, and library, it wasn't overly large, and was, in my opinion, not nearly as luxurious as the residence at Camp David.

The White House Army Signal Agency (WHASA) provided the communication for the Secret Service as well as for the presi-

Glen Ora residence, Middleburg, Virginia

dent. They brought in a trailer and placed it near the stables where we had established our Secret Service Command Post. Inside the trailer, they set up a telephone switchboard that had the capability of connecting to any telephone in the world. It also provided secure typewritten messaging and radio communication. Although our person-to-person communication was limited due to the size and weight of equipment available in those days, our car-to-car and car-to-base radio communication was excellent. All provided by WHASA.

Another issue was how to handle the

press. The isolation and quaintness of Middleburg that Mrs. Kennedy found so appealing was not at all desirable to the White House press corps. The only lodging near Glen Ora was the Red Fox Inn, a historic tavern that dates back to 1728, and it had a limited number of rooms available, which meant that the reporters were forced to share twin-bedded rooms — something they weren't used to and weren't happy about. WHASA worked with the local telephone company to install additional telephone lines at the inn, while Western Union provided the necessary lines for the reporters to file their stories. But beyond the limited communications and lodging, for the young and social press corps, Middleburg was just plain boring. It was small, rural, and quiet. Nightlife was nonexistent. Outside of monitoring the infrequent comings and goings of the Kennedys and their visitors, there was nothing to do, and nowhere else to go. The press hated Middleburg.

The rooms at the Red Fox Inn ran fourteen dollars per night, which was way too expensive for the Secret Service agents, so we commuted. Every day Mrs. Kennedy was in Middleburg, I drove back and forth on U.S. Route 50 between my home in Arlington and Glen Ora. The fifty-mile drive simply added to the length of my workday. Up bright and early for the one-hour drive. Home late — well after dinnertime — tired and hungry. The lightly graveled dirt roads became a quagmire of mud and slush, freezing as hard as stone at night, and during the daytime, sloppy and soft, as the sun melted the snow, leaving huge puddles of water in every low spot in the terrain. Helicopter was the preferred means of transportation, but only the president, first family, and high-ranking government officials or official guests qualified. Those of us who drove just did the best we could not to get stuck. Because I was the second man on the detail I worked weekends, while Jeffries took Saturdays and Sundays off. This meant that I spent a lot of time in Middleburg, along with the children's agents, Bob Foster and Lynn Meredith.

Both Bob Foster and Lynn Meredith were great guys — and the three of us got along famously. We were all three about the same age, married, and had young children. Foster was a proud and staunchly loyal Ohio State graduate who had a wonderful sense of humor. Lynn Meredith was an accomplished pianist who had an endless repertoire of upbeat songs that ranged from ragtime to jazz to anything modern. Anytime there was a piano around, he would sit down and have everybody singing in no time. John was still an infant at this time, but Caroline adored both Mr. Meredith and Mr. Foster.

All the reporters knew who I was by this time, and that I was assigned to Mrs. Kennedy, so whenever I went into the little town of Middleburg, word would get around and suddenly I'd be surrounded: "Clint, where is Mrs. Kennedy?" "Does she have any plans to leave the estate?" "What on earth does she *do* all day?"

I tried to be as friendly and respectful as I could without providing any of the information they were seeking. In fact, Mrs. Kennedy was usually doing what she loved — spending time with her children and riding, and always trying to keep out of the public eye.

When I had done my research on Mrs. Kennedy I learned that she was an accomplished horseback rider. She had ridden in competitions since early childhood, and now that she had rented this place in the Virginia hunt country, it was clear that she planned to ride more frequently for sport and relaxation. This was a bit of a problem for the Secret Service because we were responsible for protecting her — and nobody on the White House Detail was as skilled a rider as the first lady.

She boarded her horse, a bay gelding named Bit of Irish, at the nearby farm of her good friends Eve and Paul Fout. The Fouts would bring the horse by trailer to Glen Ora so she could ride him as she pleased when she was in residence there. The Fouts were also members of the Orange County Hunt Club, which had extended an invitation for Mrs. Kennedy to join.

When I first heard her talk about "riding the hunt" I envisioned a group of friends trotting on their horses across the rolling hills of the fenced estates, stopping for tea and crumpets after an hour or so. There was talk at Secret Service headquarters of sending me and a couple of other agents to riding school so that we could adequately protect Mrs. Kennedy on these outings. It soon became clear, however, that that was not a feasible option.

Fox hunting in Virginia, it turned out, was a serious sport. It was well organized, highly structured, and very expensive. The participants were all excellent riders, seriously chasing an elusive fox across the countryside, jumping over hedges and fences, surrounded by a pack of well-trained foxhounds that barked and yelped all along the way, making a tremendous racket. I had never seen or heard anything like it.

The hunt clubs were organized like a well-run business, with the master of the hunt at the top of the organizational chart. The master of the hunt organized the sporting activities of the club, maintained the kennels for the dogs — always referred to as "hounds" — and was responsible for accounting for the money raised by the club. Next came the kennelman, who looked after the hounds and helped with the kennel, and the huntsman, who was responsible for directing the hounds. Assisting the huntsman were the whippers-in. These riders carried long whips and had the job of keeping the pack together to prevent straying or "rioting" — the term used when the foxhounds chased something other than the fox. Finally, there were the followers, who rode at the back of the group.

Special attention was paid to the type of equipment one used, and proper attire was mandatory. The official hunt season in Virginia is between October and March, and during this time the huntsman, masters, former masters, and whippers-in wear scarlet-colored coats. They are sometime called pinks. The rest of the riders wear black or dark blue jackets, with the ladies' jackets distinguished by colored collars. Tight-fitting britches and knee-high leather boots are worn to prevent getting caught up in the branches; brown or black leather gloves are worn to protect the hands; a helmet to protect the head; and a tie, which can double as a bandage in case of injury. During the off season, "rat catcher," or informal, attire is allowed. That means a tweed jacket, natural or tan britches, shirt with colored tie or shirt with collar and stock pin, and a tattersall vest.

I couldn't imagine myself in one of these getups, and after seeing Mrs. Kennedy ride I sure as hell knew I couldn't keep up with her. This was a brand-new problem for the Secret Service. Mrs. Kennedy realized this as well, and it seemed to amuse her.

"Mr. Hill, there is some concern that there will be Secret Service agents riding along with the hunt, and this presents a variety of problems. First, there are time-honored rules and traditions that go along with the sport — and no one is allowed to ride, who is not a member. I don't want any exceptions to be made for me, simply because I'm the wife of the president."

"Yes, Mrs. Kennedy, the issue of your protection while riding is something we are trying to address."

"I know you have experience riding, Mr. Hill," she said, as she tried to suppress a smile, "and I'm certain you would find a way to keep up with us, but I'm not so sure that any of those other agents would have a chance."

I couldn't help but laugh. I could tell that she had something up her sleeve. "Do you have any suggestions as to how we might handle this?"

"Actually I do think I have a solution to the problem. Eve and Paul Fout are both highly experienced and I trust them completely. Perhaps you could assign them the role of being my 'guardians' during the hunts. They could ride on either side of me, thus blocking me from view of anyone who might try to sneak up on us."

It wasn't an altogether bad idea. "Let me discuss it with my supervisors, Mrs. Kennedy, and perhaps we can give it a try. We certainly want you to be able to do the things you want to do, without imposition."

In the end, it was decided that the Secret Service policy would be not to ride with Mrs. Kennedy but rather to surveil her from a vehicle, utilizing the existing network of roads and trails to attempt to keep up with the horde of riders as they participated in the "hunt." If Eve and Paul Fout were willing to also ride on either side of Mrs. Kennedy, that was fine, but nobody expected them to take protective measures should a problem arise. Proximity was going to be a major problem and just keeping up with the pack was going to be a challenge. This was far from an ideal situation, and I knew I had my work cut out for me.

The decision had been made mostly because of the cost issue. The purchase or rental of horses, and you had to have more than one, was only the beginning expense. There was the housing, feeding, and other maintenance costs. The cost of equipment, including proper attire. The expense and problem of transporting the horses to the various locations from which Mrs. Kennedy would ride. It would have required training not only for me, but several other agents as backup. Then there was the possibility of an accident and injury to the agent. All of these things weighed into the decision to go with vehicular surveillance when Mrs. Kennedy went riding. I was somewhat disappointed that I wouldn't get to participate in what was certainly a thrilling and adventurous sport, but it was the most sensible option.

The perimeter security at Glen Ora was provided by Secret Service agents brought in on temporary assignments from field offices all over the country, and so when they were off-duty they didn't have the option of returning home. A few of them searched the area for sleeping rooms they could afford, and became acquainted with Bill and Jane Waddell, a wonderful couple who owned a large home on the western edge of Middleburg. The property was right on Route 50 with a large yard, and the house was set back a considerable distance from the highway. The long driveway provided ample room to accommodate the vehicles agents drove to and from Glen Ora. They had a number of extra bedrooms and agreed to rent them to the agents at an acceptable rate. Those of us who were in Middleburg on an almost continuous basis — the drivers for the president, the agents assigned to the children, and me — decided it was better to stay at the Waddells' than to endure the daily trips to and from the Washington metropolitan area to Glen Ora. This also provided us with the rapid-response capability required in the event that became necessary. Most of the agents had to share rooms, but I was fortunate to have a room to myself.

President Kennedy was not nearly as enamored with Middleburg as Mrs. Kennedy was, so his visits were usually a quick in and out. He would fly in by helicopter on a Saturday afternoon and leave on Sunday after attending Mass at the Middleburg Community Center. Saturday evenings would be casual dinner parties — usually with the Fouts or other friends who had arrived with the president. Mrs. Kennedy would tend to stay in Middleburg until Monday or Tuesday, depending on her obligations in Washington.

I could understand why she preferred the quiet of Middleburg, and the privacy it offered. For even though she did not encourage or invite publicity, the public was insatiable when it came to news about Mrs. Kennedy or John or Caroline. And, unfortunately, the more she resisted the spotlight, the more ravenous the press and the public became. Members of the media would rarely come out to Middleburg unless the president was in town, so when Mrs. Kennedy was there by herself, she could lead somewhat of a normal life. I was fortunate to be able to share these times with her.

Mrs. Kennedy's focus those first few months as first lady was to restore and refurbish the White House public rooms to their eighteenth-century splendor. Over the years, the White House had been modernized and there were few antiques or authentic furnishings in the mansion. Mrs. Kennedy found this almost beyond belief.

"The White House belongs to all Americans," she told me at one point. "It should be the finest house in the country — something that people will be proud of — a living museum of our nation's history. Don't you agree, Mr. Hill?"

Admittedly, I'd never given it much thought, but Mrs. Kennedy was so intent on this project, almost to the point of being obsessed with it. I also knew, from J. B. West, that the entire fifty-thousand-dollar appropriation given to incoming presidents for redecorating the White House had already been used up on the family quarters.

"I think it's a wonderful idea, Mrs. Kennedy. The problem is, getting the money to do what you want to do. The Secret Service can barely buy a new car without Congress signing off on it."

"Yes, the president has told me the same thing. But . . ." She turned to me with a glint in her eye. "I have an idea. I'm going to form a committee."

"Well, Washington loves committees," I said with a laugh. "You'll be in good company."

It turned out to be a brilliant idea. Mrs.

Kennedy developed the Fine Arts Committee for the White House, which was basically a fund-raising committee to purchase antiques and period furnishings as permanent gifts to the White House. She convinced Henry du Pont — a wealthy collector and qualified authority of American antiques who had turned his estate in Wilmington, Delaware, into a museum known as Winterthur — to be chairman of the committee. Du Pont's involvement added prestige and credibility to the project, as well as inroads to the connected people who would be interested in donating gifts and money to the cause of beautifying and restoring the White House.

Mrs. Kennedy soon learned many items that had been used in the White House at one time or another were kept in storage at Fort Washington. We would walk through disorganized rooms where furniture and boxes were stacked and shoved randomly together. Mrs. Kennedy would suddenly stop at what appeared to me to be a pile of dusty junk and point to a table stacked with boxes.

"Look at the beautiful carved legs on that table," she'd say with whispery excitement. We'd get the item pulled out so she could have a better look and it would turn out to be a table used during President James Monroe's administration or John Quincy Adams's. She had an eye for detail and instinctively knew what would look perfect in every space of the White House rooms.

In mid-March, Mrs. Kennedy informed me she would be going to New York City.

"I'm going to spend several days in New York City with my sister Lee before she flies back to London," she said. "And," she added, "I'll be meeting with some antiques dealers — for the White House restoration."

Wonderful. Shopping for antiques. I was quite sure the guys on the President's Detail would never set foot inside an antiques shop. At least she didn't mention fashion shows or the ballet.

"Great. I love New York," I said.

"Oh, have you spent much time in New York, Mr. Hill?" she asked.

In fact, the last time I had been in New York City was as part of the advance team for President Eisenhower when he went to New York to help Vice President Richard Nixon in his campaign to defeat John F. Kennedy just before the election in 1960, but I wasn't about to tell her that.

"Oh yes, I've been to New York City a number of times," I replied. "Where will you stay?"

"I'll stay at our apartment at the Carlyle Hotel."

Their apartment at the Carlyle Hotel? Who has their own apartment at a hotel?

I had never heard of such a thing.

I was glad to get this information well ahead of time so that we could alert the New York City Field Office of Mrs. Kennedy's pending visit. Protecting her on the streets of New York was going to require much more assistance than in Middleburg or Palm Beach. As soon as I had the opportunity, I notified Agent Jeffries of Mrs. Kennedy's plans.

Whenever the president or Mrs. Kennedy traveled to New York, we would rely on the New York Field Office (NYFO) for their expertise in navigating the area. Whether it was to restaurants, a Broadway show, museums, or shopping on Fifth Avenue, they knew the right people to contact in advance of Mrs. Kennedy's arrival. The NYFO was one of the largest Secret Service offices in the country and they would provide us with extra manpower, and would handle the perimeter security at the Carlyle Hotel.

On Monday, March 19, Mrs. Kennedy, her sister, Lee, Agent Jeffries, and I flew on the *Caroline* from Washington to LaGuardia Airport, where we were met by agents from the NYFO.

The Secret Service had an agreement with the Ford Motor Company, and they had provided a Lincoln Town Car to transport the first lady, as well as a station wagon for us to use as a follow-up car.

So we headed off to the Carlyle with Agent Jeffries in the front passenger seat and Mrs. Kennedy and her sister in the back of the Lincoln, while I drove behind them in the follow-up car. The previous times I had been to New York with President Eisenhower, it had been a highly publicized visit, which required a police escort. Because Mrs. Kennedy preferred to keep her trips private, most of the time we never told anybody where we were going or what we were doing. From the perspective of the Secret Service, this was the preferred way to handle a trip. The fewer people who knew your intended destination or route, the better. A police escort would have just drawn attention to us, so we kept the motorcade to as few vehicles as possible. Of course, Mrs. Kennedy's luggage was always a concern and there usually had to be an additional car and handler just for her bags. She did not travel lightly.

I had never been to the Carlyle before, and as I realized we were getting close, I noticed this beautiful structure that seemed to rise up from the city, overlooking Central Park, unobstructed by any other tall buildings. Built in the Art Deco style, the hotel has a distinct look, most notably marked by the octagonal green tiled roof that is topped with what looks like a giant gilded thimble. As we pulled up to the stunning hotel that rose forty stories high, I thought back to my youth in North Dakota wheat country where the highest structures were grain elevators standing four or five stories tall, and I thought, *That sure would hold a lot of wheat.*

Agents from the New York office had secured the area in anticipation of our arrival. The general manager of the hotel, Mr. Samuel Lewis, was there to greet Mrs. Kennedy and escort her to the Kennedys' apartment on the thirty-fourth floor.

"Welcome back, Mrs. Kennedy," said Mr. Lewis as he bowed his head slightly.

"Thank you, Mr. Lewis," Mrs. Kennedy said with a smile. "It feels like I'm coming home."

"We hope you do think of this as home, Mrs. Kennedy. And so nice to see you, too, Princess Radziwill," he added as Lee got out of the car.

The hotel's lobby had the feel of the

entryway to a magnificent home. The floor was black-and-white marble in a striking rectangular pattern that looked like a carpet of black glass surrounded by a white-and-gold border. Beautiful flower arrangements, in the simple style Mrs. Kennedy liked to have at the White House, were on every table. And as we walked in, uniformed employees were standing by to render whatever assistance we required, nodding a polite, "Welcome back, Mrs. Kennedy," as she walked by.

Directly to the thirty-fourth floor we went, nonstop. The NYFO agents had secured the apartment prior to our arrival and, as the doors opened, a New York Secret Service agent was standing there.

The apartment occupied the thirty-fourth and thirty-fifth floors, and I must say, I was really impressed. I had been in presidential suites in other hotels in New York City and all around the world, but the magnitude and majesty of this apartment residence was almost overwhelming. The spacious apartment had two terraces with fabulous views of Central Park, Manhattan, and New Jersey. The lower floor contained a living room, dining room, kitchen, and study, while upstairs there were two bedrooms with separate baths, and a glassed-in solarium. The Carlyle staff had taken great care to customize the apartment with borrowed eighteenth-century French antiques and original paintings by Pissarro, Murillo, and Degas.

We got Mrs. Kennedy and Lee settled into the apartment and then Jeffries and I went to our shared room on a lower floor. Not as glorious or splendid as the Kennedy apartment, but it was still the Carlyle. We were being well taken care of by the management. Our twelve-dollar per diem allowance would not go very far if we had to pay full price at this luxurious hotel, but fortunately they cut us a great deal. Still, we had to pay for meals, laundry, and dry cleaning out of those twelve dollars. There was no way we could afford to eat at the Carlyle, so we scouted around and found a diner not far away, where we could get a meat loaf dinner for a couple of bucks.

We took Mrs. Kennedy to art and antiques shops as she searched for acquisitions for the White House restoration project, and it wasn't long before word got around that she was in town. People would follow her as she walked down the street, and clamor to get into the shops with her and Lee. She would offer a curt smile in an effort to be gracious, but I could sense how much she

hated the attention and the inability to just go about her business.

The second morning of our visit, Jeffries notified me of Mrs. Kennedy's schedule for the day. More shopping, some deliveries by Oleg Cassini for her spring wardrobe, followed by an evening at the New York City Ballet at City Center on Fifty-fifth Street. The day had finally come, just as I'd expected when I was first given the assignment on the First Lady's Detail — fashion shows and the ballet.

Needless to say, I'd never attended a ballet before, so I really had no idea what to expect. Mrs. Kennedy was accompanied by the ambassador to the United Nations, Adlai Stevenson, and somehow the press and the public had got wind that she was going to be in attendance. By the time the performance ended, a huge crowd had gathered on the sidewalk in front of the theater, so Jeffries and I arranged to sneak her out through the rear door of City Center, on Fifty-sixth Street.

I stayed close to her as we walked to the car. She was in a wonderful mood and I could tell she had thoroughly enjoyed the performance.

"What did you think, Mr. Hill? Wasn't it a wonderful ballet?"

I paused for a moment, before replying. I had nothing to compare it to, but it hadn't been as awful as I'd expected it to be.

"I really enjoyed the music, Mrs. Kennedy. And I was surprised at the athleticism of the dancers."

"Oh, Mr. Hill," she said with a laugh. Whenever she said that, I could tell she could see right through me.

The rest of the week was filled with trying

to get Mrs. Kennedy around New York with as few people knowing our comings and goings as possible. She really seemed to enjoy and feel comfortable in the city, and I wanted to make sure she continued to have the ability to go where she wanted, and be as spontaneous as she wanted, without having to worry about her personal safety and privacy.

For me, staying at the Carlyle was the highlight of the trip. I could see why she and the president loved the hotel so much. The staff was exceptional, the service impeccable. Nothing was too big or too small for them to accommodate. I never imagined that three years later, I would again be living at the Carlyle, but in a state of emotional despair that would all but erase these fond memories.

It wasn't long before the press started questioning Mrs. Kennedy's frequent absences from the White House, and specifically her use of government helicopters to fly back and forth between the White House and Middleburg when the president wasn't with her. To avoid the controversy, it soon became our routine to drive Mrs. Kennedy in the Chrysler limousine that had previously been used by Mrs. Eisenhower. Two

Army sergeants assigned to the White House garage had been selected to drive under the supervision of the Secret Service, and they rotated the position of Mrs. Kennedy's driver. I would sit in the front passenger seat so that I had a good view of our surroundings, yet close enough to shield Mrs. Kennedy in case of emergency.

One weekend we were headed out to Middleburg and I was sitting in the front passenger seat, with Mrs. Kennedy in back, as usual. In those days, I was rarely without a cigarette in my hand, and on those drives, I typically smoked on the way, with the window cracked just enough to let the smoke out of the car, but not enough to allow the wind to rush back on Mrs. Kennedy. We were about halfway to Middleburg, far enough outside of Washington that there were hardly any other cars on the road, when Mrs. Kennedy suddenly leaned forward and said softly, "Mr. Hill, would you please ask the driver to pull over?"

I turned around to look at her and saw that she had a sly smile on her face. I had no idea what she wanted, but I asked Irv Watkins, who happened to be driving at the time, to please pull over as soon as there was a safe place to do so.

"Is everything all right, Mrs. Kennedy?" I

119

asked as I put out my cigarette in the car's ashtray. I suddenly realized that perhaps she didn't like me smoking in the car, although she had never said anything before.

"Yes, everything's fine," she answered.

Watkins found a spot where there was a clear area on the side of the two-lane road and carefully brought the car to a stop. I turned around to see what she intended to do, and she leaned forward again and whispered, "Mr. Hill, will you please come in the backseat with me?"

I presumed she wanted to tell me something in confidence and didn't want the driver to overhear. So I got out, opened the back door, and slid in to the backseat next to her.

As soon as I was situated, Mrs. Kennedy said to the driver, "Okay, carry on," and we proceeded on our way.

"What is it, Mrs. Kennedy?"

She had a look on her face like an impish child.

"Could I have one of your cigarettes, Mr. Hill?"

That's what this was about? I hadn't ever seen her smoke before, so I was somewhat surprised by her request.

I laughed and said, "Certainly."

I reached for the pack of L&M's in my

jacket pocket and pulled out a cigarette. I offered it to her, but instead of taking it from my hand, she said, "Will you please light it for me?"

I put the cigarette in my mouth and pulled the lighter out of my pants pocket. I flicked the lighter and as the flame touched the end of the cigarette, I sucked in, and then handed the lit cigarette to Mrs. Kennedy.

She held the cigarette between her index and third finger, put the cigarette to her lips, and took a long inhale. I realized she was no stranger to smoking.

"Thank you, Mr. Hill," she said coyly.

The driver continued on the road to Middleburg, and Mrs. Kennedy and I sat in the backseat and talked about everything from how the children, Caroline and John, were doing, to how the Secret Service agents were getting along with members of the staff, as we enjoyed our cigarettes. She was like a giddy teenager who was getting away with something, and I was her cohort in crime. This soon became our regular routine whenever we were in the car together.

It was the first of many such secrets we would keep with each other.

5
TRAVELING WITH MRS. KENNEDY: PARIS

Mrs. Kennedy and Mrs. DeGaulle in Paris, with Clint Hill in background

Beginning in February 1961, Mrs. Kennedy's weekends to Glen Ora became an almost weekly occurrence, with the president coming by helicopter on Saturdays and leaving Sunday afternoon. The fields were too wet and soft to permit cross-country riding and fox hunts, so I would take Mrs. Kennedy to the Fouts' farm, where she could ride on a limited basis. Other than a trip to Palm Beach in early March 1961, this was our routine. It was Middleburg, Middleburg, and more Middleburg. She obviously loved it. Even though I wasn't riding, my butt seemed to become sore from all the time Mrs. Kennedy spent in the saddle.

She absolutely adored horses, and during this time, Bit of Irish was her favorite. She would walk up to the horse, which had already been groomed and saddled, raise her hands up behind its ears, and look straight into its eyes while gently caressing the animal's long neck. She would speak to him in her soft, soothing voice and suddenly the horse would respond with a nod of his head or a nuzzle into her neck with his wet nose. She'd laugh — oh what an infectious laugh she had — and as I watched from a distance, I could see the sheer joy the animal gave her. At times it appeared as if she and her large, maned friend were having an actual conversation. She was perfectly at ease around horses, and just being in their presence gave her great pleasure.

On one of our many trips to the Fout residence — it was just the two of us driving along one of the hilly Middleburg two-lane roads — Mrs. Kennedy turned to me and asked, "Mr. Hill, have you traveled much?"

"Well, when I was assigned to President Eisenhower, I had the opportunity to travel a great deal."

"Where did you go?"

"Oh, we went throughout Europe, Asia, the South Pacific, South America . . ." I looked over to see her reaction. I thought she might be impressed, but there was no sign that she was.

"Have you been to Paris?" she asked.

"Twice," I replied.

She raised her eyebrows and asked, "Parlez-vous français, Monsieur Hill?"

I wasn't exactly sure what she said, but it was clearly French, so I took a guess and responded with my version of a French accent.

"No, Madame Kennedy, I do not speak French. But I do know where to find the best French onion soup you have ever had in your entire life."

She laughed and said, "The president is going on some foreign trips, and I'm planning to go with him on some of them. Paris and Vienna will be among the first." I hadn't heard about this yet, so I was glad to receive the information.

"I presume," she continued, "that if I go with the president, the Secret Service would send someone on my behalf, right?" she asked.

"Yes, that's right. Either Agent Jeffries or I would go along with one of the president's agents on the advance, to set up the trip."

"What do you do on an advance? I mean are there certain things I won't be allowed to do?" This was typical of Mrs. Kennedy's curiosity. She wanted to know what kinds of things would be arranged for her, so she could know what to expect.

"You can pretty much do whatever you want to do, and it's our job to make sure you can do that safely," I said. "Of course it's much more difficult when we travel internationally because we have to work with the foreign police organizations and security forces. Everything will be planned out to the minute so that hopefully there aren't any surprises along the way. Everywhere you go it will be determined who is joining you, where you sit, what you eat, how you get from one place to another. We want you to be able to enjoy the trip, and feel safe everywhere you go."

As I was talking, her face took on a rather pained expression.

"Oh, it sounds so clinical," she said with dismay. "When I was in Paris in college, I was carefree. I could stay out until three in the morning and sleep till noon; I could sit at a café along the Rive Gauche without worrying about a gaggle of photographers sneaking up to snap a photo. I suppose those days are long gone."

The wistfulness in her voice made me realize how difficult the constant attention was for Mrs. Kennedy, and I could understand completely. I saw the throngs of people that gathered around gawking and snapping photos. It was constant. I made a resolve that I would do everything I could to help her be as carefree as possible, to live as "normal" a life as she could. The best way to do this would be to keep our comings and goings as secret as possible. It wouldn't be easy, but if I could wipe that sad look off her face, it would be worth it.

By this time we had arrived at the Fout residence. I had no way of knowing whether or not I'd be assigned to the foreign trips Mrs. Kennedy had discussed, but the mere mention of Paris brought back wonderful memories, and I sure hoped I would get to go.

The first weekend of April 1961 was Easter, and it was back to Palm Beach. When we returned to Washington, it seemed that spring was finally arriving after what had been one of the snowiest winters in the capital's history.

One morning, I was in the Secret Service office when Mrs. Kennedy called on the telephone from upstairs.

"This is Clint," I said as I picked up the phone.

"Mr. Hill?" she asked. "Do you play tennis?"

"No, Mrs. Kennedy," I replied, "I must say I have never played tennis."

There was a pause on the other end of the line. Then she said, "It's such a beautiful day. I was hoping to go out on the tennis court and hit some balls."

"Well, if you have an extra racket I'd be happy to give it a try," I answered.

I have to admit I considered tennis to be a very easy sport from a competitive point of view. I always thought it was a game for "sissies" — not very manly. Having played varsity baseball in college with an excellent batting average, I was confident I could hold my own on a tennis court with Mrs. Kennedy. It was indeed a beautiful day outside, and it sounded like fun.

"Oh that would be great, Mr. Hill," she said enthusiastically. "Please meet me at the South Portico."

A few minutes later, Mrs. Kennedy came striding out of the door to the South Portico with a big smile on her face, holding two rackets in one hand and a can of tennis balls in the other. She was dressed in a pair of lightweight slacks, a short-sleeved top, and white tennis shoes.

When she saw me, she laughed. "Oh, Mr. Hill! You can't play tennis in your suit!"

I had no way of knowing tennis would be on the agenda when I dressed for work in the morning, so I was wearing my usual Washington uniform of a dark suit, white shirt, tie, and Florsheim shoes.

"It's no problem, Mrs. Kennedy. I'll be fine. Let's go."

"Okay," she said as she handed me a racket. Grinning, she added, "Let's hope there aren't any photographers around."

We walked to the tennis court and I watched as she walked to the back line of one side. I removed my suit coat and gun and placed them on the side of the court. I had no idea what all the lines meant on the court, so I just walked to the other side and stood in the middle of the white line at the back.

"Ready?" she called out.

"Ready!" I answered.

I grabbed the racket in both hands like a baseball bat and held it up as if I were awaiting a pitch. She seemed to be suppressing a smile as she served up the ball and hit it across the net.

I watched, and eager to make a good impression, as the ball came toward me I swung the racket back and whacked it with all my might.

The ball went flying over Mrs. Kennedy's head, over the fence, and into the trees behind the court.

Mrs. Kennedy watched the ball throughout its flight, saw it hit the ground, and turned back toward me. She didn't say a word. Holding the racket in one hand, she just pulled out another ball and tried again. This time, I didn't wind up nearly as much and hit the ball as if I were aiming for second base instead of trying to hit a home run.

The same thing happened. The ball went flying over the fence.

"Mr. Hill," she called from the other side of the net. "The object is to hit the ball to me so I can return it."

"Yes, Mrs. Kennedy," I said as I wiped my brow. There was very little breeze and I was already starting to sweat in my wool suit.

I got a bit better and managed to hit a few balls over the net to her, but it certainly wasn't the game that she had anticipated. I ended up spending most of the time retrieving the balls I'd hit over the fence so we could continue.

We tried a few more times that spring, with similar results. Agent Jeffries, an excellent tennis player, was really her opposition of choice on the tennis courts, because he would volley — I learned the hard way what that word meant — and give Mrs. Kennedy an excellent workout. Unfortunately, he was not always available. Most staff members she tried were not much better than I, so when she couldn't find anyone else to hit balls with it was finally decided that the best option would be to bring in a pro from a local tennis club to play with her. I certainly gained a lot more respect for the game of tennis and the skill it requires, and was thankful there was no photographic evidence of my short stint as Mrs. Kennedy's tennis partner.

The weekend of April 15 and 16 seemed

like any other, with Mrs. Kennedy going to Middleburg on Friday, and the president arriving Saturday afternoon. The public was unaware that the president was dealing with his first major crisis — a failed attempt to invade Cuba by some fourteen hundred American-trained Cuban exiles, that would forever be known as "the Bay of Pigs."

On Monday, April 17, President and Mrs. Kennedy hosted a state luncheon at the White House for the prime minister of Greece, Konstantinos Karamanlis, and his wife, Amalia, as the Bay of Pigs crisis was unfolding. Mrs. Karamanlis was thirty-two years old — more than twenty years younger than her husband — and she and Mrs. Kennedy hit it off immediately.

After the departure of the Greek couple, Mrs. Kennedy asked me, "Mr. Hill, have you ever been to Greece?"

"Yes, I was in Athens with President Eisenhower."

"Oh, really?" she answered, wide-eyed. "The prime minister and Mrs. Karamanlis invited the president and me to visit them in Athens. The president can't make it, but he suggested I go anyway. I've always dreamed of visiting the Acropolis and the Parthenon."

"That's wonderful," I said. "I'm sure

you'd love Greece. You should definitely take advantage of the opportunity."

Shortly thereafter, SAIC Jerry Behn called me into his office in the East Wing of the White House and informed me that I would be doing the advance for Mrs. Kennedy in Paris and Greece.

"Tish Baldridge will be the senior staff advance person, so you'll be working directly with her," Behn said. "She used to work in Paris — knows everybody and all the locations — and she speaks fluent French."

Tish Baldridge was extremely organized and paid close attention to detail. She was exactly the kind of person I liked to have with me on an advance because I didn't have to worry about things falling through the cracks. She would handle everything with regards to Mrs. Kennedy's agenda, gifts, seating arrangements, and menus, so that I could focus on logistics and security. This was a huge relief because I had seen how involved visits to foreign governments could become. Protocol always played a big part in these visits and the further I could stay away from those issues, the better. The last thing I needed was to become involved in a squabble over someone's hurt feelings because they weren't seated at the table with the president and first lady.

I had been in Paris twice with President Eisenhower — the first time in December 1959, and again during his failed summit meeting with Khrushchev in May 1960 — and I was excited for the opportunity to return. Paris had enchanted me like no other city I had visited. There was something about the way its architectural and cultural history had been preserved and maintained that really appealed to me. From the grandeur of the Champs-Élysées to the meandering side streets lined with sidewalk cafés that were filled with couples lingering over a glass of Bordeaux at lunchtime, Paris had matchless charm.

In 1959, I had flown directly from Athens to Paris, a few days ahead of President Eisenhower, along with a few other Secret Service agents and some of the president's staff. We weren't there on advance, but had been sent ahead due to space limitations as the president traveled from Athens to Tunis to Toulon, and finally by train to Paris. Thus we had some rare free time. A member of the French police took us under his wing and gave us the "locals" tour of the city. He took us down to Les Halles — which was an open-air farmers' market where all the farmers came into the city at three o'clock in the morning to set up and sell their produce. There was one vendor who sold homemade onion soup that was piping hot, layered with thick slices of baguette, and mounds of Gruyère cheese that crusted over the top. We would go down to Les Halles around 4:30 or 5:00 in the morning, and have the soup for breakfast. The mere thought of it made my mouth water with anticipation.

"Sounds great," I replied to SAIC Behn. "When do we leave?"

"The trip is scheduled for the end of May, so you and Tish will go the week before. The president and Mrs. Kennedy will spend three days in Paris, followed by a trip to Vienna, where he's going to meet with Premier Khrushchev. After that, they're going to London for a few days. The president will return to Washington, but Mrs. Kennedy is going to Athens with her sister, Lee, and Lee's husband, Prince Radziwill."

Mrs. Kennedy's younger sister Lee had married Stanislaus "Stash" Radziwill, who was a Polish prince. I had never met him before. It sounded like an ambitious trip, to say the least.

Behn continued, "I'm going to need you to go directly from Paris to Athens to do the advance for Mrs. Kennedy."

"Yes, sir," I answered. I remained cool on the outside, but inside I was already getting excited about the trip. Going to Europe as an agent on the First Lady's Detail wasn't something I had anticipated — especially just a few months into a new administration.

"I'm going to have Ken Giannoules do the advance with you."

Giannoules was a Special Agent on President Kennedy's detail. I had worked with him a few times when the president was in Middleburg, and we got along.

"He'll be in Paris with the president," Behn said, "so the two of you can fly directly to Athens from there. He's fluent in Greek and apparently has relatives still living in Athens, so he should be a big help."

"Yes, sir," I said. "We'll take care of it."

"Okay. Thanks, Clint. Stay loose."

Stay loose. That was one of Jerry Behn's favorite expressions and it sure was descriptive of the attitude you had to have as a Secret Service agent. Don't be too rigid. Expect the unexpected and be ready to adjust to the situation. You never know what's around the corner.

Just a few weeks later, I was headed to Paris with Tish Baldridge and a couple of agents from the President's Detail to conduct the complex advance for President Kennedy's first trip to Europe since taking office. There were a million details to work out, and we had just one week to have all the logistics solidified before President and Mrs. Kennedy arrived.

Ever since this trip to Paris and Vienna had been announced, anybody that had ever been associated with the White House was vying for a place on Air Force One or the press plane. It was not just President and Mrs. Kennedy's arrangements that needed to be worked out, but hotel and transportation for the dozens of accompanying staff that included Provi, National Security Advisor McGeorge Bundy, and everybody in between. I worked with Tish and conferred with members of the U.S. Embassy, but mostly dealt with government officials, especially the Sureté Nationale — France's national police force.

The biggest problem I had was that I could not speak the language. When Tish and I were in meetings together, she would carry on in fluent French while I sat there and tried to pick up the gist of what was being said from hand gestures and various common words. In most cases, I wouldn't find out until after the meeting was over what had actually been agreed upon. Fortunately, when I dealt with the law enforcement officials, the U.S. Embassy provided an interpreter. There were times when I felt at an extreme disadvantage, but I had no choice other than to rely on the people who could translate for me.

The Sureté Nationale was extremely competent, but they were very set in their ways. The French slang for their own presidential bodyguards was "gorillas" and I was fearful that their intense and smothering approach to personal protection would completely overwhelm Mrs. Kennedy. Over the previous six months, with all the time we had spent together, I had learned that the best way to deal with Mrs. Kennedy was to give her as much space as possible, so that she almost forgot you were there. Sometimes Agent Jeffries would hover a bit too close, and it had become evident to me that she wasn't nearly as comfortable with his style as she was with mine. The last thing I wanted was for something to happen on this trip that would hinder the trust she had in me. I explained to them her shy nature and desire for as much freedom as possible. They seemed to understand and I could only trust that the interpreter was being accurate when he translated, "Yes, Mr. Hill, we will do as you suggest." They could just as easily have been saying, "Hell no, you can shove it up your ass" and I wouldn't have known the difference.

The details and logistics were endless, so there was little time for anything other than work. I never did get a chance to get back to Les Halles for that French onion soup, but finally, with all the minor details worked out, and everyone satisfied with the plan that had been laid out, we were ready for President and Mrs. Kennedy's arrival on May 31, 1961. The biggest concern was on the diplomatic side. President de Gaulle had a reputation of being distant and arrogant with foreign leaders, and it was feared that he would be tough on President Kennedy, largely because the new American president was so much younger, and had limited political experience. I was glad I didn't have to worry about that — I just had to make sure nothing happened to Mrs. Kennedy.

There was a chill to the air, but the sun was shining when President and Mrs. Kennedy arrived at Orly Airport promptly at 10:30 A.M. Thousands of enthusiastic spectators stood behind the fence line waving American flags as President and Mrs. Kennedy descended the stairs of Air Force One to full military honors. A police motorcycle escort that numbered at least one hundred strong led the motorcade through the streets of Paris. Waiting at the Place des Pyramides were a hundred Republican Horse Guards in full regalia to replace the motorcycles and lead the procession the rest of the way to the Quai D'Orsay, where President and Mrs. Kennedy would be staying in the royal suite. It was a sight to behold. The French put on an incredible spectacle that rivaled any state visit I had seen. But nobody loved it more than Mrs. Kennedy.

More than two hundred thousand Parisians lined the streets, most of them waving little American flags. There were people hanging out of windows and packed on balconies, eager to catch a glimpse and snap a photo of the handsome American president and his glamorous wife. All along the route people held up welcoming signs and cheered, "Vive le président Kennedy!" But more frequently you would hear the voices in the crowd yelling, "Vive Jac-qui! Vive Jacqui!" She waved graciously, smiling the entire way, and the French fell madly in love with her.

After a formal luncheon and a visit to a child care center, Mrs. Kennedy returned to the Quai d'Orsay so that she could have a rest and prepare for the state dinner at the Élysée Palace a few hours later. She was tired, but elated.

"Oh, Mr. Hill, wasn't it magnificent? All the horses and the pageantry! Can you believe they have done this just for us?"

Mrs. Kennedy wasn't someone who sought the limelight, but the fact that the French had welcomed her with such enthusiasm clearly meant a lot to her.

Meanwhile, President Kennedy and President de Gaulle rode down the Champs-Élysées in another grand motorcade, to the Arc de Triomphe. The blue skies that had greeted the Kennedys in the morning, suddenly turned gray and in the pouring rain, President Kennedy laid a large wreath at the Tomb of the Unknown Soldier, in front of the eternal flame.

This trip to France was like a homecoming for Mrs. Kennedy. She had studied in Grenoble and at the Sorbonne in Paris, and had lived with a French family, which enabled her to immerse herself not only in the language but the culture as well. I watched in awe as she spoke comfortably in French to President and Madame de Gaulle, as well as everyone else with whom she came in contact. I had known, of course, that she spoke fluent French, but to watch her in action only increased the respect and admiration I had begun to have for her.

In the past, first ladies were seen, but seldom if ever heard. With the exception of Eleanor Roosevelt, most had not contributed a great deal except for their visual appearance at the necessary functions. Mrs. Kennedy seemed to realize on this trip to Paris that perhaps her growing celebrity status could be used for a great deal of good.

She went to an *école de puériculture,* a child care and training center, visiting the children and raising awareness about problems associated with the health and well-being of children throughout the world. She accompanied the president to the Hôtel de Ville — Paris's City Hall — and helped translate as her husband met with French officials. She met with female members of the press corps. Agent Jeffries accompanied Mrs. Kennedy to all of these events, while it was my job, as the advance man, to be at every venue ahead of time, making sure everything was secure and ready for her arrival. Everything went like clockwork, and it was satisfying for me to see how much Mrs. Kennedy was enjoying the trip.

She would see me standing in a doorway as she entered and even if she were in deep conversation with whomever she happened to be walking with, she would make eye contact with me. I had gotten to the point where I could read her mood by her eyes, and she was clearly having a wonderful time.

The event that captured her most was the spectacular white-tie dinner at Versailles. As is customary for Europeans, the evening event didn't begin until 8:00 P.M. I was waiting at Versailles — about a thirty minute drive outside of Paris — to be there when the President and Mrs. Kennedy arrived. As she stepped out of the limousine, I thought she looked like a queen. She had on an ivory silk overcoat that she removed as soon as she entered the palace, revealing an exquisite sleeveless floor-length dress that had been hand embroidered with pastel flowers on the bodice. She had arranged for a Parisian hairdresser to style her hair in a bouffant piled on top of her head, accented by a diamond hair clip. President de Gaulle couldn't take his eyes off of her, and I daresay neither could any of the other guests — men or women. My job was not to watch her, but to watch what was going on around her.

A long rectangular dining table had been set up in the Hall of Mirrors, set with beautiful flower arrangements and huge candelabras that provided a magical ambience as the flickering flames of the candles were multiplied by the mirrors on either side of the room. President de Gaulle sat between President Kennedy and Mrs. Kennedy, but spent the majority of the evening conversing with Mrs. Kennedy. Even from a distance I could see that he was captivated by her. Not only was she fluent in the language, but she was also well educated in French art and history. There was no doubt that Mrs. Kennedy's intelligence and charm, combined with her ability to converse in French throughout the previous two days, often acting as translator for her husband and the French president, made the notoriously difficult de Gaulle much more receptive to President Kennedy's ideas. The evening concluded with a ballet performance in the Louis XV Theater, a perfect ending to a night that encapsulated so much of what Mrs. Kennedy loved — history, the arts, intelligent and witty conversation — in an exquisite environment. At the time, I don't think Mrs. Kennedy realized the tremendous influence she had, but for those of us around her, it was impossible not to recognize. Jacqueline Bouvier Kennedy had become a star.

President Kennedy certainly noticed. At a

Mrs. Kennedy and Charles DeGaulle at Versailles

luncheon in which he spoke to four hundred journalists, President Kennedy began his short speech with: "I do not think it altogether inappropriate to introduce myself. I am the man who accompanied Jacqueline Kennedy to Paris. And I have enjoyed it." The crowd roared with laughter. It was typical of JFK — to point out the obvious, and find the humor in it. He would use that line again, two and a half years later, when Mrs. Kennedy accompanied him to Texas.

On June 2, as President and Mrs. Kennedy were saying their good-byes at Orly Airport, preparing to board Air Force One for the flight from Paris to Vienna, Mrs. Kennedy reached out her hands to me and said, "Oh, Mr. Hill, it was all just magical. I couldn't have imagined anything better. Thank you so much for making everything go so smoothly."

"You're very welcome, Mrs. Kennedy," I said. "I'm glad you enjoyed yourself."

"I guess I'll see you in Athens, then?" she asked.

"I'm on my way this afternoon," I replied. "I'll see you there in a few days."

What Mrs. Kennedy didn't know was that the president had made an unusual request of me regarding her trip to Greece.

Shortly before I left for Paris, I got word that President Kennedy wanted to see me in the Oval Office. I couldn't imagine what this was about. I had never been summoned to the Oval Office before.

When I walked in, President Kennedy was standing there, with his brother Bobby, the attorney general.

"Clint," the president said, "I understand you will be doing the advance for Mrs. Kennedy in Greece."

"Yes, Mr. President, that's what I have been advised."

The president glanced at the attorney general and looked back at me.

"The attorney general and I want to make one thing clear . . . and that is, whatever you do in Greece, do not let Mrs. Kennedy cross paths with Aristotle Onassis."

I had heard the name Onassis before, but I honestly didn't understand the significance, or why the president would be telling me this.

"Yes, sir, Mr. President," I answered.

"Okay then," he said. "Have a great trip." And with that, I walked out of the Oval Office.

The Paris trip really had gone off marvelously, but as I watched the presidential plane take off for Vienna, all I could think about was what President Kennedy had said to me in the Oval Office.

Whatever you do, do not let Mrs. Kennedy cross paths with Aristotle Onassis.

6
TRAVELING WITH MRS. KENNEDY: GREECE

Clint Hill (in sunglasses) with Mrs. Kennedy and Mrs. Karamanlis at the Parthenon

It was cold and blustery, with slashing rain, when Air Force One touched down at Schwechat airport, outside Vienna. Despite the dismal weather, thousands of people stood huddled in their rain slickers under umbrellas all along the motorcade route just to see President and Mrs. Kennedy drive by on their way to the Hofburg Palace, where the president would pay his respects to the president of Austria, prior to his meeting with Khrushchev.

Meanwhile, Special Agent Ken Giannoules and I were seated aboard an Olympic Airlines Comet Jet aircraft, headed for Athens. I was dying to talk to Ken about what President Kennedy had said to me regarding Aristotle Onassis, and to find out if Ken might know the reasons behind the president's instructions, but we had to be careful about what we discussed in public. You never knew who might overhear. I'd have to wait until he and I were alone to get the information.

Ken Giannoules was twenty-five years old, unmarried, had jet-black hair and an olive complexion, and judging from the way the stewardess was fawning over him, I guess it would be safe to say women found him attractive. We kept the conversation to small talk, and inquired about each other's backgrounds. I liked Ken and could tell we would work well together. He seemed to have a strong work ethic and a great sense of humor, and the fact that he could speak Greek would be immensely helpful on the advance.

When we landed at Ellinikon International Airport in Athens a representative from the U.S. Embassy was there to pick us up and drive us to our hotel near the embassy. It was much warmer in Athens than it had been in Paris, and the sky was a brilliant cloudless blue. As we drove through the busy streets of Athens, I thought about what Mrs. Kennedy would think when she arrived. Compared to the order and elegance of Paris, Athens was like the unruly, sometimes chaotic, unpredictable cousin that tempted you with adventure. I didn't know Mrs. Kennedy well enough yet to know how she would react to this environment in which she didn't speak the language. She had been so comfortable in France, and I wanted to make sure her eight-day visit to Greece was just as memorable. Prior to my departure to Paris, Mrs. Kennedy had told me some of the things she wanted to do while in Greece — go to an outdoor Greek theater and watch a play, visit some of the islands, and of course see the ancient ruins in Athens.

This would be Mrs. Kennedy's first foreign trip without her husband, and I was responsible for her protection. Even though she was being hosted by the prime minister, the visit was considered unofficial, and there would be no elaborate arrival and departure ceremonies. But, having just witnessed in Paris the intense outpouring of interest and affection for Mrs. Kennedy, and the large crowds that appeared wherever she went, I had to assume the same thing would happen in Greece.

The driver turned onto a side street that had a row of shops selling produce, meat, and seafood. People were walking everywhere with their shopping bags, purchasing fresh food for the evening meal. Outside one vendor, a row of pig heads hung from hooks, their eyes staring at the passersby.

"Oh God, Ken," I said, pointing to the heads. "That is one thing Mrs. Kennedy will not want to see," I said. "She is such an animal lover. I'm afraid that would sicken her."

Ken laughed and said, "It's not too appealing to me, either. Kind of reminds me of the meat markets on the south side of Chicago."

"Reminds me of Seoul, Korea," I said. "God, that was a mess." I shook my head as the memories flooded back. "I was there with Eisenhower in 1960 and you could not believe the crowds. Since he played a key role in ending the Korean War, the Koreans revered him as a hero."

I knew that Ken was new to the White House Detail and while he had just witnessed the huge crowds around President Kennedy in Paris, he hadn't yet experienced how a peaceful and enthusiastic gathering can turn to chaos in an instant.

"We got there and I swear, every damn person in the city of Seoul was in the streets trying to get a view of Eisenhower as he rode by in the motorcade. It was crazy — seemed like there were millions of them crawling all over each other. We had taken an official car to a palace prior to the president's arrival, but he never got there. We ended up having to change his schedule because massive crowds had blocked the streets, and when we came out — I am telling you the God's honest truth — that car had been crushed flat by people climbing over it to get a better vantage point."

"Geez," Ken said.

"I'll never forget that. That's when I learned how unpredictable a crowd can be. After seeing how the French reacted to Mrs. Kennedy, I assume there will be a similar response here. We have to make damn sure the Greek authorities are prepared to manage their people."

"I understand," Ken said, nodding in agreement.

"I know Mrs. Kennedy wants to be able to wander freely, to get a feel for Greece and the people here," I added, "but we have to create as safe an environment as possible for her to do that. And, I gotta tell you, Ken . . . I'm counting on you because this language is Greek to me."

Ken laughed at my feeble joke, but at least I felt like I'd gotten the point across to him. Protecting a public figure is a constant struggle because safety and exposure are conflicting goals. Even though Mrs. Kennedy didn't seek out the public, people were going to find her and try to get as close as possible. You never knew when someone might attempt to harm her and we had to make sure nothing happened.

The driver delivered us to our hotel, and as soon as Ken and I checked in at the reception desk, I said, "Ken, let's meet in my room in about fifteen minutes. There's something I need to discuss with you before we head over to the embassy."

"Sounds like a plan, Clint. See you in fifteen."

As soon as I got into the room, I put the suitcase on the bed and began to unpack. Suits and shirts hung up in the small closet. Underwear and socks in the drawers. Toothbrush and shaving kit went in the bathroom.

I liked to make sure everything was in its place.

I took my two-and-a-half-inch Detective Special handgun out of my briefcase, where I had stored it for the flight, and placed it firmly into the holster on my hip. Carrying the gun had become so much a part of me that when I was without it, I felt like something was missing. I had never pulled the gun on duty, but I, like all agents, was required to practice shooting at least twice a month at the underground Treasury range. We were required to be proficient with the weapon we carried and I had qualified as an expert marksman.

Just then there was a knock on the door.

I looked through the eyehole in the door to make sure it was Ken, before opening the door.

"How's your room?" I asked.

"Great," Ken said. "I see you've got a nice view of the Acropolis, too."

"Yeah, not bad," I said as I looked at the window. It was a magnificent sight.

"What's up, Clint?" he asked.

"Listen, Ken, before I left for Paris, the president called me into the Oval Office."

Ken raised his eyebrows in surprise.

"Yes, exactly," I said. "Not an everyday occurrence. The attorney general was there, too. So the president said, 'Clint, when you're in Greece, whatever you do, do not let Mrs. Kennedy cross paths with Aristotle Onassis.' "

Ken's eyebrows rose even farther. "Really? That's interesting. What's the reason?"

"I don't know. I was hoping *you* could tell *me.* All I know is that Onassis owns a shipping company. Mrs. Kennedy has never mentioned him, but believe me, the message was very clear. Keep her away from the guy."

"Well, let me see what I can find out from my contacts here," Ken said. "We should probably head over to the embassy now anyway."

"I'm ready," I said. "Let's go."

Upon arrival at the U.S. Embassy, we were introduced to Nick Damigos, a Greek national, who handled investigations and protective security matters for the embassy. Nick understood the politics related to Greek-American relations, had a great rapport with the local and federal officials, and spoke perfect English, with just the slightest hint of an accent.

"All of Greece is very excited about the arrival of Mrs. Kennedy," he said. "I am at your disposal to help in any way possible to ensure the visit is a success."

154

"That's wonderful, Nick. We sure are going to need your help."

"As you know," Nick said, "Prime Minister Karamanlis and his wife, Amalia, are the official hosts for Mrs. Kennedy's visit, but they have given up some of their responsibilities as official government hosts to one of their friends, who is a member of the parliament, Markos Nomikos. Nomikos is quite wealthy — he owns a shipping company — and has far greater resources than the prime minister. Knowing Mrs. Kennedy's desire for privacy, Nomikos has offered his villa in the seaside town of Kavouri, as well as the use of his one hundred-and-thirty-foot yacht, *Northwind,* which will allow Mrs. Kennedy to visit some of the islands."

Giannoules and I would have to check everything out, and the fact that Nomikos was involved in shipping — as was Onassis — caused me some concern, but otherwise it sounded like an ideal arrangement, both from a security standpoint and for Mrs. Kennedy to experience as much of Greece as possible.

Nick had already arranged a meeting for us with the Greek minister of the interior, who controlled the police agencies, so we headed straight to his office. After the introductions, the rest of the conversation was conducted entirely in Greek. There was a lot of laughter mixed in with serious discussions, and while I tried to remain attentive, I could not understand a single word.

Just as I had in Paris, I felt at a disadvantage because I didn't understand the language, but once we were back in the car, both Ken and Nick assured me the meeting had gone well and the minister had guaranteed the full support and cooperation of the Greek police and military agencies. You couldn't buy better publicity than having Jacqueline Kennedy visiting your country, and it was evident that all of Greece, from the prime minister at the top, to the worker cleaning the street, was going to make sure this was a successful visit.

When we were back at the hotel, Ken informed me that he had discussed Onassis with Nick Damigos, and without divulging the reasons behind his inquiry, hadn't been able to learn too much. Onassis had amassed an enormous fortune in the shipping industry, and a few years earlier had founded Olympic Airlines. He had been under investigation for some time by the Federal Bureau of Investigation and, in 1955, Onassis had been fined $7 million by the United States government for the illegal operation of U.S. war surplus ships. A criminal indictment that charged Onassis with eight counts of conspiring to defraud the United States through false statements made when buying the war surplus ships had been dropped.

We decided we'd keep our ears open for more information, but thus far, it didn't appear as if Mrs. Kennedy would have any reason or opportunity to see Aristotle Onassis, and I still didn't understand why the president was so concerned about him.

Over the next few days, as Ken Giannoules, Nick Damigos, and I worked with Greek authorities to make all the necessary preparations, Onassis became less of an issue than the language barrier. It turned out that all the official meetings were held in *catharevousa* — the formal Greek — as opposed to the everyday Greek language that had been used in the Giannoules household. At times, Ken had to rely on the body language of the Greek officials and quickly learned that an upward flick of the head meant "no" to our requests, while a roll of the head with raised eyebrows meant "but of course, you morons." As it turned out Greek was Greek to the Greek.

While we were preparing every little detail

for Mrs. Kennedy's upcoming trip to Greece, she was creating as much of a stir in Vienna as she had in Paris. The news stories contrasted her young, chic, fashionable appearance with that of the dowdy Mrs. Khrushchev, and to prove the point there was a photo of Mrs. Kennedy leaning in close to Premier Khrushchev splashed on the front page of newspapers all over the world. Taken at a formal evening event at the Schönbrunn Palace, in which Mrs. Kennedy looked as glamorous as could be in a sleek white sleeveless gown, she appeared to be whispering into Khrushchev's ear, and he had the biggest, leering, smile on his face — you could practically read what was going through his mind. By all accounts the official talks between Kennedy and Khrushchev had gone from congenial to heated, but the Soviet Premier was so taken with Mrs. Kennedy that she became the lead story.

The president and Mrs. Kennedy flew from Vienna to London to participate in the christening of Lee and Prince Radziwill's firstborn daughter, Anna Christina, and then the president returned to Washington. June 7, Mrs. Kennedy finally arrived in Greece.

Mrs. Kennedy, her sister, Lee, and Prince

Radziwill had flown by commercial jet from London to Rome, and then from Rome to Athens, where I was waiting at Ellinikon Airport to greet them upon their arrival. The weather in Athens was much warmer than it had been in Vienna, and even at six o'clock in the evening it was about 80 degrees.

"Welcome to Athens, Mrs. Kennedy," I said as she stepped out of the plane.

She looked around somewhat timidly, and then smiled and said, "Hello, Mr. Hill."

"Prime Minister and Mrs. Karamanlis are here to greet you, along with a representative from King Paul and Queen Frederika," I said. "We have a car waiting to take you and the Radziwills to the villa in Kavouri."

"That sounds wonderful," she said. "I'm looking forward to some relaxation."

When we arrived at the villa, Mrs. Kennedy was upbeat and excited. The villa had a beautiful view of the Mediterranean, and on this summer evening, the water was calm and the color of azure.

"Isn't it beautiful?" Mrs. Kennedy remarked to her sister as she looked out to the sea.

Prince Radziwill approached me, reached out his hand, and said, "I don't believe we've met. I'm Stash, Mrs. Kennedy's brother-in-law."

"I'm Special Agent Clint Hill, sir," I replied as I shook his hand. "It's a pleasure to meet you, Prince Radziwill."

"Please, call me Stash," he said with a smile. Stash Radziwill was about five foot ten, had short dark brown hair, and a well-trimmed mustache that accentuated his smile. He spoke with a slight British accent, and although he was quite distinguished, he was very informal. I liked him immediately.

I turned to Lee and said, "It's nice to see you again, Mrs. Radziwill."

She nodded and smiled.

Mrs. Kennedy walked over to me and said, "It was so nice to arrive in Athens without all the press around." She glanced at Agent Jeffries and said, "It was awful in Rome. There were photographers everywhere and all I could hear was" — she changed to a higher-pitched voice with an Italian accent — " 'Jack-ie, smile! Over here Jackie! Smile!' "

I could tell the incident bothered her, and the indication was that Jeffries hadn't done enough to protect her from the overzealous paparazzi.

"I'm sorry to hear that, Mrs. Kennedy. We've made the Greek officials aware that this is meant to be a private visit for you, and we'll do our best to keep the press at bay."

"Thank you, Mr. Hill. I do appreciate that."

I proceeded to another area of the villa to confer with Agent Jeffries about the incident, and to give Mrs. Kennedy and her guests some privacy. Jeffries explained the incident, much as Mrs. Kennedy had, without making any excuses. Mrs. Kennedy was unharmed, and that's what mattered.

I walked outside to the front of the villa, and ran into Ken Giannoules.

"Clint, you won't believe what just happened." He had a look of bewilderment on his face.

"What? Is everything okay?"

"Yes, everything's fine," Ken said. "I was standing in the doorway when Mrs. Kennedy came up to me and asked, 'Mr. Giannoules, is the lorry coming soon?' I assumed she meant the truck bringing the luggage so I said, 'Yes, Mrs. Kennedy, the luggage is on its way and will be here shortly.' "

"Did she seem upset that it was taking too long?" I asked.

Ken laughed. "No, not at all. She was just questioning. What I don't understand, and can't believe, is that she knew who I was, and she called me by name, and pronounced it perfectly. I've never met her before."

"I think I may have mentioned to her that I would be assisted on the advance in Greece by an agent named Ken Giannoules whose family came from Greece," I said. "But that was before I left for Paris. It is rather remarkable that she would remember."

That really made an impression on Ken, and from that moment on, he had a newfound respect for Mrs. Kennedy.

Agent Jeffries remained at the estate, along with another agent who stood post overnight, while Giannoules and I returned to our hotel in Athens.

We got up early the next morning and drove back to the villa. The sun was just rising, but as we got to a point where we could see the bay below Nomikos's villa, I could hardly believe my eyes.

"Oh crap," I said. "What the hell is going on?"

The *Northwind* was anchored just offshore, and surrounding it were dozens of fishing boats, small sailboats, and other small craft. The boats were filled with tourists and press, eager to snap a photograph of Mrs. Kennedy. Fortunately, the Greek navy was well aware of the situation.

The navy boats were patrolling the area,

forcing the tourist boats farther and farther away from shore. We could hear them yelling, "Not stop here! Not stop here! Mrs. Kennedy!" I was pleased that they were doing their best to deny access to the boats, but dismayed that, by announcing Mrs. Kennedy's name, they were confirming that she was indeed in the residence at the time.

At one point, one of the boats containing members of the press tried to ignore the navy's orders and the navy boat responded by ramming into the press boat. Later, members of the press complained to me about the "excessive aggressive behavior" by the Greek security forces.

I was pleased with the way the Greek navy had handled the situation and responded to the press, "Don't try to enter areas in which you are not wanted, and you won't have any more problems."

They were not so pleased with my response.

By the time Mrs. Kennedy awakened, the navy had pushed the intruding boats a mile away from shore. She and her guests were able to relax at the villa, sunbathing and swimming in privacy, before it was time to board the *Northwind.*

The 130-foot *Northwind* was a magnificent motor yacht with polished teak decks and five staterooms for its onboard guests. Ten crew members took care of the yacht and the needs of the guests. Agent Jeffries would remain aboard the yacht with Mrs. Kennedy, while Giannoules and I would travel on the mainland by car on this portion of the trip to ensure the security of the area to be visited.

The first stop was Epidaurus, on the Peloponnesus, and which had the best-preserved open-air theater in Greece, dating back to the fifth century B.C. Epidaurus was just thirty-five nautical miles from Kavouri, but by car it was close to one hundred miles, along windy, seaside roads. It was a beautiful drive, but both Giannoules and I would have much rather been on the yacht.

We arrived at the harbor to find the mayor of Epidaurus and the entire village waiting for Mrs. Kennedy's arrival. Even though Mrs. Kennedy would only be in Epidaurus for a few hours, the villagers had white-washed all the buildings and had strewn flowers throughout the streets to welcome her.

A special rehearsal of a Greek tragedy had been arranged for her and her guests. We were just a few small figures in the enormous amphitheater, which could hold more than fourteen thousand people. Mrs. Kennedy seemed awestruck as she sat on the 2,400-year-old stone bench absorbed in the play, while I sat nearby, not understanding a word that was being said.

Later, as we walked back to the yacht, Mrs. Kennedy said, "What did you think of the play, Mr. Hill?"

"Well," I laughed, "I must say I didn't understand one word, Mrs. Kennedy. Did you enjoy it?"

She laughed and said, "Oh, I loved it. I couldn't understand a word, either, but I'm familiar with the play, and just being able to see it in that ancient theater, of which I've read about since I was a girl, was just so special."

"That's what matters, then," I said. "I'm glad you enjoyed it."

Agent Jeffries and I boarded the *Northwind* with Mrs. Kennedy and the Radziwills, and we prepared to depart Epidaurus. Ken would now have some free time, while we were on the yacht with Mrs. Kennedy for the rest of the trip. Ken's grandmother had recently died, so he was able to attend her fortieth day memorial service. The Greek government was so willing to do anything to help us, that they provided Ken with a Renault convertible with royal license plates to attend the service.

We had mapped out an itinerary prior to Mrs. Kennedy's arrival, but she had her own ideas. I got the feeling that she and Jeffries were often at odds, largely due to the difference in their personalities. He was a rigid, play-by-the-rules fellow, and she was free-spirited and spontaneous.

She came to me and said, "Agent Hill, you told me that the job of the Secret Service is to allow me to do the things I want to do."

"Yes, Mrs. Kennedy, that is correct."

"Well, not everyone seems to understand that."

I knew what she was trying to tell me, yet it wasn't my place to tell a supervising agent how to do his job.

"Mrs. Kennedy," I said, "as long as you let us know what you want to do, we will make sure you are safe. If you want to change your plans, we will adjust."

"I'd like to go water-skiing."

"Then, Mrs. Kennedy, if you want to go water-skiing, you will go water-skiing."

And that is what she did. For nearly an hour, Mrs. Kennedy water-skied off the back of a small motorboat, expertly weaving back and forth across the wake on a single ski, while I sat in the back of the boat, hoping I didn't have to go in after her. Having learned how to swim by being thrown into the Missouri River at the age of six, I had never water-skied in my life, nor had I seen anyone do it up close.

The Greek navy ships managed to keep the press boats far enough away so she was able to water-ski in relative privacy, with no photos.

She had a constant smile on her face, her eyes squinting from the sun and spray, and when she finally had had enough, she simply let go of the rope and slowly sunk into the water. The Greek crew member that was driving the small craft steered the boat around quickly and pulled alongside her.

She was slightly out of breath, and dripping wet, as I helped her into the boat and handed her a dry towel.

"Thank you! That was so much fun!" she exclaimed as she wiped her face with the towel. Her eyes were sparkling with amusement as she added, "Mr. Hill, why don't you have a go?"

I laughed. "No, thank you, Mrs. Kennedy. I'd need a few lessons before I could compete with you."

She laughed and we sped around, back to the *Northwind,* where Stash and Lee had been watching from the deck. Mrs. Kennedy seemed so relaxed, and I was happy we had been able to accommodate her desires to water-ski in the Aegean Sea.

Despite Ken Giannoules's concern that his formal Greek wasn't up to par, the Greek government couldn't have been more cooperative, even going so far as closing off to tourists the tiny island of Delos, where according to Greek mythology, Apollo was born, so Mrs. Kennedy could wander the ruins in privacy. We sailed to the charming island of Poros, and on to Hydra, where enthusiastic crowds waved and church bells rang as the yacht entered the quaint harbor.

We had planned to sail from Hydra to Mykonos at 6:00 P.M., but Mrs. Kennedy and Prince and Princess Radziwill were having such a good time at a local *taverna* that they decided they wanted to stay. Jeffries and I sat at a table nearby, trying to remain as unobtrusive as possible.

A group of locals in native costume were singing folk songs and the entire restaurant was clapping and singing along, Mrs. Kennedy included. As they started to dance the *kalamatianos,* Mrs. Kennedy jumped out of her seat and joined the circle, laughing, and singing and dancing. We finally left Hydra at midnight, bound for Mykonos.

The next morning, we awoke at anchor in the picturesque harbor of Mykonos, where the turquoise sea and the cloudless azure sky framed the freshly whitewashed buildings stacked on the hillside like an exquisite painting. Mrs. Kennedy was enchanted. Finally, the yacht and the small flotilla of navy ships returned to the villa in Kavouri.

After four days on the yacht, Mrs. Kennedy was eager to see the sights for which Athens was so well-known — the Parthenon and the Acropolis. With the prime minister's wife, Mrs. Karamanlis, as her tour guide, Mrs. Kennedy walked up the rugged rocks and steps that led to the Parthenon, the classic Greek temple that was built in honor of the goddess Athena. As the late afternoon sun cast a warm glow on the Doric columns, Mrs. Kennedy smiled graciously for the tourists and press who snapped photographs constantly during her hourlong visit. I followed closely behind her, barely noticing the historic ruins as I scanned the swarm of people, looking for anybody or anything unusual. When somebody would get just a bit too close, I'd reach out my arm as a barrier, ready to push someone if needed, but fortunately, the people were friendly and we had no problems at all.

"I hope these sights are retained forever," Mrs. Kennedy remarked to Mrs. Karamanlis. I could tell that she was sincerely impressed, and despite the curious onlookers, she had truly enjoyed herself.

On Tuesday, June 13, Mrs. Kennedy and Prince and Princess Radziwill went to the Tatoi Palace for a private luncheon hosted by King Paul and Queen Frederika. The ten-thousand-acre royal summer residence was located just outside of Athens. After an exchange of gifts, we were preparing to leave the estate when Prince Constantine, the twenty-one-year-old heir to the Greek throne, drove up in his brand-new, dark blue convertible Mercedes sports car.

"Would you like to go for a ride, Mrs. Kennedy?" he asked.

"I'd love to!" she said. She glanced quickly at me, and without saying anything, hopped into the car, and the prince sped off.

Oh God.

Ken Giannoules had rejoined us for the mainland security portion of the trip and was waiting near the follow-up car. "Get in the car," I said calmly to Giannoules, as I strode to the car. Nick Damigos was already in the driver's seat with the engine running, so I jumped in the passenger seat, while Giannoules climbed into the back.

The king's military aide, a colonel, had been standing nearby, and shouted, "I'm coming with you!"

170

The colonel jumped in the back and Nick stomped on the gas.

"Whatever you do, don't lose him," I said. The prince was driving so fast that we had already lost sight of the blue convertible, but we finally caught up just as he was turning onto the main road outside the palace.

I could see Mrs. Kennedy laughing as the car turned and the prince once again put it into high gear.

We had no idea where the prince was taking her, so we simply followed the racing blue car around the curving roads toward the port of Piraeus. Fortunately, Nick Damigos knew these roads well and was able to keep up with the prince and Mrs. Kennedy, so they were never out of our sight.

After stopping at the Royal Yacht Club to show her his sailboat, in which he had won a gold medal in the 1960 Olympics, Prince Constantine drove Mrs. Kennedy back to Nomikos's villa at Kavouri.

We pulled up behind the convertible and Mrs. Kennedy had an enormous grin on her face. She knew she had put us to the test, and she loved it.

The colonel, however, was furious. He stormed over to Prince Constantine and bawled him out. I couldn't understand the

Mrs. Kennedy and Prince Constantine of Greece

exact words in Greek, but there was no mistaking the message he was sending to the young man. Sheepishly, the prince got out of the car and said good-bye to Mrs. Kennedy as the colonel got into the passenger seat of the sports car, the veins in his neck still bulging. I felt sorry for the poor kid and was quite sure his ride back to the palace wouldn't be nearly as much fun.

I knew it wouldn't be the last time she tried something like this. She despised schedules and loved to live spontaneously. For the agents who protected her, it was our job to react to whatever situation developed.

On June 15, we all boarded a commercial flight back to Washington and as the wheels went up, I finally breathed a sigh of relief. We had managed to keep the press at bay, the gawkers were kept under control, and I would be able to report to the president that Mrs. Kennedy had not crossed paths with Aristotle Onassis. Not yet, at any rate.

7
A SUMMER IN HYANNIS PORT

President and Mrs. Kennedy leave church in Hyannis Port, escorted by Clint Hill (right)

In the seven months since I had been assigned to Mrs. Kennedy, I had spent eighty percent of the time away from Washington, D.C., and from my family. Palm Beach, Middleburg, Paris, Greece. Now I had to tell my wife, who was pregnant with our second child, that I would be gone all summer, with Mrs. Kennedy, in Hyannis Port. This did not go over well.

I had come to realize that the Kennedy family had a regular routine when it came to holidays. Christmas, New Year's, and Easter were always in Palm Beach; May 29, the president's birthday, was usually celebrated in Hyannis Port, marking the beginning of the summer; Labor Day weekend was often spent at Hammersmith Farm in Newport, Rhode Island, the home of Jacqueline Kennedy's mother and stepfather; then, Thanksgiving it was back to Hyannis Port.

The summer months were all about Hyannis Port. For the extended Kennedy family, this was home, and this was where all the activity took place. And boy was there activity. Rose and Joe, their children, and God knows how many grandchildren — the number was always rising — were gathered together, and there was always something going on. Touch football, waterskiing, swimming, tennis, golf, sailing. I had never seen such a close family, or a family with so much energy and competitiveness. Their laughter and cohesiveness was contagious, and there I was, right in the middle of it all.

Hyannis Port is a sleepy village on the south side of Cape Cod, about seventy miles from Boston. President Kennedy's father owned a large, rambling, white shingled house that was the centerpiece for the family's gatherings. Located at the very end of Marchant Avenue, overlooking the entrance to Lewis Bay off Nantucket Sound, the home was three stories, plus a lower basement level that opened to the expansive lawn leading down to the beach. A covered porch wrapped around the house from the front door to the ocean side of the house, providing an outdoor living area with a great view of the frequent family football games, sailing, and beach activities. There was a circular driveway with a tall flagpole in the middle, where the American flag was proudly displayed, constantly flapping with the ocean breeze. When the president was in residence, the presidential flag was also raised. Alongside the driveway was a large, flat piece of lawn that was ideal for landing the presidential helicopter.

Just behind the main house was a smaller — yet still quite large — Cape Cod–style gray shaker home that belonged to Bobby Kennedy, his wife, Ethel, and their seven children. Backing up to Bobby's house was the president and Mrs. Kennedy's house —

Ambassador Kennedy residence, Hyannis Port

smaller, yet in the same style as Bobby's house. Next door to JFK's house was the Shriver home, which belonged to the president's sister, Eunice Kennedy Shriver, her husband, Sargent "Sarge" Shriver, and their

177

three children. The four houses all backed up to each other, and the kids of all the families were constantly running from one house to another. Jointly the properties became known as the "Kennedy Compound."

My first visit to Hyannis Port was on June 30, 1961, which was Mrs. Kennedy's first trip there since becoming first lady. The agents had been notified that Hyannis Port would be designated as the "Summer White House" because President Kennedy planned to spend nearly every weekend there during the summer months. Like the residences in Palm Beach and Middleburg, the Secret Service had to set up semipermanent security for the frequent comings and goings of the president and his family, and the agents had to find accommodation that fit our budgets.

The press set up headquarters at the Yachtsman Motor Inn and someone found a group of small cottages nearby that the agents got together and rented for the summer. We shared expenses and chores — it was kind of like summer camp with shared bathrooms and bedrooms. We had to make do on our twelve-dollar per diem, so we all chipped in on food and other necessary items to make our money go as far as possible. Having grown up during wartime, we all had similar values and strived to live within our means. Fortunately, a couple of the agents were good cooks and would make home-style meals, leaving leftovers in the fridge for the on-duty agents. We all worked as a team, whether on duty or off.

The First Lady's Detail was provided two cars — a Lincoln convertible and a Mercury station wagon — so as one of the two agents assigned to Mrs. Kennedy I had the luxury of an automobile at my disposal most of the time. One car would be used to transport Mrs. Kennedy and the other was used as a security car or transportation for advance assignments in the area. The agent going to the compound early in the morning would take the car to be used by Mrs. Kennedy so that vehicle was available throughout the day, while the other car was shared getting agents to and from the compound and other necessary errands and assignments.

We set up the Secret Service Command Post in a little guest cottage between Bobby's and the president's house. I'll never forget that first Fourth of July weekend, when President Kennedy brought the agents several cartons of clam chowder from Mildred's Chowder House. I had never had clam chowder before — there wasn't a whole lot of seafood in North Dakota — but from the first taste, I realized why the president loved it. The creamy soup was loaded with fresh clams with a hint of bacon and potato chunks, and on a cold, damp afternoon, nothing tasted better. From that point on, Mildred's chowder became a dietary staple for the Secret Service agents in Hyannis Port.

After the Fourth of July holiday weekend, the activity for the rest of the summer was fairly predictable. From noon Mondays to noon Fridays, the president would be in Washington, while Mrs. Kennedy, John, and Caroline stayed in Hyannis Port. Mrs. Kennedy would spend part of each day doing some kind of physical activity — usually playing tennis or waterskiing. Much of the rest of the time, she'd be in her house on the phone with her staff arranging future White House events, or following up on fund-raising and specific antiques for the White House renovation project she had initiated.

Mrs. Kennedy had the company of her sisters-in-law at Hyannis Port, and while she was closest to Jean Kennedy Smith, her husband's youngest sister, she got along well with all the Kennedy women. There was a beautiful, well-maintained tennis court behind Ambassador Kennedy's house, where I spent many hours watching the Kennedy women compete. Mrs. Kennedy most frequently played singles with Jean, but often there would be doubles matches with Eunice and Ethel, Bobby's wife. The Kennedy sisters were fiercely competitive, but Ethel beat them all in terms of her desire to win. The competitive nature of the family seemed to annoy Mrs. Kennedy at times, but she did her best to hide it. She was much more relaxed and happy while playing for fun or exercise. She was not a blood-and-guts player hoping to leave her competition completely annihilated on the courts, as some of the ladies were. She loved the give-and-take of long volleys and the way strenuous exercise gets your heart pumping and your blood flowing.

On the water, Mrs. Kennedy was a daring water-skier and excellent swimmer. Jim Bartlett, a U.S. Navy enlisted man, took care of the boats the Navy provided for us to use in water sports. We used jetboats as security patrol units and Jim drove one of them as the tow for Mrs. Kennedy's water-skiing adventures, while I'd ride in the back, ready to jump in should she require assistance. Truth be told she was a far better swimmer than me. In those days, water-skiers didn't wear life jackets, and at the time, I had had no in-water lifesaving training. It wasn't until partway through the Kennedy administration that someone realized, with all the time the first family spent in the water, the agents protecting them should probably be capable of saving someone if they were drowning. Fortunately, the Kennedys all seemed to be born with gills, and we never had any incidents that caused concern.

Mrs. Kennedy loved to slalom water-ski and was always seeking a partner to ski in tandem. One day we were out in the boat on a beautiful sunny day, when the waters were fairly calm. We were in the back of the boat — both of us in our bathing suits — when she turned to me with a glint in her eyes and said, "Mr. Hill, why don't you ski with me? It would be a lot of fun."

I had never been on water skis in my life and when I had seen her water-ski in Greece, it was the first time I'd ever seen this sport in person.

"Mrs. Kennedy, I hate to tell you, but I have never water-skied before."

She looked at me incredulously. "Oh my goodness, I thought everyone water-skied."

She was dead serious. I laughed and said, "There wasn't a lot of water for such activities where I grew up, but after watching you, I really would like to learn."

At the helm, Jim Bartlett was snickering, trying to pretend not to listen to our conversation. Mrs. Kennedy turned to him and said, "Mr. Bartlett will help you learn, won't you Mr. Bartlett?"

Grinning, Jim said, "Well, I'm not sure that Clint is teachable, Mrs. Kennedy, but I'll certainly give it a try."

With that I became the student and Jim Bartlett became the instructor. After I was off duty for the day, Jim and I practiced and practiced. My first attempts were disastrous. Mrs. Kennedy made it look so easy, I had thought for sure I'd pop right up out of the water just as she did. When Jim put the boat in gear, however, instead of being pulled upright, I fell forward and ended up holding on to the rope for dear life, being dragged on my stomach, as the salt water hit my face like a fire hose. My feet came out of the skis, and when I finally let go of the rope, it was all I could do to tread water before Jim came around to pick me up. I wasn't about to give up so I tried it again and again, but still I was unable to get up on the water and glide along like I'd seen Mrs. Kennedy do — and she did it on one ski. It was humiliating. Fortunately, Mrs.

Kennedy was not a witness to my learning experience.

Jim had been patient for a long while, starting the boat, then stopping and coming back around when I let go of the rope and slapped down in the water, my arms flailing as I tried to remain afloat, with the skis feeling like awkward, heavy appendages. Finally, his frustration started to show.

"Clint, damn it! Keep the tips of the skis above the waterline when you start, or you're going straight to the bottom."

Somehow, something finally clicked. It was a great moment when I finally got the gist of it, popped up out of the water, with my two skis gliding along behind the jet boat.

"Way to go, Clint!" Jim yelled from the boat.

"Yee ha!" I yelled as I edged in my skis and cut across the wake, the speed picking up dramatically as Jim turned the boat. I loved the feel of the wind on my face, the adrenaline pumping through my body as we sped around the cove. It was thrilling. I couldn't stop smiling. Now I understood why Mrs. Kennedy enjoyed it so much. It was just plain fun.

The next time we went out, I attempted to ski on one ski. I assumed that since I'd mastered two skis, getting up on one would be no problem. Wrong again. Poor Jim Bartlett. He was so patient with me, working overtime trying to teach a Secret Service agent to water-ski. I finally managed to get up on one ski and was able to hold my own.

I tandem skied with Mrs. Kennedy several times, but I was no match for her. I fell far more frequently than she did and I finally told her that, as the person responsible for her protection, I was probably better off staying in the boat. I sure as hell didn't want to get in a situation where she had to come rescue me.

Every so often Ethel would come and ski with Mrs. Kennedy, and on one occasion the astronaut John Glenn skied in tandem with her, as the president — and the press — watched with delight. But usually, when we were water-skiing in Hyannis Port, it was just Jim, Mrs. Kennedy, and me.

During the weekdays when the president was in Washington, Mrs. Kennedy spent a considerable amount of time with Ambassador Kennedy, the president's father, who was then seventy-two years old. Joseph P. Kennedy had been the U.S. ambassador to Great Britain during Franklin Delano Roosevelt's administration, and while he no longer served in that capacity, as is custom-

185

ary, he was still referred to as "Ambassador." He was a jovial man, with a great smile, and while he had plenty of enemies, he and Jacqueline Kennedy had a tremendous fondness for each other, a special relationship of mutual respect and admiration. They would spend hours sitting on the big porch of the ambassador's residence talking and laughing, just the two of them.

On noon Friday, the whole routine changed. For the next forty-eight hours, activity on the compound was at its maximum. Almost like clockwork, President Kennedy would arrive at Otis Air Force Base on Air Force One. From there he would transfer to an Army or Marine helicopter — military green with a white top denoting it was a presidential chopper — and fly to Hyannis Port, landing in the front yard of Ambassador Kennedy's residence.

The helicopter arrival was a huge event for the children. What a thrill to have a helicopter land at Grandpa's house! They also knew what would happen next. The kids would all come running when they heard the distinctive sound of the rotors getting louder and louder overhead. We would have a golf cart waiting in the driveway. As soon as the chopper touched down, the door would open and the president

would bound down the steps. Caroline
would be first in line, followed by all her
cousins, running to meet him. President
Kennedy would be laughing, a look of sheer
joy on his face, as if the sight of the children
and his beloved Hyannis Port made all the
worries of his office disappear for one brief
moment. He would stride straight to the
golf cart, hop behind the wheel, and yell,
"Anyone for ice cream?"

"Yay! Ice cream!" the kids would yell, as
they piled onto the golf cart around him.
There might be ten or twelve piled onto that
cart, sitting, standing, hanging off the sides.
The president would take off down the
driveway, a huge grin on his face, and cut
across the lawn behind Bobby's house,
toward his house, in an effort to lose the

Secret Service follow-up car. He'd end up in the driveway of his own house, which fed onto Irving Avenue, hang a right, and then a left onto Longwood.

You could hear the kids screaming, "Go faster! Go faster!" from two blocks away.

At the corner of Longwood and Wachusett Avenue, next door to the post office, there was a tiny news store that had ice cream and candy. Everybody would pile out and order their ice-cream cones.

Saturday meant going aboard the *Marlin,* Ambassador Kennedy's personal yacht, for lunchtime cruises. The fifty-two-foot motor yacht was just large enough to accommodate the president, Mrs. Kennedy, a few guests, a small crew, and a couple of Secret Service agents. Lunch meant clam chowder or fish chowder, from a favorite family recipe made by the Kennedys' cook. The aroma drove me crazy, and the whole time I was out on the boat, I'd be hoping one of the agents had gone to Mildred's that day and there'd be some leftover chowder in the fridge at the cottage for my dinner.

We would put a security perimeter around the yacht, consisting of one or two Coast Guard boats and two Navy jetboats, all operated by military personnel under the direction of Secret Service agents on board.

President and Mrs. Kennedy on the Marlin, *Hyannis Port*

I always worked one of the speedy jetboats with Jim Bartlett at the helm ready to intercept someone when necessary or to take Mrs. Kennedy water-skiing if she so desired. The press would usually have a charter boat of their own, to follow and observe the presidential party. We kept them outside the security perimeter, much to their dismay.

Just prior to that first trip to Hyannis Port, shortly after Mrs. Kennedy and I returned from Greece, Mrs. Kennedy was taking her usual morning walk on the oval driveway on the White House south grounds. As always, I was in close enough proximity in case anything were to happen, yet trying to be as unobtrusive as possible. She had been walking in silence, as she often did, her pace brisk, her head held high and her posture erect. When she was silent like this, I knew she had something on her mind that she was trying to sort out. Suddenly she stopped and turned to me with a look of excitement in her eyes, like she'd just come up with a brilliant idea.

"Mr. Hill?" she asked. "Do you know if there has ever been a state dinner held away from the White House?"

The question took me by surprise. I could practically see the wheels spinning inside her head.

"I don't know for sure, Mrs. Kennedy. Why do you ask?"

"Say we were to have a state dinner somewhere like Mount Vernon — would that be an issue for the Secret Service?"

"I don't see that it would be a problem from our perspective. It would require some advance planning, but we would do everything we could to secure the area and make the location as safe as having a function on the White House grounds."

"Oh good," she said, with excitement in

her voice. "The dinner that President de Gaulle held for us at Versailles was so magical, I have been trying to think where we could do something just as special. I think George Washington's home would be perfect."

With that, she resumed her exercise pace, and spoke not another word about it.

I had no idea as to exactly what she had in mind, or when or for whom she had this dinner planned. However, just like when she had told me about Middleburg, I alerted Jerry Behn's office about the conversation, and added, "Knowing Mrs. Kennedy as I do, unless the president vetoes the idea, there is going to be a state dinner at Mount Vernon sometime in the not too distant future."

Thus it was not a surprise to the Secret Service when the announcement was made that an official state dinner was going to be held on July 11, 1961, for the visiting president Mohammad Ayub Khan of Pakistan — not at the White House, but at Mount Vernon, the historic home of President George Washington. Situated on the banks of the Potomac a few miles south of the nation's capital, the setting was stunning. It was also a logistical nightmare.

Mrs. Kennedy's interest in history and

keen sense of pageantry was never so evident as it was, fresh on the heels of her visit to Paris and the spectacular dinner at Versailles, when she proposed and planned this elaborate state dinner — the first one ever held off White House grounds. Mrs. Kennedy saw the dinner as an opportunity to remind people of the revolutionary beginnings of the United States and how we as a people had fought to acquire freedom and independence. She wanted this occasion to be so different, so special, that it would be long remembered, and set a standard for future state dinners. From the moment she got the idea into her head, it was like she was directing a Broadway play, preparing for opening night.

The eighteenth-century estate of Mount Vernon was not equipped to accommodate such a large, elaborate event, as there was no electricity or indoor plumbing. But Mrs. Kennedy had a vision, and once she put her mind to something, there was no stopping her. From the guest list to the menu to the entertainment, she had specific ideas as to how everything should look and feel.

"We're going to have a reenactment of a Revolutionary War battle with muskets and bugle players," she informed me at one point.

Great, I thought. *A bunch of costumed actors with guns will be within shooting distance of you and the president.* I made a mental note to alert the Agent in Charge.

"And the president made a brilliant suggestion that the guests could arrive by boat. Wouldn't that be magical?" she asked me.

"Magical," I replied. "How many guests are you expecting?"

"Oh . . . probably between one hundred thirty to one hundred fifty."

One hundred and fifty people — presumably including many high-ranking government officials — cruising slowly down the Potomac. This was going to be a major undertaking for the Secret Service, not to mention a menagerie of government services.

A cast of hundreds would be required to pull it off. Mrs. Kennedy's vision for an early American historical state dinner required cooperation and coordination between various people and organizations that were not necessarily used to working together, including Tish Baldridge's staff, the office of the Military Aide to the President, the National Park Service, the State Department, the White House usher's office, the Mount Vernon Ladies' Association, the Secret Service, and René Verdon, the White

House chef.

Every day Mrs. Kennedy would come up with a new idea, sending people scurrying around to get the necessary permits. If anyone raised the possibility that something might not be able to be accomplished, Mrs. Kennedy would reply softly, in her most convincing tone, "Of course it can be done." She was in complete control of the countless details to make her production come together, and had steadfast confidence in her staff and their willingness to do whatever it took. I don't think she ever knew how several behind-the-scenes incidents nearly turned the evening into a disaster.

The guests were split up between the *Sequoia,* the *Honey Fitz,* a PT boat, and a Navy yacht. They boarded at the Washington docks and sailed down the Potomac to the Mount Vernon dock. It was decided that they would make the return trip by car, which in and of itself was confusing and logistically difficult, as there needed to be far more cars than boats. Then there was the mosquito infestation problem. There had been a lot of rain, and the mosquitoes were rampant. So, on the day of the event, the area was sprayed with mosquito repellant once in the morning, once around midday, and again one hour prior to the guests' arrival.

Chef Verdon had worked with Mrs. Kennedy to come up with a menu that could be prepared largely at the White House and then transported in military vehicles to the estate. As the food was being offloaded, he saw the repellant being sprayed and became concerned that the noxious spray would poison the food. He was terrified that the guests would become ill and he would be blamed. It was too late to prepare more food. René was beside himself. Fortunately, Tish Baldridge came up with a solution.

"Why don't we have some Secret Service agents taste the food?" Tish suggested. "If they don't become sick and die, then we know the food is fine for our guests."

René acquiesced so two agents were given the task of gorging themselves on samples of every item of food that was to be served. They started with the *George Washington Mint Julep,* then the *Avocado and Crabmeat Mimosa Salad,* moved on to the *Poulet Chasseur,* to the *Couronne de Riz Clamart,* to the *Framboises à la Crème Chantilly,* and finally the *Petits Fours Secs.* There wasn't much time, so they had to eat and drink quickly. As it turned out, the food was not tainted, but the agents felt sick simply from the mass quantity of food they had each consumed. This satisfied René that all was well and he could safety serve the president, first lady, and all the guests without danger of his reputation being damaged beyond repair.

It was a beautiful evening and by the time the guests arrived, everything was in place. Mrs. Kennedy looked regal in a white lace sleeveless Oleg Cassini dress with a wide green sash around her waist and elbow-length white gloves, as she and President Kennedy escorted President Ayub Khan and his daughter, Begum Nasir Aurangzeb.

After a tour of Washington's home, it was time for the battle reenactment. The Army's Colonial Color Guard and Fife and Drum Corps performed a military drill, and then a group of musket-carrying soldiers, wearing powdered wigs, aimed their muskets and fired. It just so happened that the sixty or so members of the press corps were right in the line of fire, and even though the guns were loaded with blanks, the noise and smoke were realistic, causing more than a few members of the press to jump at the sudden gunshots. I glanced at Mrs. Kennedy, and when I saw the smile on her face, I had little doubt that the placement of the press, directly in the line of fire, was all part of her master plan.

I stayed off to the side, always near Mrs. Kennedy, observing everything going on around her. I had noticed the table settings with several forks, spoons, and knives, of different sizes, lined up in a particular order outside the plates. Growing up in Washburn, North Dakota, I had never been to a restaurant or event that required so many different types of cutlery. As I watched Mrs. Kennedy confidently choose the appropriate utensil for each course, I took mental notes should I ever be in a situation myself that would require me to know which fork was for salad, and which spoon was for dessert.

Everybody commented on the ambience, the delicious food, and the extraordinary theater of the evening. By all accounts the dinner for President Ayub Khan was a smashing success. President Kennedy knew how much effort his wife had put into the occasion and he seemed particularly proud of her.

Mrs. Kennedy was beaming the entire evening. She was seated next to Ayub Khan, and while I couldn't hear the conversation, it was clear they were truly enjoying each other's company. She later told me that they spent much of the evening discussing a shared passion — their love of horses. Mrs. Kennedy was enthralled with Ayub Khan's

Mrs. Kennedy and Ayub Khan at Mount Vernon dinner

captivating stories of life in Pakistan — and intrigued by this part of the world that she had never visited. Naturally, Ayub Khan had offered an open invitation to President and Mrs. Kennedy to visit him in his homeland. As crazy as it sounded, I had a feeling that Mrs. Kennedy might find a way to take him up on the invitation.

8
FALL 1961

Family photo at Hammersmith Farm

During the summer of 1961, from the time we first went to Hyannis Port at the end of June, Mrs. Kennedy spent the better part of four months away from the White House. She did return on a few occasions to participate in official functions such as the Mount Vernon dinner in July, and another state dinner on September 19 for President Don Manuel Prado of Peru, but those were the only times during the summer that I was able to go home.

After a brief stay in Washington for the state dinner for President Prado, we were off to New York City on September 24, so Mrs. Kennedy could attend the president's speech to the United Nations the next day. Of course we stayed at the Carlyle — the president and Mrs. Kennedy in their luxurious apartment — with all the agents spread around the building, some of them three or four to a room due to lack of availability, and to cut down on expenses.

The day after the president's speech, we flew to Newport, Rhode Island, and on to Hammersmith Farm, the home of Mrs. Kennedy's mother and stepfather, Hugh Auchincloss. The children, John and Caroline, had been driven there earlier by their Secret Service detail.

I had been to Newport with President Eisenhower, so I was familiar with the area. Having been to Ambassador Kennedy's stately homes in both Palm Beach and Hy-

Hammersmith Farm, Newport, Rhode Island

annis Port, I expected that the Auchincloss estate would be on par with those residences. But as we drove up the long curving driveway to Hammersmith Farm for the first time, I was honestly taken aback by the grandeur of the home in which Mrs. Kennedy had spent many of her childhood years.

The home was a Victorian-style mansion that looked like something straight out of the English countryside. Weathered shingles gave it a cottage-like feel, but you could hardly call this a cottage. Twenty-eight rooms were spread out among three levels; countless brick chimneys stuck out of the

201

roof; and there was even a turret. The mansion was set on a rise in the middle of forty-eight acres — about eight times the size of the entire Kennedy compound in Hyannis Port — that overlooked Narragansett Bay. Most of the acreage was lawn, and I figured it had to take a whole staff of gardeners just to keep that grass mowed. Off to one edge of the property was a beautiful stable — plusher and much larger than the two-bedroom house in which I'd grown up in Washburn — with multiple stalls for the family's horses.

In between the stables and the main house was the tennis court. Gravel paths dissected the lawn, meandering around the property, leading from the house to the tennis court to the stables, and down to the dock, where there was a small, rocky beach. I could just imagine how it must have looked on September 12, 1953, when twelve hundred people attended the wedding reception for Jack Kennedy and Jacqueline Bouvier. It must have been spectacular.

One of the presidential yachts, the *Honey Fitz,* had been sailed to Newport prior to the president's arrival. It was berthed at the Newport Naval Station and brought to the dock at Hammersmith Farm every morning for the president's use. This ninety-two-foot

Navy yacht had been commissioned for use by the sitting president. During the Eisenhower administration, it was named the *Barbara Anne,* after one of the Eisenhower granddaughters. President Kennedy had it renamed the *Honey Fitz* after his maternal grandfather, John Frances "Honey Fitz" Fitzgerald. Taking the *Honey Fitz* out for a lunchtime cruise became a daily activity, and just like in Hyannis Port, I would always be out on one of the jetboats, securing the area around the yacht.

It was September, and the weather had turned from summer to fall, so that a light jacket or sweater was required when you were out on the water. One morning, as we were getting the boats ready to go out, Mrs. Kennedy called to the Secret Service Command Post.

"Mr. Hill, I was hoping to go out water-skiing this afternoon. Will you please make sure you have my skis on the jetboat?"

"Water-skiing? Are you sure? Do you realize how cold the water is, Mrs. Kennedy?"

"Oh, yes, that doesn't bother me," she answered. "I've got a skin-diving suit. I'll be fine."

I laughed and said, "Mrs. Kennedy, I hope you realize that the press will be dying to get a picture of you in that wet suit. You are the first wife of a president to go water-skiing. I can tell you Mamie Eisenhower and Bess Truman never went water-skiing, with or without a wet suit."

She laughed. "Well, now you know I have to go, Mr. Hill."

Sure enough she put on a black neoprene wet suit, and we pulled her around with the jetboat. The calmest waters were in Potter Cove or near Bailey's Beach, a private beach club, and you could practically see the word getting passed around as the people on the beach stood up and stared. Some members of the press had rented boats, and while we did our best to keep them away, there was not much we could do as long as they remained outside the security perimeter we would establish. Mrs. Kennedy didn't like the attention, and neither did I. I kept thinking about how cold that damn water would be if I had to jump in after her. I didn't have a skin-diving suit. Fortunately, she didn't require my assistance, and I didn't see any pictures in the newspaper the next morning.

Around this time Mrs. Kennedy also decided to take up golf. I accompanied her to the Newport Country Club, where she took some golf lessons and practiced with her longtime friend Bill Walton. As with almost any sport she tried, Mrs. Kennedy was a natural. She hit the ball long and straight, and her form was so good she reminded me of some of the female pro golfers I had observed. She was determined to do well, and you could see it in her attitude that she really wanted to improve and was going to work hard to do so.

The weather in Newport had been very pleasant with crisp temperatures, and a mixture of sun and clouds. But as is typical along the New England coast, the weather can change rapidly, and in the early evening hours of Friday, September 29, a cold, dense fog settled in, and decided to stay.

We had just returned to Hammersmith Farm from an outing when I got a call that my wife had gone into labor and had been taken to Alexandria Hospital in Alexandria, Virginia. I was taken by surprise because the baby wasn't due for at least another two weeks.

I immediately informed Mrs. Kennedy.

"Mrs. Kennedy," I said, "I just got word that my wife has gone into labor, so I'm going to need to get back to Washington as soon as possible."

"Oh, Mr. Hill," she said with a look of sincere concern, "yes, absolutely. You must get there right away. Don't worry about a thing."

Unfortunately, getting back to Washington on this particular night was going to be next to impossible. The closest commercial airport was in Warwick, but the fog was so dense that flights were grounded. The next option was the Naval Air Station at Quonset Point, which handled a variety of aircraft. They weren't flying, either. We contacted the U.S. Coast Guard and they said they could see what they could do, but they got back to me with the same report: nothing was coming in or going out. There was nothing anybody could do. I was stuck in Newport.

The next day, the weather cleared, and I was finally able to get a flight out. An agent from the White House Detail met me and we raced to the hospital, where I got to see and hold my son, Corey Jonathan, for the first time. He was a bit premature, but healthy, and I was thrilled to now be the father of two sons.

The Kennedys' hectic schedule was difficult for all the agents and their families. President Kennedy traveled far more than Eisenhower had, so the agents on his detail were often gone, too. The difference was that Mrs. Kennedy was rarely in Washington, which made my absences lengthier and more frequent. Fortunately the Secret Service wives had a good support network, and I was thankful for that. Many of us lived in the same area and had children around the same ages, so when the guys were traveling, the women stuck together.

When we returned to the White House on October 27, I presumed our time in Newport and on the Cape was pretty much finished for the year. Only Thanksgiving left. I was really looking forward to sleeping in my own bed each night for a month, and spending some time with my family. But, that wasn't to be. It was back to Hyannis Port the next weekend, and then back to Newport, before returning to Washington for a few days to entertain the visiting prime minister of India, Jawaharlal Nehru, and his daughter, Indira Gandhi. I was realizing that Mrs. Kennedy made every effort to be away from the White House as much as possible. It turned out that she no more wanted to attend ladies' luncheons and tea parties than I did. She really abhorred being in the spotlight, and having to make small talk. She would pick and choose which events were important to her, yet there were plenty of times she committed and then changed her mind. It was frustrating to Tish Baldridge, who would have to find replacement hostesses when Mrs. Kennedy told her she felt ill or had changed her plans — only to learn that we had gone off to Middleburg.

When it came to visiting heads of state, however, Mrs. Kennedy would throw herself into the planning of an event. I think the success of the dinner at Mount Vernon really boosted her confidence, and also showed her that she could think big when it came to entertaining on behalf of the White House. One of the most important and memorable events was the night Pablo Casals came to play.

"Mr. Hill, do you enjoy music?" Mrs. Kennedy asked me one day when we were up in Newport.

"I love music, Mrs. Kennedy," I replied. "In fact, one thing you probably don't know about me is that I used to sing in a quartet in college."

"Really?"

She looked like she was about to burst into laughter, as if the idea of me, the tough Secret Service agent, singing in a quartet was beyond her comprehension.

"Yes, really," I said, with a smile. "And I also played the trumpet. I wasn't bad, if I do say so myself."

She laughed and said, "I'm sorry, Mr.

Hill. I don't mean to laugh, but you are always so serious — I never thought of you as being someone who would sing and play an instrument."

"I am serious about my job, Mrs. Kennedy, that's for sure. But I can have fun every now and then, too, you know."

"I didn't mean to insinuate that you don't have fun, Mr. Hill," she said, laughing. "But now that I know you appreciate music, you'll have to make sure you're on duty for the state dinner for the governor of Puerto Rico."

I was aware that Governor Luis Muñoz Marin and his wife were being honored at a state dinner, but I couldn't figure out what this had to do with whether I enjoyed music.

"And why is that, Mrs. Kennedy?"

"We're going to have a very special after-dinner concert. Pablo Casals, who is perhaps the world's greatest cellist, has agreed to play for us. He hasn't played in the United States in thirty-three years. Isn't that exciting?"

Her subtle enthusiasm was contagious. "I'm sure it will be fantastic," I said. "I guess I better take my tuxedo to be dry-cleaned."

On November 13, 1961, I did wear my tuxedo, and while I wasn't an invited guest,

I did stand at the back of the East Room when eighty-four-year-old Pablo Casals played the cello, accompanied by pianist Mieczyslaw Horszowski and violinist Alexander Schneider, in what was the most moving concert I had ever heard.

Being able to showcase the very best talent in the world to emphasize the importance of the arts was one of Mrs. Kennedy's favorite things to do, and she was very successful at getting the most sought-after performers to come to the White House. For this spectacular evening, she and the president had invited people who truly appreciated this once-in-a-lifetime chance to hear Casals perform in the United States. The guest list included composers Leonard Bernstein; Aaron Copland; Eugene Ormandy; and Leopold Stokowski; as well as Henry Ford II; Thomas J. Watson, the founder of IBM; oil tycoon Edwin Pauley; and Alice Roosevelt Longworth, the daughter of President Theodore Roosevelt, who had been in attendance the last time Casals played at the White House in 1904. Thus it was not just Casals himself, but also the collection of guests that made the night so memorable. I was privileged to have been one of them.

Mrs. Kennedy was in her glory and as

usual, she looked ravishing. It was a white-tie event and everyone in the room was dressed in their most formal attire, but Mrs. Kennedy stood out among everyone with the way she carried herself, and the smile that lit up her face the entire evening.

There had been a lot of publicity surrounding Casals's performance at the White House, and while Mrs. Kennedy thoroughly enjoyed the event, when it was over she was eager to get out of Washington. So the next day we headed to Middleburg, for a few days at Glen Ora.

Still beaming from the success of the Casals performance, Mrs. Kennedy had a stack of newspapers she brought with her. As I drove, she sat in the front passenger seat and read some excerpts of the rave reviews to me.

"It really was a marvelous evening, Mrs. Kennedy," I said. "You should be very proud of what you've accomplished."

"Thank you, Mr. Hill," she said with a smile. "I'm so glad that you were able to enjoy the evening. I know it wasn't the same as if you had been a guest, because you were working, but I wouldn't have wanted you to miss such a special experience."

"I do appreciate that, Mrs. Kennedy. That's very thoughtful of you."

"I hope you know that I appreciate everything you do for me, Mr. Hill. You've certainly changed my view of the Secret Service."

On Friday morning, November 17, I drove Mrs. Kennedy from Glen Ora to ride with the Piedmont Hunt, while her horse Bit of Irish was transported by trailer.

It had been a long time since she'd ridden and she was excited to be back in the Virginia hunt country. Dressed in jodhpurs, a blazer, and boots, with not a stitch of makeup on, she looked even more beautiful than she had in her fancy gown at the Casals concert. This was the Mrs. Kennedy I had come to know — at ease and comfortable in her own skin, away from the public eye.

"We might have quite a long ride today," she said. "I'll be joining everyone for the hunt breakfast when we are through so I may be longer than usual."

"That's fine, Mrs. Kennedy. Just enjoy yourself and I'll catch up with you when you're ready to leave."

Behind her, the riders were assembling, as the hounds scattered around barking. I noticed the handler seemed to be having a bit of difficulty with her horse.

"Bit of Irish looks anxious to go," I added. "Be careful out there."

She glanced at the horse and said, "Oh, he can be a handful, but I'll be in control. Don't worry, Mr. Hill." Then she broke into a grin and said, "You be careful driving over all that rough terrain trying to keep up with me!"

I laughed and watched as she walked toward the rest of the riders who had gathered in the meadow.

"Good morning, Jackie!" they called. "So great to see you!"

"Good morning!" she replied. She was so relaxed in this environment. Here she was just another rider in the Hunt Club. They didn't treat her any differently than anyone else, and that is what she loved. Here she could shed the first-lady moniker and just be Jackie.

I watched as she put her foot into the stirrup and mounted the horse. Then I drove the station wagon to place myself in a position where I could observe the group as they started on their ride across the rolling hills of the Mellon property. The whips were cracking, the hounds were yelping, and I wondered how the hell they thought they could sneak up on a fox with all that racket.

The riders set out along the course for the

day and one by one they would jump over the rail fences and hedges at various points. Mrs. Kennedy loved to jump, and she was very good at it. I drove slowly along the country roads trying to keep the group in sight, but it wasn't always easy.

Things were going along well on this particular morning, when I noticed a man crouched down in the field, just ahead of the riders.

Oh crap. As I got a bit closer, I recognized the man as Marshall Hawkins, a local photographer noted for his pictures of horses and the various hunt clubs in the area. He had positioned himself near a fence the group was about to jump. The hounds were running silently, and the only sound you could hear was that of the horses' hooves hitting the ground as they galloped closer and closer. I was on the road, a good hundred yards from the fence, too far away to do anything other than yell. Yelling, though, I figured, could potentially make matters worse. I didn't think Mrs. Kennedy was in any danger, but I knew she would be furious if Hawkins managed to get a photograph of her.

I got as close as I could and stopped the car, just as the group began jumping the rail fence, one by one. Hawkins was still

crouched in the grass, not making a sound. Then, just as Mrs. Kennedy approached the fence, he suddenly stood up and started snapping away.

The sudden movement and sound of the camera caught Bit of Irish by surprise, and the horse reacted by digging in his front feet in an abrupt stop.

I watched in horror as Mrs. Kennedy went flying off, over the head of her horse, and over the rail fence, headfirst.

I jumped out of the car, and was about to leap over the property fence that bordered the road when Mrs. Kennedy got up, remounted, and rode away with the rest of the group without saying a word. She had put her arms out in front of herself to break her fall, and thank God she appeared to be all right. Now my fear for her safety turned to fury at the photographer.

I ran across the meadow, adrenaline coursing through my body.

"What the hell are you doing?" I screamed.

He hadn't realized I was watching and seemed startled to see me coming toward him in a rage.

Seconds later I was standing eye to eye with him.

"What the hell are you doing?" I repeated.

"What I always do," he answered caustically. "Taking photos of the hunts in the field."

"Damn it! You could have got Mrs. Kennedy seriously injured."

I reached for his camera and said, "Give me that goddamn film, Marshall."

"Oh no," he said as he clutched the camera to his chest. "This is mine and I'm keeping it."

Unfortunately, this was a personal issue, not a matter of national security, and I was pretty sure he knew that. I would have to bluff him into giving me the film.

"You don't want to embarrass Mrs. Kennedy, do you?" I asked. "If you use that photo of her falling, she will be humiliated. Is that what you're after?"

"I'm not giving you this film, Clint."

I tried to convince him but realized it was futile. He knew he had a valuable shot, and he wasn't falling for my efforts to get the film. I had to get back to the car and catch up with the hunt, so I just shook my head in disgust and walked away.

"Tell Mrs. Kennedy I'm sorry if I caused her to fall," he called after me. "I'll print a copy for her, if she likes."

I felt like turning around and punching him in the face, but I knew that wasn't going to solve any issues, so I broke into a jog and made my way back to the station wagon.

I drove down the road that surrounded the Mellon property and saw the hunt just as they were dismounting. Everybody was gathered around Mrs. Kennedy.

Oh God, I hope she's not hurt. I couldn't see her facial expression, but she was at least standing.

I jogged up to her just as she was taking off her helmet. With her helmet in one hand, she used the other hand to run her fingers through her hair.

"Mrs. Kennedy, are you all right?"

She turned toward me, and smiled.

"Yes, Mr. Hill, I'm fine," she said softly.

Then, concerned, she asked, "Did you talk to the photographer? Did you get the film?"

"I'm afraid he won't give it up. I'm going to see what I can do about it after I get you back to Glen Ora. I'm just glad to hear you're not hurt. That was quite a fall."

She laughed and said, "Oh it wasn't the first time I've fallen off a horse, and I'm sure it won't be the last."

Her friends laughed and somebody said, "Who wants breakfast?"

"Enjoy your breakfast, Mrs. Kennedy," I said. "I'll be standing by."

"Thank you, Mr. Hill," she said as I started to walk away. "I really am all right. But I sure would like to get that film."

Yeah, me too. I was so relieved she wasn't hurt, but I knew that I would be typing up a lengthy report on the details of what happened, and I wasn't looking forward to it.

I contacted Marshall Hawkins several more times, but his position remained the same. The last time we spoke he said, "I'll print a copy for you, too, Clint."

I knew he would be attempting to sell that photo to the highest bidder, and that is exactly what he did. Mrs. Kennedy was embarrassed when it came out in *Life* magazine, and I felt terrible that the incident had happened on my watch and I wasn't able to confiscate the film.

A few weeks later a poster-sized framed photo of Mrs. Kennedy falling off the horse arrived at the White House to my attention. I didn't know what to do with it, so I took it home and stuck it in a closet.

The press, and probably many Americans, seemed to think that President Kennedy was on a permanent vacation when he was in Hyannis Port or Newport, when in reality the responsibility of the job never leaves the occupant of the office of president. The international situation had deteriorated as the Soviets, together with the East Germans, had begun to tie a noose around West Berlin, tightening the borders and building a wall which caused great concern throughout the Western world. The United States promptly called up some 150,000 reservists to active duty. Then 40,000 regular Army troops were sent to Europe, increasing U.S. strength on the continent to 290,000. Cuba remained a major concern after the Bay of Pigs disaster earlier in the year, while the situation in Southeast Asia including Laos, Cambodia, and Vietnam was heating up and required concentrated attention. Domestically, attempted hijacking of commercial airliners necessitated the placing of armed federal personnel on board some flights as air marshals. And racial segregation had become an issue that could no longer be ignored.

Mrs. Kennedy was well aware of the tremendous responsibility and the constant and continued attention the job required. She tried very hard to make the time the president spent with family and friends as comfortable and relaxing as possible. She might invite Paul "Red" Fay and his wife, Anita, for a weekend at Middleburg or an intimate dinner at the White House. Red and JFK had been friends since the president's Navy days and they shared a similar sense of humor, along with a love of sailing. Chuck Spalding and his wife, Betty, were frequent guests. Chuck had been an usher at the Kennedys' wedding and had worked on the president's campaign.

And then there was Lem. Lemoyne "Lem" Billings and Jack Kennedy had known each other since their prep school days at Choate, and they were almost like brothers. Lem seemed to be a permanent fixture at the White House, and would often be with the president when he arrived by helicopter to

Middleburg, Hyannis Port, or Palm Beach. He was a tall, lanky guy, rather effeminate, and he just always seemed to be around. Mrs. Kennedy tolerated him, much like a somewhat annoying sibling, but Lem's antics and quick wit made the president laugh, and that was worth a lot.

On November 22, 1961, it was back to Hyannis Port for Thanksgiving with the president's parents, Rose and Ambassador Kennedy, along with as many members of the extended family as could possibly make the annual event. I wondered what the family would do in the cooler weather since so many of the summer activities revolved around the water. They were such an active, competitive family. I soon found out that Thanksgiving on the Cape meant touch football games and ice-skating at the Kennedy Memorial Skating Rink in Hyannis.

The Lieutenant Joseph Patrick Kennedy Jr. Memorial Skating Rink was built in honor of Ambassador and Rose Kennedy's oldest son, who had been killed in World War II. Most of the family would go on daily outings to the rink, skating and laughing, just enjoying being together. It was such a wonderful sight to observe, and I so wished I could join them.

Growing up in the frozen plains of North

Dakota, ice-skating had been one of my favorite after-school activities. There was a vacant dirt lot in Washburn, about half a block in length, that was flooded at the first freeze in the fall and stayed frozen until Easter, and that was our skating rink. When I wanted to be alone I would head to Painted Woods Creek, and skate for miles and miles in peaceful solitude. My mother worried about me when I'd go to the creek, though, because you had to watch out for air pockets, where the ice was thin. There had been a few kids who had drowned. I never worried about my own safety, but if I was with my sister or some friends, I wanted to be the one in the front of the pack, looking out for the soft spots ahead.

It didn't matter the outdoor temperature — 20 degrees below zero was commonplace for me — skating gave me energy and brought a smile to my face. I saw that same enjoyment on the faces of Mrs. Kennedy, the president, Caroline, and the rest of their family as they glided across the frozen surface with sheer delight.

Weather permitting, it was touch football time. Somebody — usually it was Bobby who instigated a game — would start rounding up players and picking teams. Quite often they were short a player, and Bobby or younger brother Teddy would call me at the command post.

"Clint, come on down here. We need another guy for our team."

I had played football in high school and college and I loved it. They didn't have to ask me twice.

The president rarely played, because of his back problems, but Bobby and Teddy would be out there, along with their wives, Ethel and Joanie; sisters Eunice and Jean, and their husbands Sarge Shriver and Steve Smith; and any guests who might be there and willing to participate. It was great fun, and quite competitive. Ethel especially hated to lose, and boy was she tough. God, Ethel — the thought of her out there playing still makes me chuckle. She was a ball of energy.

The rough-and-tumble nature of the Kennedy football games wasn't Mrs. Kennedy's style, so she would usually be sitting on the porch with the ambassador, watching with amusement, as we huddled and scrambled out there on the lawn. They treated me just like one of them — almost like part of the family. I thoroughly enjoyed it — not just for the sport, but also because it gave me the opportunity to occasionally throw a good hard block across certain family members. Payback time for things they had done causing me extra concern and work. Like using one of the Secret Service cars on the spur of the moment without asking permission or advising any of the agents what they were going to do. We learned never to leave keys in any of the cars even within the secured area, because if we did, you could count on Eunice or Sarge Shriver or Teddy taking off with the vehicle. It always seemed to happen just before Mrs. Kennedy or the president was about to go somewhere. They were always trying to pull pranks. Believe me, it wasn't funny at the time.

At this point, I had been on the First Lady's Detail for just over a year, and it had been nothing like I'd first envisioned. What had started out as uncertainty for both Mrs. Kennedy and me, had turned into a comfortable and enjoyable working relationship based on mutual trust and respect.

It was nearly Christmastime, and once again, we were headed to Palm Beach for the holidays.

9

ANOTHER PALM BEACH CHRISTMAS

The president and Mrs. Kennedy had realized the previous year that the Secret Service somewhat hindered the activities of the rest of the family when the president stayed at his father's house in Palm Beach, so they had made arrangements to rent the nearby home of family friends Colonel and

Mrs. C. Michael Paul for the winter of 1961–62.

"It will be so much better for us," Mrs. Kennedy told me. "It has a beautiful heated swimming pool, and eight bedrooms, so there's plenty of room for our own guests. It's not far from the ambassador's house, so it will be very convenient."

"It sounds ideal," I responded. Then, teasing, I said, "You don't think you'll get bored with the peace and quiet?"

She laughed and said, "Mr. Hill, you know as well as I do that peace and quiet when the Kennedys are all together is something that is next to impossible. But at least I'll have a place to which I can escape and spend time with Caroline and John."

John had turned one year old on November 25, and had become quite active. A typical little boy, he loved to climb and jump, and as soon as he learned to walk, he rarely walked — he ran. Because John and Caroline began doing more activities separately, it was decided that an additional Secret Service agent was needed permanently on the Kiddie Detail to assist Bob Foster and Lynn Meredith. Paul Landis was the perfect man for the job.

At twenty-six years old, Paul Landis was the youngest agent on the White House

Detail, and previously had been assigned to the Eisenhower grandchildren. Born and raised in Ohio, he came from a close family with a strong work ethic, and he took his protective duties extremely seriously. Even though he was unmarried and had no children of his own, he had a warm, playful personality that endeared him to the children. He was five foot, nine inches tall, slender, and physically fit — as all of us were required to be — had sandy brown hair, brown eyes, and a boyish look about him that made him appear younger than he actually was. The rest of us couldn't help but tease him about his youth — and when he joined the Kiddie Detail, he was given the code name "Debut."

As a matter of security, code names were used for all radio communication. To make them easier to remember, each group of people had names beginning with the same letter, and we tried to come up with names that described the individual in some way. Each administration had code names designated beginning with a letter used only for that administration, chosen at random, with no significance. The Eisenhowers had been "S," while the code names for the Kennedys all began with the letter "L." JFK was "Lancer," Mrs. Kennedy was "Lace," Caroline was "Lyric," and John was "Lark."

Not all the Secret Service agents had code names — only the chief, the supervisors on the president's detail, and those of us with Mrs. Kennedy and the kids. The code names for the Secret Service all began with the letter *D*. Bob Foster on the Kiddie Detail was "Dresser" — because he was always impeccably dressed and took great care with his appearance; Lynn Meredith was "Drummer" — he was the musician in the group. My code name was "Dazzle." I have no idea who came up with it, or why, but from the time I started on Mrs. Kennedy's detail, I was "Dazzle" and that remained my code name for the rest of my Secret Service career.

The sun was shining and the temperature was pleasantly balmy when we landed at Palm Beach International Airport at 7:30 A.M., Monday, December 18, after a whirlwind three-day visit to South America and Puerto Rico.

"Look, Jack, your father came to meet us," Mrs. Kennedy said as she waved out the window.

Ambassador Kennedy was standing on the tarmac, and when he saw Mrs. Kennedy wave, he broke into a huge smile and waved

Paul Landis comforts John after a fall

back. They adored each other and in many ways, I thought the senior Kennedy had a closer, more intellectual connection to his daughter-in-law than to his own daughters.

It was obvious he was the boss, the patriarch of the family. No question about it. His children loved and respected him, and always made the effort to spend time with him whenever possible. All three of his sons frequently went to him for advice and listened to what he had to say. Because there had been a lot of scrutiny surrounding Joe Kennedy's influence over Jack's election to the presidency, the ambassador rarely came to the White House. Thus he relished the time he could spend with the president and Mrs. Kennedy at Hyannis Port and Palm Beach.

By the time we hit the ground in Palm Beach, however, President Kennedy was really under the weather. It seemed the pressure from the frequent take-offs and landings had caused him a great deal of pain in his ears, due to a head cold — and he wanted to go directly to the Paul residence to rest. Dr. George Burkley, the president's personal physician, had accompanied us to South America, and was concerned enough that an ear, nose, and throat specialist was called to examine him.

When we arrived at the Paul residence, the president went straight to bed. The children were still at the ambassador's house, and I presumed Mrs. Kennedy would also want to rest.

I was exhausted but remained on duty while Agent Jeffries went to Woody's Motel to check in. A few hours later, Mrs. Kennedy called down to the command post.

"Mr. Hill, I want to go to Worth Avenue and do some shopping. I haven't had a chance to do any Christmas shopping, and I'd like to see what is in the stores this season. The press is concerned about the president's health at the moment, so hopefully no one will pay any attention to me."

"Okay, Mrs. Kennedy. I'll get the car ready."

The spur-of-the-moment shopping trip was typical of her. I knew there was no chance she would go unnoticed, but I sensed that she just wanted to go out and try to be a "normal" person. She knew that Agent Jeffries was not on duty, and I realized that, more and more, she would call me specifically for things, rather than following the protocol of going through Jeffries, who was the Agent in Charge of her protection. It was pretty evident to everybody that she and I had a comfortable rapport, while she and Jeffries just didn't connect.

We drove to Worth Avenue, and I parked the car on a side street, hoping to at least avoid immediate attention. I got out, walked around to the passenger side, and opened the door for her, taking her hand gently as she stepped out of the car.

"Thank you, Mr. Hill," she said with a smile. "I do hope I can raise John to be such a gentleman."

The sun felt good as we walked down Worth Avenue. I stayed close to her to make it appear as if we were a couple, which would look less conspicuous than if she were walking a few steps ahead of me. My eyes, hidden behind dark sunglasses, constantly scanned the other people on the street. At first no one noticed us, and I thought maybe she was right after all.

She stopped in front of a store window and asked, "What do you think of that dress, Mr. Hill?"

It looked like something she would wear, and would look attractive on her tall, slim figure.

"It's very nice. That color would look great on you. Do you want to go in?"

"Yes, let's go have a look."

I opened the door, scanned the store quickly, and then allowed her to walk in ahead of me.

As soon as she walked in, the woman behind the checkout counter dropped whatever she was holding and put her hands up to her mouth, gasping in utter shock. There was a chain reaction, and within seconds, everyone in the store was staring at us — at her.

It's Jackie!

Oh my God! Jackie Kennedy is in the store!

Mrs. Kennedy tried to ignore the gasps and stares, going from one rack to the next, but soon it became too uncomfortable for her. She grabbed my arm and whispered, "Let's go."

We proceeded to walk into a few more shops, but everywhere we went the reaction was the same. Word spread like wildfire and soon there were people gathering on the sidewalk. I felt sorry for her and wished there was something I could do.

It wasn't long before we were back in the car, headed back to the Paul residence, having got very little shopping done.

President Kennedy was supposed to have flown back to Washington right away to prepare for a critical meeting in Bermuda with Prime Minister Harold Macmillan of the United Kingdom, but because of his severe cold, he decided to stay overnight in Palm Beach.

The next morning, the president felt well enough to return to Washington, and the ambassador, never able to get enough time with his son, joined the president in the car for a last-minute chat on the way to the airport.

A short while later, Mrs. Kennedy informed me she wanted to go to the ambassador's residence.

"The ambassador has gone golfing and I'm going to go swimming with Caroline," Mrs. Kennedy said.

"I'll get the car," I said. Paul Landis came along for Caroline's protection.

The ambassador's residence was still well secured, so Paul and I tried to give Mrs. Kennedy and Caroline as much space as possible, while staying within eyesight in case there were any problems.

Not long after we arrived, Ambassador Kennedy returned to the residence.

I knew he couldn't have finished a round of golf in that time, and he appeared to be walking more slowly than usual, like he was completely worn-out.

He walked toward the house and Mrs. Kennedy called out to him, "You're home early. Is everything all right?"

"I'm just feeling very tired," the ambassador said. "I'm going to go upstairs and lie down."

Shortly after one P.M., Mrs. Kennedy called the command post and said, "Please call an ambulance right away. Something is wrong with Mr. Kennedy."

An ambulance arrived within several minutes and the president's father was whisked to St. Mary's Hospital in Palm Beach.

I could tell Mrs. Kennedy was deeply concerned about her father-in-law. She kept her thoughts to herself, but there was worry written all over her face.

When we got to St. Mary's Hospital, we were notified that the ambassador had suffered a stroke, a blood clot in the brain. He was partially paralyzed and his speech was severely impaired.

Mrs. Kennedy's eyes welled with tears as she walked into the ambassador's hospital room to join Rose Kennedy and his beloved niece Ann Gargan by his bedside.

Mrs. Kennedy stayed in there for nearly an hour, conferring with the doctors. When she came out of the room, I could see the emotional strain on her face, and I sensed that the ambassador's condition was even worse than she had expected. She looked so incredibly sad, standing there alone, and it pained me because I knew what a special relationship she had with her father-in-law. I walked toward her and looked into her eyes. I didn't know what to say. I wanted to reach out and hug her, like I would any friend in a time of need, but I knew it wasn't appropriate.

"It's going to be okay, Mrs. Kennedy. It's going to be okay."

Her lips quivered as a tear streamed down her face. Closing her eyes, she nodded faintly, but I could tell she didn't believe it at all.

It was hard for all of us to comprehend how just hours earlier, the ambassador had been a vibrant, energetic seventy-three-year-old man, proudly accompanying his son, the President of the United States, to Air Force One, and now he lay helpless in a hospital bed, completely dependent on the assistance of others. I couldn't help but think how ironic it was that the president's severe cold had resulted in his being able to see his father one last time while the ambassador was still fully communicative. Those memories would have to sustain him for the rest of his life.

Life can change in an instant, I thought. *Just like that. In an instant.*

The president had returned to Washington and was now obviously eager to get back to Palm Beach as soon as possible. Unfortunately, a heavy fog had blanketed the area and he was unable to depart for several hours. We were waiting at the hospital when the president; his brother Bobby, the attorney general; and their sister Jean arrived later that evening. None of them said a word as they walked through the corridor of the hospital to their father's room, but their faces revealed grave concern.

Throughout the evening the president together with his mother, siblings, and Mrs. Kennedy alternated between the ambassador's hospital room and the hospital chapel. There had been some hopeful moments when it was clear that the ambassador recognized his family members, but he wandered in and out of consciousness. Finally, after midnight, one of the nurses urged everyone to go home and get some sleep, and allow the patient to do the same.

I got back to my room at Woody's sometime after 1:00 A.M. It had been an emotionally draining day for everyone, and I should have been able to sleep, but somehow sleep evaded me. I kept seeing Mrs. Kennedy's sad eyes in my mind, and feeling like I should have been able to do something to ease her pain.

The next day, it was back to the hospital, as the rest of the Kennedy children arrived one by one. Another long, emotional day.

In the days that followed, Ambassador Kennedy's condition did not improve a great deal. The president and Mrs. Kennedy visited him daily, with stops at St. Ann's Church or the chapel at St. Mary's in between. The responsibilities of the president do not cease during periods of personal crisis, however, and on Thursday, December 21, President Kennedy flew to Bermuda to meet with Prime Minister Macmillan, as previously planned. He remained in Bermuda overnight, returning to Palm Beach on Friday, December 22.

While the president was away, I was in the Secret Service Command Post at the Paul residence when a call came through the switchboard.

"Call for Mr. Hill," said the switchboard operator.

While all calls to the president or Mrs. Kennedy went through the switchboard, Mrs. Kennedy had requested that calls from certain people go through me.

"This is Clint Hill," I said.

"Mr. Sinatra on the line for you, Mr. Hill." I had anticipated he would call.

"Put him through," I said.

"Hi, Clint. It's Frank."

"Hello, Mr. Sinatra, what can I do for you?"

"I heard the terrible news about the ambassador and I wanted to see how Jackie is doing. Is she there?"

"No, she isn't available now," I said. The same thing I always said.

"Well, it's just terrible, isn't? How serious is Joe's condition?"

I told him what I could about Ambassador Kennedy's condition — basically the information the family had already made public.

"And how is Jackie?"

"She's doing very well, Mr. Sinatra. As well as can be anticipated under the circumstances."

The conversation went on for about twenty minutes, as it usually did, with Sinatra trying to find out what he could about Mrs. Kennedy's activities, and me giving him the barest of information in return. I didn't enjoy these conversations, but I knew that I was saving Mrs. Kennedy the uncomfortable position of having to go through them herself.

"Well, please tell Jackie I called," he said, as he always did.

"Oh, yes, I will, Mr. Sinatra."

I hung up the phone and called Mrs. Kennedy.

"I just got off the phone with Mr. Sinatra, Mrs. Kennedy."

"Oh? What did he say?"

"We had a very pleasant conversation and

he wanted me to relay to you his concern about the ambassador as well as his concern for you and the president."

"Thanks for letting me know, Mr. Hill. I'll talk to him myself one of these days."

The approaching Christmas Day caused Mrs. Kennedy some concern regarding gifts and the appropriate attitude considering the Kennedy patriarch's condition. She decided to once again venture out to Worth Avenue, hoping to regain the celebratory feeling of a normal Christmas. Once again the store employees were in awe and soon people were gathering and gawking through store windows. Agent Jeffries and I worked as a team, with one of us walking in front of Mrs. Kennedy, parting the way through the crowd, constantly saying, "Excuse us, please. May we get through here please?" while the other walked behind her. We tried to be as respectful as possible, and usually people responded positively to our requests, but every so often, we'd have to extend an arm or use our body to fend off an overzealous individual trying to reach Mrs. Kennedy. We managed to keep the people away so that she could purchase some gifts for Caroline and John, and other family members, but it was not the pleasant experience she had hoped for.

Later she pulled me aside and said, "Mr. Hill, it seems I can't go anywhere anymore without causing a scene. It is so difficult to do the rather simple things I enjoy, like buying a gift, without it becoming a front-page story."

She wasn't complaining, just stating the facts. Then she looked up at me with wistful eyes and asked, "Isn't there something you can do about it, Mr. Hill?"

A thought entered my head, but rather than respond right away, I paused and said, "Let me think about the problem, Mrs. Kennedy, and I'll see what I can come up with."

Thus it was that I became a frequent shopper on Worth Avenue, buying swimwear for the president, toys for the children, and personal items for Mrs. Kennedy. This was not in the job description the Secret Service had for me, but it was just one more way to make life a lot easier and less confrontational for Mrs. Kennedy. She appreciated my efforts, and I considered it a good protective move to remove her from public exposure as much as possible.

Christmas came and went, as the remaining time in Palm Beach became somewhat routine, day after day. Go to St. Mary's

Hospital to see the president's father; stop by the chapel and pray or go to St. Ann's Church in West Palm Beach or St. Edward's in Palm Beach; have a lunchtime cruise aboard the *Honey Fitz;* back to St Mary's Hospital in the afternoon. The days were long, and the laughter that had once been constant in the bustling Kennedy household had all but disappeared.

Late one evening, Paul Landis and I were driving back to Woody's Motel together, discussing the day's events and how incredibly sad the situation was. By this point the doctors had said there was nothing they could do. Ambassador Kennedy would be paralyzed and confined to a wheelchair for the rest of his life. They said that he had retained full cognizance and intellectual capacity, but it was unlikely he would ever speak again. He would be a prisoner in his own body, unable to have the influence that he had thrived upon, and on which President Kennedy had relied.

It seemed like there was nothing to feel good about, when Paul suddenly remembered a bright spot in the day.

"I did see the president smile one time today," Paul said.

"Oh really?" I asked. I couldn't imagine what could have possibly made the president smile throughout this terrible ordeal.

"He had just taken Caroline in to visit the ambassador, and when we walked out of the elevator, on the ground floor, there was a gumball machine there. Caroline saw it and asked, 'Daddy, may I please have a gumball?'

"The president looked at her and said, 'Oh, Buttons, I'm sorry, you need a penny for the gumball machine. I don't have a penny.' "

I shook my head in amusement. It was so typical of JFK — he never carried money. Here he was the President of the United States and he didn't have a penny for the gumball machine.

Paul continued, "Poor Caroline looked like she was going to crumble. So the president turned to me and asked, 'Mr. Landis, do you happen to have a penny?'

"I pulled out the change in my pocket, and fortunately, I did have a penny.

" 'As a matter of fact I do,' I said as I handed Caroline the penny.

"Her eyes got big and she said, 'Oh, thank you, Mr. Landis!'

"You'd think I had given her a diamond ring," Paul added with a laugh.

We were both laughing now. I could see little Caroline, just as excited as could be over such a simple thing as a gumball.

Paul continued. "So she struggled a bit to get the penny into the machine, but she finally did it, and the president helped her turn the knob, and when the gumball rolled out, she just grabbed it and popped it in her mouth, and began chewing away, a big smile on her face.

"I turned to look at the president and he had a big grin on his face.

"Then he said, 'Thank you, Mr. Landis. I owe you a penny.'"

Even after the president returned to Washington, Mrs. Kennedy stayed in Palm Beach with John and Caroline, and continued to visit the ambassador in the hospital on a daily basis. It was clear to me that these visits were not out of obligation, but came from her deep love and devotion to her father-in-law. She would often bring Caroline, whose innocent, exuberant spirit was uplifting not only to Mr. Kennedy, but to members of the hospital staff as well. Caroline would help the nurse push her grandfather's wheelchair down the hospital corridor, chattering on about what had happened on the morning's walk on the Lake Trail, completely undaunted by his inability to respond.

It was a rough Christmas on all of us — for the Kennedy family, who were struggling to understand what the future would be like without Joe's ability to offer advice; for Mrs. Kennedy, trying to deal with the ever-growing pressures of being in the public eye; and for the agents, spending another holiday away from our own families.

Everybody was looking forward to turning a new page in 1962. Little did we know it would be one of the best years of our lives.

■ ■ ■ ■

PART THREE:
1962

■ ■ ■ ■

10
TRAVELING WITH
MRS. KENNEDY:
INDIA

Mrs. Kennedy at the Taj Mahal

In early February, Jerry Behn, the Special Agent in Charge of the White House Detail, informed me that, after much discussion and several postponements, Mrs. Kennedy was going to India, and Pakistan as well. I would be in charge of the advance, working closely with Ambassador John Kenneth

Galbraith.

"Mrs. Kennedy's sister, Princess Radziwill, will accompany her on the trip," Behn said, "and the tentative schedule I've been given has them traveling the entire month of March: four days in Rome, seventeen days in India, five days in Pakistan, and three days in London. But you know as well as I do, that schedule will change."

I laughed. "Jerry, with Mrs. Kennedy *nothing* is ever carved in stone."

He smiled. "Yes, I'm well aware that she prefers things to be — shall we say — unstructured?"

"Yes, you could say that," I said, with a smile.

"But listen, Clint, whatever resources you need, just let me know," Behn said. "I know it's not going to be easy."

It *was* an ambitious itinerary — and the first time an American first lady had ever visited India or Pakistan. In both countries, Mrs. Kennedy would visit a number of different cities, and each one had to be advanced. There was no way Agent Jeffries and I could adequately protect Mrs. Kennedy on our own, so I selected a team of agents from the President's Detail and other field offices, choosing men with whom I'd worked before on trips like this, and on whom I knew I could depend.

Based on my past experience in that part of the world, I knew there was a good chance some of us were going to get sick, so I assigned two-agent teams at each location to do the advances. The itinerary was so complex that the teams of agents would need to leapfrog from one city to another, without a break. Advancing Mrs. Kennedy's trip to India would be the most challenging assignment of my career thus far.

So it was that on February 16, 1962, I and fourteen other Secret Service agents boarded a Pan Am flight at New York City's Idlewild Airport headed to New Delhi. It would take us nearly two days to get there, with stops in London, Frankfurt, Munich, Istanbul, Beirut, and Tehran.

For the guys who hadn't been on Eisenhower's India trip, New Delhi was an eye-opening experience. The U.S. Embassy security officer met us at the airport with a bunch of cars and drivers to take us to our hotel. As we drove through the streets of New Delhi, I watched the expressions on the faces of my colleagues as they saw what we were going to be dealing with.

Sharing the road with trucks and cars were horse-drawn carts, stray cows, pigs, goats, rickshaws, tractors, and every so often, a camel strutting along, all seemingly oblivious to the traffic around them. Darting in and out of this chaos, were people on bicycles. Everywhere you looked there were bicycles. And there wasn't just one person to a bicycle. More often than not, there would be two, three, or even four people pressed together, balancing with their legs dangling as the driver pedaled with all his might to propel the bike with the extra weight.

Along the side of the road, vendors with street carts were selling fruits, vegetables, clothing, pots and pans, fabrics, tires, and sandals. People were cooking over open fires, as small, naked children with protruding bellies wandered amid stray animals and mounds of garbage. The dust and dirt created smog that made your eyes tear, while burning cow patties and elephant dung gave off an almost unbearable stench. Dotted throughout this slumlike environment were bright splashes of turquoise and pink and yellow as women in flowing saris and veils carried huge baskets of grass or clay pots of water on their heads. It was like we were in the middle of a traveling circus.

Everywhere I looked, I thought of what Mrs. Kennedy would think, how she would react, and most important, what we were going to have to do to protect her in this unsanitary and unpredictable environment. She was scheduled to arrive on March 1, eleven days later, and we still didn't have the final itinerary. Pakistan had its own set of problems, and I was going to have to fly to Karachi as soon as we got the India portion squared away.

I pulled out a notepad and jotted down thoughts as they came to me: purified water, imported fruits, soap, medical supplies, *gloves*. Mrs. Kennedy wore gloves to church and often to formal banquets, but here I thought she could wear them not just for fashion, but also to keep her hands clean. She would need plenty of gloves.

I had worked with the State Department to arrange hotel rooms at the elegant Ashoka Hotel in the diplomatic section of New Delhi for the duration of our stay there. The rooms were luxurious, and due to the favorable exchange rate between the dollar and the Indian rupee, were well within our per diem, which had recently been increased to sixteen dollars per day.

Colonel Gordon Parks from the White House Communications Agency (WHCA) — we called it "Waca" — had come with us to set up a secure telephone and radio system so that we could communicate directly with the White House. It never ceased to amaze me how, even in a third-world country like India, he could pull out a stainless steel case filled with wires and electronics, piece it all together, and *voilà!* — we had a phone line to the White House. While this was normal procedure when the president traveled, it was highly unusual for a first lady's solo trip. But there was a specific reason WHCA came along.

Shortly before I left on the trip, President Kennedy had called me into his office.

"Clint," he said — he always called me Clint — "I want you to stay in touch with Jerry Behn's office and Tish, and make sure any changes Ken Galbraith wants, you clear with us before they're put on the schedule. He's trying to make this jaunt to India last forever, and I don't want Mrs. Kennedy overscheduled."

So, shortly after checking in, while Gordon was setting up the secure phone connection in a hotel room at the Ashoka, my first order of business was to meet with Ambassador Galbraith at the U.S. Embassy.

I had heard that Galbraith was extremely tall, but still, when he approached me with his lanky, six-foot, seven-inch frame, I was somewhat taken aback. He had to bend down to shake my hand, and I felt like I needed to stand on my tiptoes to look him eye to eye.

"Welcome to India, Mr. Hill," he said with a kind smile. His voice was gravelly, and somewhat high-pitched for a man. "We are all very excited for Mrs. Kennedy's visit." He laughed and added, "It has been the talk of the country for three months now."

"I can assure you, she is very much looking forward to this trip, Ambassador."

As it turned out, when he showed me his plans for Mrs. Kennedy, nothing was the way it had been presented to me when I left Washington two days earlier. I quickly understood the problem President Kennedy had predicted. Ambassador Galbraith wanted Mrs. Kennedy to be able to see as much of the country as possible during her stay, and he had her crisscrossing from New Delhi to Calcutta to Bombay and all the way down to Bangalore and Hyderabad, up at 7:00 every morning and going nonstop until midnight.

The ambassador was so enthusiastic, I almost felt sorry for him. This was somewhat ironic since besides towering over me physically, the ambassador was also intellectually intimidating. He was a renowned economist and one of President Kennedy's most trusted political advisors, and here I was in the middle of these negotiations. One wrong move would not only be the end of my career, but could easily turn this trip into a full-blown international disaster.

"Why don't we plan to meet every afternoon, say around five o'clock at my residence," Galbraith said at the end of the meeting. "That way we can brief each other and handle any problems before they arise."

"That sounds great, Ambassador. I'll see you tomorrow at five."

The meeting had gone well, and I liked Ambassador Galbraith. He really had the best of intentions and wanted nothing more than to show Mrs. Kennedy the India he had come to know and love. But if he had his way, she would be trekking from one end of India to the other for six weeks. I had to get on the phone to Washington right away.

There was a ten-and-a-half-hour time difference between India and Washington, D.C. — I had never heard of time zones in half hour increments but so it was in India — so when it was daytime in Washington, it was nighttime in New Delhi. Later that night I called SAIC Jerry Behn, while Gordon worked the frequency. Unfortunately, the shortwave radiophone connection was terrible — not by any fault of Gordon's; it was just that international telecommunications at that time were still rather primitive. There were echoes and delays and often we would just get cut off completely. With all the stops and starts, I didn't get to bed that night until after 3:00 A.M.

So that became my routine. Early evenings at Ambassador Galbraith's residence, followed by a midnight call to Washington that usually lasted two or more hours, catch a few hours sleep, up at dawn to work logistics, meet with Indian security officials and political representatives. Then report back to the ambassador's residence and start the cycle again.

I would get the ambassador to remove two stops from the schedule, and then he'd come back the next day with one more. It was two steps forward and one step back. The White House staff was the source of another major problem — they kept changing Mrs. Kennedy's departure date.

Frustration reigned on all sides and it was a bit like I was in the middle of a diplomatic game of tug-of-war. Just when it seemed the trip might not happen at all, President Kennedy called Ambassador Galbraith himself. I don't know what was said, but after the phone call, the ambassador rather sheepishly accepted everything I had proposed and the schedule was finally set. What had started as a seventeen-day itinerary in India alone, had been successfully whittled down to nine days.

There wasn't a cloud in the sky as Mrs. Kennedy stepped off the plane at the New Delhi airport on Monday, March 12, 1962. Dressed in a bright pink silk coat and matching hat, she looked absolutely stunning. The crowd of three thousand people that were standing behind fence lines on the tarmac broke into a welcoming roar.

A group of about twenty press people had accompanied Mrs. Kennedy and her sister Lee on the flight, including Frances Lewine from the Associated Press, Sander Vanocur from NBC, Marjorie Hunter from the *New York Times,* and Barbara Walters from NBC's *Today* show. They were eager for comments from Mrs. Kennedy, but she largely ignored them.

Prime Minister Jawaharlal Nehru and his daughter, Indira Gandhi, together with Ambassador Galbraith and an array of government officials were there to greet her and as she went down the receiving line, I could tell by the enthusiastic smile on her face that she was truly excited to be here. After greeting her hosts, she looked around and saw me. Our eyes connected and she mouthed, "Hi, Mr. Hill," before carrying on with her hosts.

Agent Jim Jeffries had accompanied her from New York, along with another agent from the New York Field Office. As the Special Agent in Charge, Jeffries would be with her throughout the trip, while I would continue supervising the other agents conducting the advances throughout India and Pakistan. At least that was the original plan.

More than one hundred thousand people lined the roadway as we proceeded by motorcade into central New Delhi. I couldn't believe it. Mrs. Kennedy and Lee sat in the back of a convertible Mercedes sedan, provided by the Indian government, with Agent Jeffries in the front seat, while I rode in the follow-up car. Snake charmers, men on the backs of camels, bullock carts and their drivers, all lined the route waving and shouting, "Jackie! Jackie! Welcome Mrs. Kennedy!"

I had seen this kind of reception in Paris and South America, but on those trips she had been with the president. Here, all of these people had come out *just for her.*

We took her to the guesthouse arranged by the U.S. Embassy, where she had a short time to relax. Her first official visit was with

President Rajendra Prasad at his 350-room presidential mansion, the Rashtrapati Bhavan. As it turned out, President Prasad had just addressed Parliament and as was the custom, would be traveling in a grand procession filled with pomp and circumstance from Parliament back to his mansion. Upon arrival at the airport, Prime Minister Nehru had mentioned this to Mrs. Kennedy and suggested that she might like to see the parade prior to her meeting with Prasad.

She of course loved the idea. Agent Jeffries immediately tried to squash the improvised plan because it hadn't been advanced.

"Let her do it, Jim," I urged my supervisor. "We'll get her in a safe position and make sure she's covered."

I had told Mrs. Kennedy the first time I met her that our job was to allow her to do the things she wanted to do, and keep her safe at the same time.

Jeffries acquiesced and we got her to a viewing platform where she could watch. The seventy-seven-year-old president arrived riding in an open, horse-drawn carriage surrounded by spear-carrying horse-mounted bodyguards in scarlet tunics and high turbans. It was like a scene out of a movie and Mrs. Kennedy loved it. She really enjoyed pageantry of this sort — people in traditional costumes, showcasing their country's history and civilization. Like her husband, Mrs. Kennedy was a history buff, and this seemed to bring history to life. She couldn't thank Nehru enough for suggesting it.

After a brief formal meeting with the president, our entire entourage of Indian security officials, dignitaries, an army of press, and our small contingent of Secret Service agents headed to Old Delhi to the site where Mohandas K. Gandhi had been cremated, after his brutal assassination in 1948. Hundreds of women and children, all dressed in bright colors, lined the gravel path that led to the tomb, and they applauded as Mrs. Kennedy walked past.

Prior to her trip, Mrs. Kennedy had studied the history of India and Pakistan so that she would be knowledgeable in her discussions with the country's leaders. She was well aware of Gandhi's significance to the country, and how his life had ended so suddenly, at the hands of a lone gunman, just fourteen years earlier. I remember how she so carefully took the wreath of white roses someone handed to her and gently placed it on Gandhi's simple tomb. And then she stood there, silently, in prayer, for

a full minute of respectful contemplation.

The next couple of days were nonstop: lavish luncheons and dinners interspersed with cultural tours and poignant visits to children's hospitals, and a ceremony in which she presented to Indira Gandhi a portable American classroom equipped with art materials, known as the "Children's Carnival of Art."

Everywhere we went Mrs. Kennedy caused a sensation. At one point, a baby elephant was paraded in front of her and she asked, "May I touch him?"

Agent Jeffries said, "No, Mrs. Kennedy that's not a good idea," at the same time the elephant's handler said, "Yes, it's fine."

Mrs. Kennedy reached right over to touch its trunk, and the little elephant reacted as if it were being tickled, wrapping its stubble-covered trunk around her hand. She was laughing hysterically — she just loved animals — while Jeffries looked like he was about ready to physically remove her from the situation.

He wasn't much happier when Mrs. Kennedy showed up in full riding attire — jodhpurs, boots, blazer, and helmet — to go riding at the exercise grounds of the President's Bodyguard. The President's Bodyguard is the elite cavalry regiment of the Indian army, and they had magnificent horses and exquisite training grounds. Mrs. Kennedy was in her element as they brought out a mare named Princess for her to ride around the beautiful jumping course. I had no worries at all as I watched her expertly take the jumps, her eyes shining, and a look of sheer exhilaration on her face. I had convinced Ambassador Galbraith to arrange this respite in the itinerary for her, and she loved it.

After three successful days in New Delhi, I was off to Karachi, to set up everything in Pakistan, while Mrs. Kennedy was off to Agra and the Taj Mahal, Benares, and Udaipur. The press followed her everywhere, and from the daily newspaper articles, it appeared as if everything was going smoothly.

She would tell me later the details of what I had missed — watching the spectacle of the young men diving fifty feet into the water tank at Fatehpur Sikri in their underwear, spending hours at the Taj Mahal with a mob of tourists and photographers who wouldn't leave her alone, riding an elephant with Lee at the Amber Fort in Jaipur, riding down the Ganges in a riverboat as thousands of people ran to the shores to watch her go by.

At the time, however, I had no way of knowing what was happening with Mrs. Kennedy and the trip after I left India, and I didn't have time to worry about it. Pakistan was going to be a whole different set of problems.

The capital of Pakistan had been moved temporarily from Karachi to Rawalpindi in the late 1950s and was in the process of being permanently moved to Islamabad, but most of the U.S. Embassy business was still being handled in Karachi in 1962. Located on the Arabian Sea, Karachi was one of the most squalid places I had ever visited. When I was there with Eisenhower, we actually brought in a U.S. Navy ship and kept it anchored offshore, and that's where the Secret Service agents and staff slept and ate. I was working the midnight shift and will never forget the sight of trucks patrolling the streets in the predawn hours, as a laborer poked at the bodies lying on the side of the road to see which ones were alive and which were dead. They'd throw the dead ones into the back of the truck and continue on. The poverty was mind-numbing.

Fortunately, Pan Am had made arrangements with one of the hotels in Karachi, in which they had a completely separate area for their flight crews. It was very basic, but Pan Am brought in all the food, water, and linens so it was up to American standards — and they graciously allowed me to stay there while I advanced Mrs. Kennedy's trip.

Meanwhile, as I ironed out the wrinkles in the proposed schedule for Pakistan, I was confident that Mrs. Kennedy was being well taken care of by her hosts in India, and that the agents I had assigned to each place were capable of handling any problem that should arise. I had no way to communicate with them, except through the embassies.

One night, shortly before Mrs. Kennedy was due to arrive in Pakistan, I was sound asleep in my room when I heard someone pounding on the door.

"Mr. Hill! Wake up! Mr. Hill, wake up!"

I jumped out of bed and opened the door. One of the Pan Am staff was standing there with a piece of paper.

"What's going on?" I asked, groggy-eyed.

"Mr. Hill, we just got a call from the U.S. Embassy. You need to report there immediately. There is a top secret message for you at the command center. They said it couldn't wait until morning. I've already arranged a driver to take you there."

I had no idea what could be going on, but I quickly got dressed and headed to the embassy.

When I got there, there was not one, not two, but three messages addressed to me, all labeled "Top Secret."

One was from Secret Service Chief James Rowley, one was from Secretary of State Dean Rusk, and the third was from the National Security Council on behalf of the President of the United States.

All three said the same thing:

PROCEED FIRST AVAILABLE FLIGHT TO LAHORE, PAKISTAN. UPON ARRIVAL OF MRS. KENNEDY IN LAHORE ON MARCH 21

FROM NEW DELHI, YOU ARE TO ASSUME COMMAND OF FIRST LADY'S PROTECTIVE DETAIL.

There was no additional explanation. Something had gone terribly wrong in India.

11
TRAVELING WITH
MRS. KENNEDY:
PAKISTAN

Ambassador McConaughy, Ayub Khan's military aide, Clint Hill, and Mrs. Kennedy

When I read the three top secret messages, I was stunned. I called Paul Rundle, the senior agent I had assigned to the advance in Lahore, explained the situation, and told him I'd be on the next flight from Karachi to Lahore.

When I arrived at the Lahore airport to greet Mrs. Kennedy on March 21, I could hardly believe the crowd of people that had already gathered for her arrival. Agent Rundle had done an excellent job of working with the Pakistani security forces in creating a roped-off area for the people, but there had to be at least *eight thousand* people waiting to greet Mrs. Kennedy. It was like a carnival with balloons and welcome banners, children in school uniforms waving little American flags, and a mass of people packed behind the rope lines waiting just to see Mrs. Kennedy get off the plane.

"My God, Rundle," I said to Paul. "What did you do? Put a notice in the newspaper saying she was going to hand out twenty-dollar bills?"

Rundle shook his head. "I know. It is *unbelievable.* Reminds me of the receptions we used to get for Ike, but I've never seen anything like this for a first lady."

In fact the government had declared the day a holiday. A holiday in Pakistan for the arrival of America's first lady. Unbelievable.

President Mohammad Ayub Khan had sent his personal Vickers Viscount turboprop airplane to pick up Mrs. Kennedy in New Delhi and to have available for her use throughout her stay in Pakistan. When the door of the plane opened and Mrs. Kennedy stepped onto the portable stairwell, dressed in an exquisite blue silk coat with oversized buttons and a straw hat in the same color, the crowd went absolutely nuts.

She had a bubbly smile on her face and I could tell by the look in her eyes that she was thrilled by the enthusiastic reception. There was no hint that anything was wrong. Since receiving the confidential messages, all I had learned was that Jeffries had been called back to Washington. I could only assume that the ongoing personality conflicts between him and Mrs. Kennedy had reached a boiling point and she had requested his removal.

President Ayub Khan and other dignitaries were lined up at the bottom of the steps to greet her. As she walked carefully down the stairwell, she turned to look where she knew I would be, and her eyes said, *It's wonderful to see you, Mr. Hill.*

I remained in close proximity to her as she went through the receiving line and entered the waiting convertible Oldsmobile with President Ayub Khan. Mrs. Kennedy and the president got into the backseat, while I squeezed into the front bench seat, between the driver and the president's military aide.

The lead vehicle in the motorcade was a press truck — an open flatbed truck with rails around the outside — filled with about a dozen photographers. This was typical when you expected large crowds along a motorcade route for a *president,* but I'd never seen it, prior to this trip, for a first lady. Behind the press truck were six Pakistani policemen on motorcycles, and then the presidential car. Our two Secret Service guys followed in another open-top car, along with the president's security men, while Princess Radziwill, the U.S. ambassador Walter McConaughy, other officials, and still more press were scattered in cars and trucks behind.

It had rained earlier in the morning, and then, shortly before Mrs. Kennedy's plane landed, the clouds parted, the rain stopped, and the sun came out. As we drove from the airport to the residence of the governor of West Pakistan, where Mrs. Kennedy would stay, the weather remained clear and pleasant.

The crowds along the route to the governor's residence were large, dense, and enthusiastically noisy. Bands with booming drums and bagpipes played along the way, as the people cheered and thousands upon thousands of schoolchildren waved small, handheld American flags. The cars were going about ten miles per hour, and the president convinced Mrs. Kennedy to stand up so the people could see her better. So there she was, behind me, standing in an open-top car as we drove through Lahore. The Pakistani flag hung alongside the American flag over the street at one point, and at another, a huge banner read: LONG LIVE THE AMERICAN FRIEND-SHIP.

All along the way, people were throwing handfuls of flower petals at the car — well, mostly they were petals, but every so often I'd see a whole damn bouquet coming at her and have to rise out of my seat to fend it off so it didn't knock her in the head. By the time we reached the governor's house, the inside of the car was ankle-deep in a rainbow of flower petals. Mrs. Kennedy was completely taken by surprise by the outpouring of affection from these people more than 7,200 miles from her home. She was ebullient.

Touching Ayub Khan's arm, she said, "Mr. President, the people in your country are so warm and friendly. Thank you for convincing me to come and visit. It is just wonderful to be here."

One of the things Mrs. Kennedy had most wanted to do was visit Lahore's famed

Shalimar Gardens, but shortly after arriving at the governor's residence, the skies opened up with a violent thunderstorm. Mrs. Kennedy took the opportunity to rest, while Agent Rundle and I went to work rearranging the schedule, postponing the visit to the gardens until the next day.

By the next morning, the weather had cleared, and it was going to be a busy day. The schedule called for Mrs. Kennedy to accompany President Ayub Khan to the grand climax of the National Horse and Cattle Show, which was West Pakistan's biggest social event of the year. When it was first discussed, I had no doubt that Mrs. Kennedy would thoroughly enjoy this — anything that had to do with horses was always at the top of her list — but I had no idea of the surprise President Ayub Khan had planned for her.

Mrs. Kennedy's entrance to the Horse and Cattle Show was an event in and of itself. Dozens of trumpeters sounded a fanfare as Mrs. Kennedy arrived at the ancient fortress stadium in a gilded, horse-drawn carriage seated next to President Ayub Khan. The president's elite mounted security force, dressed in bright red military jackets with brass buttons, white jodhpur-type pants, and colorful turbans fashioned high atop their heads, surrounded the carriage in perfect formation, each horse stepping in line with the others.

Satisfied that Mrs. Kennedy was well protected by the presidential security, I watched from the stands, constantly scanning the crowd for anything unusual. The entire audience seemed spellbound by the beaming Mrs. Kennedy, who was wearing an ice-blue long-sleeved silk coat with a matching whimsical beret. As Mrs. Kennedy took her place of honor in the stands, I moved in to be as close but unobtrusive as possible. It was a warm day, and although this was a Muslim country in which the local women dressed conservatively, no one seemed to mind when Mrs. Kennedy took off her coat to reveal a formfitting dress with cap sleeves that exposed her arms and was cut into a deep V that exposed an ample portion of her back.

Sitting with Lee and President Ayub Khan by her side, Mrs. Kennedy watched the spectacular show that was filled with such pomp, ceremony and tradition, it rivaled the show put on by the French during her visit to Paris with President Kennedy the year before. As the red, white, and blue American flag fluttered high above the stands next to the green Pakistan flag with the crescent moon and white star, a huge marching band of bagpipe players and drummers performed along with dancing horses and camels, and mounted troops carrying spears and riding in intricate formations. As specially groomed cattle and show horses of all varieties were paraded in front of the grandstand, Mrs. Kennedy chatted comfortably with the president, who shared her love of horses and animals in general.

Then came the moment of high drama. President Ayub Khan escorted Mrs. Kennedy from the stands onto the grounds, and led her to a beautiful chestnut-colored horse that had been brought out by two of his red-coated guards.

"My dear Mrs. Kennedy, on behalf of the people of Pakistan, I present to you 'Sardar.' It is my hope that every time you ride Sardar, you will remember with fondness the time you spent in Pakistan."

Mrs. Kennedy was stunned. He was beautifully marked, a bay gelding with a diamond-shaped white spot on his forehead, and as she reached her gloved hand up to stroke the horse's nose, she broke into a huge smile and said, "He is magnificent."

It was love at first sight. President Ayub Khan explained that he was ten years old, and an award-winning jumper that was a

Clint Hill holds Mrs. Kennedy's coat as Ayub Khan presents Sardar

descendant from the horses of Agha Khan. He couldn't have chosen a more perfect gift for her. As she stood caressing the horse, thanking the president over and over for his thoughtfulness and generosity, all I could think was *how the hell are we going to get this damn horse back to Washington?*

There was no time to deal with that problem just yet. After one last spectacular military demonstration on the field, it was time to get Mrs. Kennedy out and on to the next event. Our departure was not going to be as easy as the arrival.

While we had been watching the show, outside the arena hundreds of thousands of people had gathered to see Mrs. Kennedy as she left the horse show. Fortunately we had planned to leave by car rather than horse-drawn carriage. At one point, a group of people became unruly and began fighting among themselves to get a better vantage point as the car approached. I rose up out of the front seat, ready to fend off anybody who got too close to Mrs. Kennedy. However, the police responded to control the people and our driver was able to maneuver us out of the situation with no incident. I looked back to make sure Mrs. Kennedy wasn't affected by the disruption, and with my eyes I asked, *Are you okay?*

I could see that she had stiffened up a bit, but as soon as our eyes met, she relaxed and held my gaze as if to say, *Thank you.*

Along with the press, seven thousand local citizens had shown up to greet Mrs. Kennedy at the Shalimar Gardens when we arrived just before sundown. Covering more than forty acres, the exquisite seventeenth-century terraced gardens were built by Shah Jahan, the same Mughal ruler who had commissioned the Taj Mahal in Agra, India, and they were truly impressive. Marble pavilions stood like thrones amid manicured flower beds overflowing with countless varieties of trees, fruit-bearing plants, and seasonal flowers, all of which were watered by an ingenious canal system. It was truly an oasis on the outskirts of Lahore, with more than four hundred fountains, cascading water, and shallow pools mirroring the brilliant fuchsia, violet, and yellow flowering plants and well-tended lawns.

As the sun began to set, the trees lit up with thousands of twinkling lights, and the effect was magical. President Ayub Khan had walked with Mrs. Kennedy through the gardens and urged her to say something to the people who had come to see her. I was surprised when she obliged, and stepped up to a microphone that had been set up under one of the pavilions.

"I'm so happy to be here today," she said. "All my life I dreamed of coming to the Shalimar Gardens. I never thought I'd be lucky enough to have it happen, especially after yesterday's thunderstorms. I thought fate would never get me here, but it is even lovelier than I'd dreamed. I only wish my husband could be with me and that we had something this romantic to show President Ayub when he came to our country."

The press was furiously taking notes and frantically setting up cameras as this was the first public statement Mrs. Kennedy had made since beginning the trip eleven days earlier. She seemed to be very much at ease as she continued to speak to the appreciative crowd that had gathered in the gardens.

"I must say I'm profoundly impressed by the reverence which you in Pakistan have for your art and for your culture and for the use that you make of it now. My own countrymen too, have a pride in their tradition so I think that as I stand in these gardens, which were built long before my country was born, that's one more thing that binds us together and which always will. We'll always share an appreciation for the finer things. Thank you."

Later, at the dinner reception, Mrs. Kennedy couldn't stop talking about everything that had happened throughout the day, and how it would always remain in her memory.

"Today at the horse show, I was so impressed with the daring riding which took place — all the qualities I have always admired, so daring and brave." She seemed to be somewhat melancholy, and added, "I bring a message of esteem and friendship from my husband, and I hope I will be forgiven if I say that he has those qualities, too. I am only sorry that he is not here in your country, where he would feel so much at home."

I was so proud of her. I knew how much she hated being in the spotlight. She would have much preferred to attend the horse show and walk through the Shalimar Gardens as an ordinary tourist, but she accepted her role graciously, and the result was that she had created a respect for America that hadn't existed before. In the eyes of the Pakistani people, Jacqueline Kennedy represented all Americans. And they loved us.

We were all exhausted by the time we got back to the governor's residence. But Mrs. Kennedy had one last request of me.

"Oh, Mr. Hill, wasn't today just wonderful?"

"Yes, Mrs. Kennedy, it certainly was special."

Her eyes were weary, and her makeup had all but been worn off.

"May I ask you to do something?"

"Of course. What do you need?"

"Can you please clear the schedule for tomorrow morning? I just want a day to sleep a little bit late, and more than anything I want to ride Sardar just once before I have to leave him. It's all I can think about."

"No problem, Mrs. Kennedy. I'll take care of it."

She grabbed my hands and said, "Oh, Mr. Hill, I haven't had a chance to tell you this, but I'm so very glad you're now the Agent in Charge. You understand me."

"I just want you to be happy, Mrs. Kennedy. Happy and safe."

"Good night, Mr. Hill."

"Good night, Mrs. Kennedy."

The next morning, Mrs. Kennedy slept late, got dressed in her riding attire, and rode Sardar for the first time.

I had seen her ride many times, of course, on many different horses, but there was something special about the way she rode Sardar. It was truly like they had a unique connection. Sardar had captured her heart. They understood each other.

When she dismounted, she had a look of sheer joy on her face.

Rubbing his neck, she praised Sardar and kept telling him how wonderful he was.

Then she turned to me and said, "Mr. Hill, Sardar is mine, all mine. No one is going to be allowed to ride him except me."

The next stop was Rawalpindi, the temporary capital of Pakistan. The scene in Rawalpindi along the six-mile motorcade route from the airport was literally wall-to-wall people. The four hundred thousand residents of Rawalpindi apparently had all turned out to welcome this American guest of honor. There were bagpipe bands, marching bands with drums and trumpets, and it seemed like every person along the route was waving an American flag. At various points people held up signs that said, LONG LIVE MRS. KENNEDY.

The welcome was warm, friendly, and *loud.* Her only other activity for the day was a private dinner, a garden party, with President Ayub Khan celebrating Pakistan Day, similar to our Fourth of July.

The next morning, our gracious hosts — President Ayub Khan, his military aide who had been so helpful throughout the trip, and Ambassador McConaughy — accompanied us to the Rawalpindi airport as we departed for Peshawar.

I had come to really like the Pakistani president — he was gregarious, fun, and sincere. On the day of our departure, he was wearing a black fur cap called a karakul, also known as Jinnah cap, which was common attire for Pakistani men.

"I love your cap, Mr. President!" Mrs. Kennedy exclaimed as soon as she saw it. "Why haven't I seen you in this before?"

President Ayub Khan took off the cap and

playfully placed it on her head. "It's yours, Mrs. Kennedy."

She laughed and said, "Oh, thank you. I must get one for President Kennedy, too."

"I'll take care of it," President Ayub said with a laugh. "We'll have an assortment of karakuls sent to President Kennedy."

We landed forty-five minutes later at an airport near Peshawar that was the same spot from which American Gary Powers had taken off for his ill-fated flight over the Soviet Union — the flight that ended with him a prisoner of the Soviets and the United States embarrassed into acknowledging flying spy planes over that country. It was an event that caused immense tension between our two countries and resulted in Premier Khrushchev refusing to talk to President Eisenhower at a summit meeting in Paris in 1960. This piece of history was not lost on Mrs. Kennedy.

Once again there were large crowds upon our arrival, but in Peshawar there were noticeably fewer women in attendance. The people in this region tended to be far more conservative in their Muslim traditions, and many considered it inappropriate for women to be seen in public. Thus it was the men who came out in droves to welcome Mrs.

Kennedy.

As soon as we got settled into our rooms at the governor's residence, Mrs. Kennedy came to me with a look of grave concern on her face and a piece of paper in her hands.

Ever since President Ayub had presented Sardar to Mrs. Kennedy, Ambassador Mc-Conaughy had a staff of people working on the necessary arrangements to get the horse to the United States as soon as possible with as little muss and fuss as possible. To make matters more complicated, I also learned that just prior to Mrs. Kennedy's departure from India, she had been given two tiger cubs, courtesy of Air India. According to the ambassador, she envisioned keeping them on the White House lawn.

Tigers roaming freely on the White House lawn. I hadn't yet broached that subject with her or anybody back in Washington.

"Mr. Hill," she said as she handed me the paper with her handwritten notes on it. "I need to get this message to the president — I think he is in California, in Palm Springs. I don't want anyone to know about it, but I need him to get it as soon as possible."

"Sure, Mrs. Kennedy, I'll take care of it right away."

I went straight to the embassy, found the ambassador, and requested he send the secure message to President Kennedy immediately.

FROM: THE FIRST LADY
TO: THE PRESIDENT
///SECRETEYESONLY///

DEAR JACK,
IT SEEMS SO RUDE TO PAKISTANIS TO SUGGEST THAT THEIR BEAUTIFUL HORSE HAS HOOF AND MOUTH DISEASE WHEN OBVIOUSLY HE HASN'T A GERM IN THE WORLD.

HE IS SO BEAUTIFUL AND HIGH STRUNG IT WOULD BE CRUEL TO QUARANTINE HIM IN NEW YORK FOR THIRTY DAYS. CANNOT BEAR TO BE PARTED FROM HIM THAT LONG AS COULD SHOW HIM THIS SPRING AND START SCHOOLING HIM IMMEDIATELY.

COULD YOU NOT HAVE VETERINARIAN EXAMINE HIM IN NEW YORK AND SAY HE WAS FREE FROM ALL DISEASE AND HAVE HIM GO STRAIGHT TO GLENORA.

IT WOULD BE LIKE LEAVING LEE IN QUARANTINE TO PART WITH HIM — ESPECIALLY AS HE

HAS BEEN SO FRIGHTENED PAST
FEW DAYS BY PHOTOGRAPHERS
— AND PLANE TRIP WILL UPSET
HIM.

YOU CAN LEAVE TIGER CUBS IN
QUARANTINE AS THEY ARE TOO
FEROCIOUS TO PLAY WITH — SO
WARN CAROLINE. PLEASE GET
ORVILLE FREEMAN TO LET HIM
IN QUICKLY — THEY HAVE
PRINCE PHILLIP'S POLO PONIES.
PHILLIP TOOK THEM RIGHT
HOME — SO REALLY THINK
THERE WOULD BE NO CRITICISM
AND IT WOULD BE (UNFAIRLY)
CRUEL TO ANIMALS IF YOU LET
HIM BE LOCKED UP IN NEW YORK
FOR THIRTY DAYS. HE WILL GET
SICK THERE. ALL PRESS WILL SAY
YOU WILL LOSE ASPCA VOTE FOR-
EVER IF HE CAN'T COME
STRAIGHT TO GLENORA.

                    LOVE JACKIE

I could just picture President Kennedy
getting this message. He would read it and
by the end he'd be laughing hysterically.
Leave it to Mrs. Kennedy to find a political
reason to convince the president to inter-
vene on behalf of her beloved horse. He

would read the note again, shaking his head in comic disbelief, and then he would do exactly what she wanted. There was no doubt in my mind that Sardar would be grazing at Glen Ora within a week. Hell, the damn horse would probably be in Washington before I was.

The next morning, we were off to the legendary Khyber Pass. We traveled from Peshawar up to the pass with a motorcade convoy of about ten cars occupied by staff and press. Riding in one of the cars near the back was Mrs. Kennedy's personal assistant, Provi Paredes. Poor Provi had a difficult time with heights, so when we began traveling up into the mountains on primitive roads with sheer thousand-foot drop-offs, she panicked. I was told later that she was screaming and carrying on so badly that the driver had no choice but to turn the car around and return her to Peshawar. She never saw the Khyber Pass.

Mrs. Kennedy, on the other hand, thoroughly enjoyed the thirty-four-mile thrill ride through the rugged mountains. Accompanied by the governor of West Pakistan and President Ayub Khan's military aide, she was in a cheerful mood as we carefully navigated the hairpin turns. She thought it was a fantastic adventure.

We first arrived at the mud-walled Jamrud Fort, where bearded tribal leaders, wearing gun belts and daggers, greeted Mrs. Kennedy. Our two advance agents had worked out the details of our short visit with the Pakistan government representatives and the tribal leaders, and had agreements as to exactly what would happen. In honor of Mrs. Kennedy's visit they had erected a large, multicolored tent at the point where the tribal territory began, and had a traditional welcoming ceremony in which they presented Mrs. Kennedy with some special gifts.

Agent Ron Pontius was one of the agents I had assigned to advance this portion of the trip. He was from the south side of Chicago, tough as nails, and I figured his previous experience was as good as any for dealing with these tribesmen. Just as the gift presentation was about to begin, Pontius pulled me aside.

"Clint," he said. "We have a bit of a problem."

"What's up?" I asked.

"Well, they had told me they were going to present Mrs. Kennedy with some gifts. They're going to give her an antique dagger in a decorative case . . . and a lamb. A baby lamb."

"Oh crap. Not another damn animal to get back to the United States," I said.

"Well, that's what I thought. But I just found out that they're going to present her with the lamb and then sacrifice it in front of her."

"Oh, God. *Kill the lamb in front of her?*"

"Yeah. That's what they said. They consider it an honor."

If that happened, I'd be on the next plane to Washington, following in Jeffries's footsteps.

"Ron, listen. We absolutely cannot let that happen. You've got to tell them they can present the lamb to her, but they cannot kill the damn thing until after we leave. You guard that lamb with your life, and do not let her know what is going on."

I stood close to Mrs. Kennedy as they presented the dagger and she accepted it graciously. *What the hell do they think she is going to do with a dagger?* I thought.

Then they brought out the lamb, all dressed in a colorful silk costume. She touched it on its nose and then thanked them for their thoughtfulness as the tribal chieftain led the animal away.

I hurried Mrs. Kennedy into our car, and

as we started back onto the winding road to
the Khyber Pass, I could hear the poor
animal bleating as it was sacrificed in her
honor.

As we progressed over the winding mountain roads, armed tribesmen and members

of the Khyber Rifles, the Pakistan army's paramilitary force responsible for securing the border, escorted us. It was a crystal clear day and you could see for hundreds of miles across the rugged terrain that formed the border between Pakistan and Afghanistan. Our convoy was being carefully watched throughout our journey to the Khyber Rifle outpost, and off in the distance, at various intervals, I could discern men with rifles standing guard as we passed the various checkpoints. The Pakistan government wanted to make sure that nothing would happen to mar the visit to the Khyber Pass.

We drove through the town of Torkham, to the border separating Pakistan and Afghanistan, to the Khyber Pass, where the Pakistan and Afghanistan military faced each other eyeball to eyeball. It was here that the Khyber Rifles maintained control. Looking out from this point at the Hindu Kush mountains, one can feel the presence of Genghis Khan and his horde of Mongol tribesmen as they rode through these mountains. The soldiers of Alexander the Great had passed this way, and based on the number of blue-eyed people we saw along the way, it was apparent they had left descendants behind.

Mrs. Kennedy was wearing the cap President Ayub Khan had given her, and I was sure it was the first time anyone had ever worn the cap with a tailored jacket, skirt, and pumps.

Mrs. Kennedy commented on what a beautiful sight the view was and we then went to Landi Kotal, the headquarters of the Khyber Rifles, to have lunch at the Khyber Rifles Mess. Ron Pontius and I exchanged glances when they brought out a big platter of roast lamb — thankfully not the same animal that had been presented as a gift a few miles back.

Our last night in Pakistan was spent back in Karachi and there was one last thing Mrs. Kennedy wanted to do. The year before, Vice President Lyndon Johnson had visited Pakistan and made a big deal out of meeting a camel cart driver named Bashir, whom he had stopped to shake hands with by the side of the road. In typical LBJ fashion, the vice president casually remarked, "Why don't y'all come see me sometime?" Bashir accepted the invitation, and the friendship between the American vice president and the Pakistani camel cart driver turned into a media spectacle as Bashir toured the United States and became an overnight celebrity.

Mrs. Kennedy had brought a letter from

Vice President Johnson and wanted to personally deliver it to Bashir. So it was arranged for Bashir to bring his family and his now famous camel to visit her at the president's residence in Karachi, with the full ranks of press in attendance.

Of course the press wanted a photo of Mrs. Kennedy with Bashir and the camel. They were snapping away like mad when Mrs. Kennedy suddenly turned to Bashir and asked, "May we ride your camel, Bashir?"

Oh dear God. Riding the camel was not in the program. Mrs. Kennedy and Lee were both wearing knee-length sleeveless dresses with high heels — not exactly camel-riding attire — and I thought, *that's all we need is for you to fall off a camel with the press catching it all on film.*

Bashir looked nervously at the president's military aide for permission. Then the military aide turned to me. "What do you think? Is it okay, Mr. Hill?"

Mrs. Kennedy and Lee were laughing and having such a good time, I thought, what harm can it do?

"If Mrs. Kennedy wants to ride the camel, go ahead and let her ride the camel," I said.

So Bashir got the camel to kneel, and while Lee required some assistance getting on the camel's back sitting sidesaddle, Mrs. Kennedy turned her back to the camel, put her hands on the saddle, and effortlessly hoisted herself up. Sitting side by side, Lee and Mrs. Kennedy were just laughing and laughing. But this wasn't enough for them. No, they wanted to ride the camel, not just sit on it.

"Up, up!" Mrs. Kennedy said as she motioned with her hands to Bashir. "Make him stand up!"

Bashir was so nervous he was sweating. He knew that a camel does not get up very gracefully and with the two women sitting sidesaddle, they were perched rather precariously on the camel's back. He looked at me again, and I nodded.

"Go ahead," I said.

As the camel slowly got up — first its back legs, and then its front legs — I called out to Mrs. Kennedy, "Hold on!"

So there they were high atop the camel, Lee in front and Mrs. Kennedy at the back, laughing and just having the best time as the photographers were snapping away like crazy. Bashir led the camel around at a slow pace, and then Mrs. Kennedy said to Lee, "Hand me the reins, Lee."

Fortunately Bashir did not let go of the lead, and despite Mrs. Kennedy's best ef-

forts to get the camel to take off in a gallop, Bashir retained control. I stood there and watched with amusement, not saying a word, as Mrs. Kennedy laughed and laughed.

The trip to India and Pakistan had been tremendously successful for Mrs. Kennedy personally as well as politically. Ambassador McConaughy would write a note to President Kennedy expressing the enormous impact she had: "She has won the confidence and even the affection of a large cross section of the Pakistani populace who feel that they know her and know that they like her. I believe benefits to our relations with Pakistan will be reflected for a long time in ways intangible as well as tangible."

12
ANDRÉ MALRAUX AND MARILYN MONROE

Mrs. Kennedy and André Malraux at White House dinner

The trip to India and Pakistan had truly been an adventure and Mrs. Kennedy couldn't stop talking about it. For three days, she stayed in London, at Lee and Stash Radziwill's posh townhouse at No. 4

Buckingham Place, not far from Buckingham Palace, and while there was one official visit with Queen Elizabeth, mostly it was meant to be a few days of relaxation before returning to the United States.

Mrs. Kennedy and Lee regaled Stash with stories of their adventures, and when Stash would be disbelieving about something, Mrs. Kennedy would turn to me and say, "Tell him, Mr. Hill. Didn't it happen just as we said?"

She seemed to recall every detail of every fort and palace she had visited, and was still in awe over the magnificent Islamic architecture, the splendor of the Taj Mahal, the opulence of the Indian president's residence. During one of these conversations, I must not have responded in the way she expected to something she had said, because she suddenly turned to me and asked teasingly, "Doesn't anything ever impress you, Mr. Hill?"

I remember looking at her lounging on the sofa in casual slacks, a cigarette in her hand, laughing, so relaxed with her sister and Stash. I wanted to say, "You know what impresses me, Mrs. Kennedy? You. Everything you do impresses me. The way you handle yourself with such grace and dignity without compromising your desire to enjoy life and have fun. You don't even realize the impact you have, how much you are admired, how you just single-handedly created bonds between the United States and two strategic countries far better than any diplomats could have done. And you did it just by being curious and interested and sincere and gracious. Just by being yourself. No politics. No phoniness. Just you being you."

But I was there to do my job, and my job did not entail saying things like that to her. So all I said was "I guess it takes a lot to impress me, Mrs. Kennedy."

When we returned to Washington on Thursday, March 29, the president was waiting at Washington National Airport to greet Mrs. Kennedy. There were lots of press and it was a heartwarming homecoming. As it turned out, Sardar had not yet arrived, but arrangements had been made for the horse to be delivered on a Military Air Transport Services (MATS) plane a couple of weeks later. Somehow President Ayub Khan had convinced someone to allow Sardar's trainer to accompany the horse on the long journey, with specific instructions not to leave Sardar until he was delivered to Mrs. Kennedy. So when Sardar showed up at Andrews Air

Force Base in the middle of the night, poor General Godfrey McHugh, President Kennedy's military aide who had been charged with handling the rather delicate arrangements, was in for quite a shock when the trainer, all decked out in his military attire — the red jacket with brass buttons, white jodhpurs, boots, and turban — got off the plane with the damn horse.

When we returned from the India and Pakistan trip, it was back to our normal routine of Middleburg on the weekends, with Mrs. Kennedy returning to the White House for special functions.

After ten days in Palm Beach for Easter, we returned to the White House the day before another historic dinner honoring Nobel Prize winners from the Western Hemisphere. Impressive as it was to host forty-nine Nobel laureates in her home, Mrs. Kennedy was far more concerned with and excited about a dinner two weeks later honoring André Malraux, the French minister of culture.

While many Americans might not have been familiar with Malraux, he was one of Mrs. Kennedy's idols, and she had become enamored with him during her trip to Paris the year before. Malraux had led an extraordinary life: he was an adventurer/explorer, a

Spanish Civil War veteran, a World War II resistance leader who had escaped from a Nazi prison, and had served in the de Gaulle administration since its inception. But Mrs. Kennedy, with her degree and interest in French literature, knew him best for his prizewinning writings.

Malraux had escorted Mrs. Kennedy through several Paris art museums during the 1961 trip, and even though I was merely on the sidelines at the time, there seemed to be a strong connection between the two of them as they chatted comfortably together in French. Tish called their relationship a mutual "intellectual crush" and that, I think, summed it up perfectly. During one of our many discussions about the Paris trip Mrs. Kennedy said, "Mr. Malraux is so interesting. He has been everywhere, knows everyone, and has done so many things. He is a real hero of France." Mrs. Kennedy wanted this dinner to be the most special one yet, and the guest list was the top priority.

Mrs. Kennedy had a yellow legal pad devoted to the Malraux dinner on which she kept all her notes and ideas, and as the date drew nearer, she would be so excited to tell me which guests had replied and would be attending.

"Oh, Mr. Hill, you won't believe it. Listen to who we have now." She would rattle off names of the writers, poets, artists, and actors who had responded: "Arthur Miller, Thornton Wilder, and Tennessee Williams; Lee Strasberg, Julie Harris, and Geraldine Page; Andrew Wyeth and Mark Rothko; George Balanchine and Leonard Bernstein!"

President Kennedy had made one specific request for the guest list: Charles Lindbergh — who would soon celebrate the thirty-fifth anniversary of his solo, nonstop flight to Paris from New York City — and his wife, an aviator and author herself, Anne Morrow Lindbergh. When Mrs. Kennedy found out that the Lindberghs had accepted the invitation, she was over the moon.

The dinner was a huge success. Mrs. Kennedy appeared in a strapless shocking pink ball gown with white gloves up to her elbows, and from the moment she walked into the East Room, it seemed no one could take their eyes off her. I had never seen her look more lovely. She was the belle of the ball, and once again she had orchestrated an event the likes of which had never before been seen at the White House.

Despite the amazing collection of people representing the arts, however, Charles

302

Lindbergh was the big hit of the party, and he and his wife ended up staying overnight at the White House. For Mrs. Kennedy, the highlight of the evening was when Malraux promised to bring a collection of French masterpieces to the United States for a special exhibition at the National Gallery of Art.

"He even promised *La Giaconda* — the *Mona Lisa!*" she told me the next day. "I've always felt that I was so fortunate to be able to see these great works of art, and now the American public will have the same opportunity. Isn't it wonderful, Mr. Hill?"

The *Mona Lisa* had never before been outside of France. And now she was coming to America. I was impressed.

It was now back and forth between the White House and Middleburg, and since I was now the only agent permanently assigned to the First Lady's Detail, it was just Mrs. Kennedy and me. The weekend of May 18, we were back at Glen Ora, as usual. The weather was beautiful this time of year, and Mrs. Kennedy longed to take advantage of every opportunity to ride Sardar. Additionally, she had entered the Loudon Hunt horse show and was scheduled to ride the Sunday of that weekend. The president had been opposed to her competing in the show, thinking it wouldn't look good politically, but in the end he had acquiesced. Thus far it had been kept a complete secret from the press, and she was really looking forward to it. She was in a particularly happy mood.

As we were driving along one of the secluded country roads, smoking and talking, as usual, Mrs. Kennedy told me about her upcoming plans.

"I'm thinking of spending some time in Italy this summer," she said casually.

"Oh? Where in Italy?"

"Perhaps on the Amalfi Coast. I have some friends there, and I've never been. There's a village on the coast called Ravello I've been told about. Have you been there?"

"I've been to Italy, but no, never to the Amalfi Coast. I would imagine it is beautiful."

"Yes, Lee and I are talking about taking her son, Tony, and Caroline with us. Caroline is old enough to travel abroad I think, and it would be a wonderful experience for her. What do you think?"

"Summer in Italy? The Amalfi Coast? What's not to like?"

She laughed and said, "Oh, Mr. Hill. I know *you* will enjoy it, but do you think it will be all right for Caroline?"

"Oh, I think it would be a great experience for her," I said. "And very relaxing for you, too. Just let me know when you finalize your plans because the sooner I know, the better."

Typically, President Kennedy would join Mrs. Kennedy at Glen Ora on Saturday, but this particular weekend he was in New York City, and wouldn't arrive until Sunday evening. A Democratic fund-raiser had been organized at Madison Square Garden on Saturday night, May 19, in which fifteen thousand donors paid $100 to $1,000 for a ticket to see a lineup of entertainment that included Ella Fitzgerald, Jack Benny, Harry Belafonte, and Marilyn Monroe. President Kennedy's forty-fifth birthday was ten days later, and the show was billed as a birthday celebration. Mrs. Kennedy despised these kinds of functions, and it was not at all surprising for her not to attend. She was much happier spending the weekend at Glen Ora with her hunt country friends than making shallow conversation with political donors.

The morning after the event, it was reported in newspapers across the country how Marilyn Monroe had sung a "sultry rendition" of "Happy Birthday" to the president, after which he had quipped to the audience, "I can now retire from politics having had 'Happy Birthday' sung to me in such a sweet, wholesome way."

I read the article and I'm sure Mrs. Kennedy did, too, but neither of us ever brought up the subject. It was never discussed.

I was pleasantly surprised to find out that the president and Mrs. Kennedy and the children were going to spend the Fourth of July weekend at Camp David. We had just returned from a highly successful trip to Mexico, where more than *two million* people had lined the streets in Mexico City to see President and Mrs. Kennedy. After one night at home — just enough time to unpack and repack my suitcase — I was back at the White House the morning of July 2.

Mrs. Kennedy and the children would fly ahead to Camp David, and the president would join them the evening of the Fourth, after some events in Philadelphia.

Maud Shaw had brought John and Caroline down to the Diplomatic Reception Room to wait for the helicopter that would be landing shortly on the South Lawn. Little John was twenty months old at this time, and boy did he love helicopters. He was bouncing around the room, so excited he could hardly contain himself. It wasn't often that he got to ride in the chopper, so today was a special day.

"Hey, John," I said, as I squatted down next to him. "You ready to ride in the helicopter?"

"Yeah!" he squealed in his little-boy voice, jumping up and down. Just then the unmistakable sound of the helicopter rotors could be heard overhead, and he ran toward the doors. "Copter!" he yelled. "Copter!"

It *was* quite a spectacular sight — to see a helicopter land in your backyard.

Watching John's reaction as we lifted up and flew away from the White House toward the Washington Monument was a joy in itself. Sitting on his mother's lap, his nose pressed against the window, he could barely sit still. His innocent enthusiasm was precious, and a reminder of just what a privilege this was.

I had spent considerable time at Camp David during the Eisenhower administration and for me it was like going home. All familiar territory. Mrs. Kennedy had been there only briefly the previous year, and I had come to learn that one of the reasons she hadn't been enthusiastic about spending time at Camp David was that there were no stables for her horses. So, as was her way, she managed to have stables built at the presidential retreat. Sardar and Caroline's pony, Macaroni, were transported by trailer and were there waiting upon our arrival.

As we were walking along one of the pathways through the woods on the property, Mrs. Kennedy said, "Oh, Mr. Hill, you were right. Camp David is wonderful. It is so secluded and private."

"I thought you would like it here," I said. "It's a great place to relax and get away from the Washington scene."

"Yes, and you know how much I need that," she said with a laugh. "That reminds me, I have finalized the dates I'll be in Italy. Caroline and I will leave during the first week of August, and I think we may be gone three weeks. Lee, Stash, and their children will be joining us in Ravello."

I had been wondering if the trip was going to materialize, since I hadn't heard anything since she'd first mentioned it to me in Middleburg.

"Three weeks in Italy. Sounds wonderful," I said with a smile. "I better brush up on my Italian."

She laughed and said, "Oh, is your Italian as good as your French?"

"I'm afraid not." I laughed.

"Well, I'm not worried about that," she said. "I have decided, however, that the only staff I'm bringing with me is Provi."

She stopped and turned toward me to make a point. "You know, Mr. Hill, I realized that I really don't need anyone but you — you handled everything so well on the trip to India and Pakistan. I'd much rather have you deal with the press and take care of personal things that come up. You understand how I like things done. Do you think you can handle that?"

I was somewhat surprised by this — that she wanted me to handle the kinds of details normally taken care of by her personal and social secretaries — but I also understood why. It gets tiresome having people around you all the time, and she wanted this to be a very private vacation.

"Of course, Mrs. Kennedy. I'll do the best I can."

She smiled and said, "I know you will, Mr. Hill. You always do. There is never any question about that."

13
ANOTHER SUMMER
IN HYANNIS PORT

After the Fourth of July weekend at Camp David, Mrs. Kennedy and the children spent the rest of July 1962 in Hyannis Port, with the president joining the family every weekend. Having a separate residence in Palm Beach away from the hubbub of the ambassador's house during the winter months had worked out so well that this summer they had rented the home of singer Morton Downey, on Squaw Island, which was just about a mile away from the Kennedy compound. Squaw Island wasn't really an island, but was connected to Hyannis Port by a narrow beach road that was used only by the small group of residents who lived there. The Downey home was larger than President Kennedy's own house on the compound, was much more secluded, and with little or no traffic between the two locations, it was ideal.

Lunch on the *Marlin* or the *Honey Fitz* was almost a daily routine. But frequently the president would sail the *Victura,* the twenty-six-foot Wianno Senior sailboat that his parents gave him on his fifteenth birthday. He loved that boat. He could maneuver it with such grace and ease that it was almost like it was an extension of himself.

One day at the end of July, the president and Chuck Spalding were sailing the *Victura* close to shore, just off the dock from the ambassador's residence. It was a cool summer day, and both were dressed in chino pants and cardigan sweaters. They were in the midst of a deep conversation and didn't realize they were coming upon some rocks. Suddenly the boat stopped dead in the water, as it got wedged in between the rocks.

I was in a jetboat nearby, watching the scene unfold, fully expecting the president to get the boat moving again with ease, but the boat wasn't budging. President Kennedy dropped the mainsail to let the wind out of it, stood up, and turned toward me.

"Hey Clint, can you give us a little help? We seem to be stuck."

"I'll be right there, Mr. President," I said as I jumped into the water.

We were so close to shore that the water was only up to my thighs, so I waded over to the stuck sailboat.

There was a glare on the water such that you couldn't see the problem from above, so I took a deep breath and went under the boat. Sure enough, the hull was jammed into some boulders.

"Looks like you're wedged in between two big rocks, Mr. President. Let me see if I can rock the boat to get it moving. You may want to sit down."

The president laughed and said, "Good idea. But I'm more concerned about the boat than Chuck and myself."

I placed my feet on top of one of the boulders and squatted with my back against the bottom of the hull.

"Hang on, Mr. President," I said. "Here we go."

I began to rock up and down and as the boat started to move, I gave one big thrust upward with my body while simultaneously pushing down with my legs. As I did so, the *Victura* slid off the rocks, causing my feet to slip down each side of the rock on which I was standing. The rock was shaped somewhat like a cone, and that final thrust caused me to go straight down, with the cone-shaped rock crashing into my groin area.

I gritted my teeth to keep from yelling out in pain, as the president immediately raised the sail and turned the tiller.

The boat began drifting away.

"Thanks, Clint!" the president called back to me, completely unaware of what had just occurred under the water.

"No problem, sir," I replied. "Glad I was able to help."

I walked gingerly through the water back to the jetboat, and as I climbed over the side, I noticed blood running down my legs. I had almost crushed a very important part of my anatomy. Pained and bloody, I continued on for the rest of the day.

I was completely unaware that Cecil Stoughton, one of the White House photog-

For Clint Hill — "The Secret Service are prepared for all hazards" John Kennedy

raphers, happened to catch the ordeal on film, and apparently word got back to the president that I had been injured. A few days later I received an 8×10 photo of the president and Chuck Spalding standing on the *Victura* as I waded through the water toward the stuck boat. The president had signed the photo with the inscription:

For Clint Hill
"The Secret Service are prepared for all hazards"
John F. Kennedy

It was a very nice gesture, and that photo is a treasured memento. The *Victura* and her passengers were unharmed, and while I did walk a bit funny for the next couple of days, I healed without any permanent damage.

It was easy to see why the Kennedys loved Hyannis Port so much. It was quaint and comfortable, and despite the big houses on the ocean with the boats and yachts, it was unpretentious. The Kiddie Detail agents — Bob Foster, Lynn Meredith, and Paul Landis — and I were there the entire time, and we really began to feel like part of the family. If things needed to be hauled onto the boat, we'd grab the baskets of food or towels or whatever needed to be brought aboard. There always seemed to be dozens of children around, and they all knew us by name — it was always "Mr. Hill" or "Mr. Landis." I often wondered if the younger ones thought we were just a few more uncles. Every Friday afternoon the president would arrive in the helicopter, with even more Secret Service agents, and more activity, and then by Monday morning he would return to Washington and we would return to our more casual routine. Summer in Hyannis Port was a very special time.

In between the constant activity, I was working with Mrs. Kennedy and Secret Service headquarters on plans for her upcoming trip to Italy. Once again I needed to assemble a team of agents to handle the

Clint Hill holds John, watching Mummy and Daddy aboard the Marlin

advance, perimeter coverage, vehicles, travel arrangements, and boats, as well as to assist with the personal security coverage of both Mrs. Kennedy and Caroline.

When President Kennedy was in Hyannis Port, he tried to spend as much time with John and Caroline as possible, even though so many others were always vying for his attention. Caroline was now four and a half years old and the president seemed to want to share his passions with her more and more. They had a very close father-daughter relationship and it was precious to see the two of them together. The Saturday prior to our departure for Italy, President Kennedy spent all morning with Caroline. He took her to Hyannis Country Club to watch the golfers tee off, shopped in the pro shop, and then, walking hand in hand, they went to visit the ambassador at his residence. Because we had secured the perimeter of the property, the Secret Service agents tried to give the president and his family as much space as possible when they were on the compound.

As was typical, a lunchtime cruise was planned aboard the ambassador's yacht, the *Marlin*. I was down on the dock with a couple of the Navy aides getting the jetboats ready when the president came walking down with Caroline.

His tan had deepened after spending so much time outdoors, and dressed in a golf shirt, trousers, and sunglasses, he looked like any other father with his daughter out here on the Cape. Sometimes in this casual environment you could almost forget he was the President of the United States.

"Clint," he said as he walked toward me, "Mrs. Kennedy will be coming out shortly with my father to go on the *Marlin*. But first, I'm going to take Caroline for a short sail on the *Victura*. Just hang close and when I give you the signal, you can come pick us up and take us to the *Marlin*."

"Yes, sir, Mr. President," I answered.

Once Caroline and the president were on the small sailboat, the Navy aides untied the dock lines and gave the boat a push-off. As I watched the president hoist the mainsail, I could see the pleasure he took in this simple, hands-on task. Aboard the *Victura* was one of the few places where the president could fully relax, his direction determined solely by the wind.

They sailed gently away from the dock and from a distance I could tell that the president was explaining to his four-year-old daughter how the sailboat worked — how to trim the sails to take full advantage of the wind, how to manage the tiller. He was so intent on sharing his love of sailing with her, and she just adored him.

After they had sailed for a while the president pulled in the sail, dropped the anchor near shore, and signaled for me to come pick them up.

I sped over and tied the jetboat loosely to the sailboat for the transfer. I stood up and the president said, "Okay, Buttons, I'm going to hand you to Mr. Hill."

The president picked up his daughter and held her toward me. I grabbed her firmly by the waist and said, "Okay, Mr. President, I've got her."

Transferring kids and dogs from one boat

to another seemed to be a constant activity itself, and Caroline knew the routine. As the president stepped into the boat with us I said, "I was watching you, Caroline. You did a good job with that sailboat."

She looked up at me with her big blue eyes and grinned. "Thank you, Mr. Hill. But my daddy did most of the work."

The president and I looked at each other and laughed.

It was a beautiful day on the waters off Cape Cod, as the president, Caroline, and I sped off to join Mrs. Kennedy and the ambassador on the *Marlin* for lunch.

"Clint," President Kennedy said to me, "I wanted to mention a few things to you before you leave for Italy."

"Yes, Mr. President?"

"You know we aren't sending staff over with Mrs. Kennedy to handle the press, but obviously there are going to be photographers there and they will be constantly trying to get pictures of her."

"Yes, sir. Unfortunately that seems to be the case no matter where we go."

"The beach is not secluded and I don't want to see photos of her at luncheons with eight different wines in full view or jet-set types lolling around in bikinis. Do what you can to remind her to be aware of that."

"I'll do what I can, Mr. President."

"Jackie has invited Benno Graziani and his wife, Nicole, to stay with her and Lee in Ravello," President Kennedy continued. "Benno is a lot of fun, but he's always got his camera in his hand."

The Italian Graziani had become good friends with Mrs. Kennedy prior to her marriage, when she was a photojournalist for the *Washington Times Herald,* and now he had become a well-known photographer for *Paris Match* magazine.

"Do not let Benno talk Lee and Jackie into letting him take pictures for the magazine," the president said emphatically. "And above all, no nightclub pictures."

I had met Benno Graziani several times before. He *was* a lot of fun — always clowning around — and I think he was a relief from the political types that dominated their circle of friends. He was one of the few people with whom Mrs. Kennedy let her guard down, and because they had known each other prior to her becoming the wife of John F. Kennedy, she trusted him.

About this time we reached the *Marlin,* and transferred the president and Caroline into the bigger yacht from the jetboat. As I slowly pulled away, the president's words played over and over in my head and I realized that while he wouldn't be joining his wife on this holiday, he was going to be aware of everything she did. With no other staff or press people on the trip, it was clear that he was counting on me to protect Mrs. Kennedy's image as well as her physical safety.

14
TRAVELING WITH
MRS. KENNEDY:
RAVELLO

Clint Hill leads Mrs. Kennedy through the constant crowds in Italy

On August 8, 1962, Mrs. Kennedy, Caroline, Provi, and I departed from New York's Idlewild Airport on a Pan American World Airways regularly scheduled overnight commercial flight for Rome. The excellent relationship that the White House transportation office and the Secret Service had with the major airlines enabled me to handpick most of the Pan Am crew. There were certain pilots and stewardesses we had flown with before who we trusted to provide not only reliable service but also a confidential environment. Mrs. Kennedy attracted so much attention wherever she went that the last thing I wanted was to have passengers and crew members bothering her on the flight. For additional privacy and comfort, we had reserved extra seats in the first-class section so that Mrs. Kennedy and Caroline could lie down across four seats. Provi and I sat across the aisle in our own first-class seats, both of us appreciative of the fact that we could never afford to travel like this on our own. There were certainly fringe benefits to our jobs.

We landed in Rome early the next morning and boarded a privately chartered aircraft for the short flight to Salerno. Agent Paul Rundle was there to greet us, along with Prince and Princess Radziwill, a group of cars, a police escort, and, thank God, no press in sight.

Ravello was only about a ten-mile drive from Salerno, but that was an adventure in and of itself over hazardous hairpin-turn roads high atop the cliffs along the Amalfi coast. There were stretches in the road where only a single car could pass, and even though the Italian police had blocked off the route to normal traffic for our arrival, it was still a nail-biter of a ride, as one minor swerve would send you careening into the sea below. The views were spectacular, however, with colorful stucco villas terraced into the steep and rugged terrain, with the sparkling acqua water below. Mrs. Kennedy loved it.

As our small motorcade entered the main piazza in Ravello, it was like we were driving into a festival — all in honor of Mrs. Kennedy and Caroline. Colorful hand-painted *Welcome Jacqueline* signs hung outside nearly every shop and restaurant, and the cobblestone streets were lined with townspeople and tourists, all waiting to catch a glimpse of Mrs. Kennedy and Caroline. We were greeted by the mayor, a group of dancing children, a live band, and, much to my dismay, an army of photographers. There must have been seventy-five or eighty photographers jostling and shoving each other to get in better position for their shots, and the police were having a difficult time keeping them behind the police lines that had been set up. While Mrs. Kennedy waved and smiled graciously, I could tell that she had the same immediate concerns that I did. Creating the privacy she desired on this trip was going to be an even bigger challenge than we had anticipated. We were going to have to do something about the press.

Finally we made our way through the chaos to the Villa Episcopio, where Mrs. Kennedy, Caroline, and the Radziwills would stay for the next two weeks. Perched high above the Mediterranean Sea, the nine-hundred-year-old stone villa was solidly built into the steep rocky hillside, like an eagle's nest, overlooking the stunning beauty of the Amalfi Coast. Originally a bishop's residence, and once occupied by King Vittorio Emanuele III, the villa with its stone archways and wrought-iron entry gates was like something out of a fairy tale.

As we walked through the cavernous living room, out to the veranda, it was like we were suspended one thousand feet above the crystal blue sea with a panoramic view of the entire area. Mrs. Kennedy turned to her sister and said, "Oh, Lee, it's just magnificent."

Lemon and orange trees grew all across the hillside, filling the air with their fragrant aroma, while red and fuchsia bougainvillea grew in long draping vines up and around the archways and gates. In all my travels, I had never seen a more beautiful setting.

While the villa had unmatched views, it was a long way from the water, so an additional house had been rented that had beach access. The Conca dei Marini beach was not an expansive strand like those in Cape Cod or Palm Beach, but a small spit of pebbly sand surrounded by high rocky cliffs. The beach house was actually more like a cliffside cottage, built into the rocks about one hundred and fifty feet above the beach, accessible by a narrow and very steep stone stairway. It was much smaller than the villa, but very comfortable, and its key purpose was to be used as a place to get out of the sun, for changing in and out of beach attire, bathroom facilities, and midday meals.

In order to get to and from the main villa and the beach house on the steep, windy roads, we had acquired the use of two open-air motorized beach buggies that held six or eight passengers. Made by Fiat, they were fun little vehicles — kind of like a cross between an oversized golf cart and a Volkswagen beetle. I'm not sure who enjoyed them more — the agents or the children.

All of the agents, meanwhile, had rooms at the Hotel Palumbo, which was conveniently located just a short walk down the street from the Villa Episcopio. Like most of the places in this elite area, the Hotel Palumbo was quite pricey, but the advance agents had arranged a deal with management that made it affordable for us. We were living with and among the rich and famous, but we had to do it on sixteen dollars a day.

Unlike the official state visits, there was no set schedule for this trip. Advances could only be conducted once Mrs. Kennedy told me what she wanted to do, and I knew often we would have no advance notice at all.

"Just come to the villa each morning, Mr. Hill," Mrs. Kennedy told me, "and we'll take each day as it comes."

I was deeply concerned about the press — especially the overly aggressive Roman freelance photographers, the original *paparazzi.* Fortunately the Italian police were just as concerned, and they immediately laid down some ground rules for the overzealous photographers: no beach, water-skiing, or swimming pictures; no photographs at the entrance to the villa; photographers will be allowed to stand in the public garden forty meters from Mrs. Kennedy; they may photograph her from a distance in Ravello or boarding a speedboat in nearby Amalfi.

I had seen how these paparazzi operated, however, and I was not convinced they

Clint Hill in working attire, Ravello, Italy

would follow the "rules."

The morning after our arrival, I got up, had a quick breakfast of a biscotti and espresso, and packed a bag to bring along with me. There would be no need for a suit and tie, but I had to be ready for waterskiing, a cruise on a yacht, or anything else Mrs. Kennedy might want to do. There was no agenda. Once we left the area of the villa there was no opportunity to go back for something you forgot or to change clothes, so I had to be prepared for just about anything. I dressed in a black golf shirt with black trousers, and filled an airline flight bag with everything I might need: bathing suit, my Secret Service Commission book, diplomatic passport, and extra ammunition. I slipped my handgun into my holster and wore my shirt on the outside to cover it, but when I wore my swimsuit, the gun would have to go in the airline bag, too. The last thing to go in the bag was a bar of chocolate and a small package of nuts I'd stashed away from the flight. One of the first things you learn as an agent is to eat whenever you have the chance, and use the bathroom whenever the opportunity presents itself. There were plenty of days you'd go for ten or twelve hours without a chance to do either, and a bag of peanuts often became lunch or dinner.

When I arrived at the villa, Benno and Nicole Graziani were there, and everybody was sitting around drinking coffee, laughing, and telling stories. It was nice to see Mrs. Kennedy so relaxed, among friends and family with whom she didn't have to put up any pretense. The group had decided to go to the beach that morning, so we called the police to let them know the plan.

Police boats would patrol the coast, and both uniformed and plainclothes officers would be scattered around the area.

We piled everybody into the umbrella-topped beach cars and headed down the steep, curvy streets to the seaside town of Amalfi, where we would then take a boat to the Conca dei Marini. The children loved the miniature cars and everybody was laughing and kidding around.

We had arranged to have a boat available for waterskiing, sightseeing, and just getting from one point to another. This boat was not your average rental boat, however. It was a Riva — a sleek Italian-made Chris-Craft type boat about twenty-four feet in length that had a highly varnished mahogany hull and an extremely powerful engine. The boat was named *Pretexte* and came with its own operator, who was on standby for the duration of our stay. He spoke very little English, but we managed to communicate in a sort of charades-type system in which I tried to act out what it was we wanted to do, and he would respond by nodding his head and rattling off in Italian. Somehow it worked.

By the time we got the beach cars down to Amalfi, word had gotten out, and there was a line of photographers waiting on the pier. Their cameras were snapping away as they called out, "Jackie! Jackie! Look here! Over here! Smile Jackie!"

It felt like we were being surrounded by a swarm of locusts.

"Just ignore them," Mrs. Kennedy whispered to Caroline. "They'll tire of us soon enough."

I knew better. Jacqueline Kennedy had become an international star — more popular than Elizabeth Taylor, Sophia Loren, and Grace Kelly all put together — and these photographers knew that a picture of the First Lady of the United States of America in a bathing suit was worth big money. The question was, how to get them to stop? Obviously the "rules" set out by the police weren't working.

When Mrs. Kennedy emerged from the beach house in a dark green one-piece bathing suit with a low-cut back, the photographers went crazy. Some were snapping pictures from balconies in villas perched above the bay, while others were hazardously zipping around in motorboats trying to get a different angle. Benno Graziani, Mrs. Kennedy, and Lee were wading in the water with the three young children trying their best to ignore the circus-like scene that was getting worse by the minute. Benno wasn't taking any pictures, but his mere presence was creating a problem.

Agent Paul Rundle had been trying to resolve the situation with the police and the photographers, and he had learned that the other photographers felt that Graziani had exclusive access to Mrs. Kennedy, which was unfair to the rest of them. They refused to back off. So Rundle and I came up with an idea. What if we got Mrs. Kennedy to give them ten minutes of photos if they would agree to back off and leave her alone after that? The photographers thought that sounded reasonable. Now I had to get Mrs. Kennedy to go for the idea.

I waded into the water to Mrs. Kennedy, who was pushing Caroline and Tony around on a raft. Her hair was pinned up in the back, with her long bangs hanging wispily in front of her eyes.

As soon as she saw me, she said, "Oh Mr. Hill, these photographers are horrible. Can't you do something about them?"

"That's what I came to talk to you about. Apparently they are upset that Benno has almost unlimited access to you, while they are restricted to distant shots. They've agreed to stop this aggressive behavior, and promise to give you some privacy if you will just pose for one good photo in your bath-

ing suit."

"Do you really think they'll do as they say with just one photo session?"

"I honestly don't know, but I will tell them that one session is what they get and then they must withdraw and quit harassing you. If they don't comply, we will make their lives miserable."

"Oh Mr. Hill, can't you make their lives miserable without me having to pose?" she asked.

I knew this was asking a lot of her, and was so outside of her comfort zone, but there didn't seem to be an alternative, other than have her spend the entire holiday inside the villa.

"I think in all fairness, Mrs. Kennedy, you have to give them something or the harassment will only continue to get worse and worse."

This still didn't satisfy her. She looked at me pleadingly.

"Can't you just round them all up and have them sent away somewhere?"

I wanted to laugh, but she was dead serious.

"Unfortunately, Mrs. Kennedy, they have a right to be here, too, because it's public property."

Remembering President Kennedy's instructions to me, I knew he wouldn't be thrilled about seeing his wife posing for the cameras in her bathing suit, but the alternative was that someone was going to get a shot of Mrs. Kennedy in an awkward position, and that would be even more embarrassing and potentially humiliating.

"All right, if you think it will work, I'll allow a brief photo session."

"Thank you, Mrs. Kennedy," I said. "I'll arrange it and we'll try to just get it over with."

A short while later, Mrs. Kennedy posed on the landing area just below the beach

Mrs. Kennedy poses for paparazzi with Tony, Caroline, and Lee

house, in front of a big *Welcome Jacqueline!* sign the locals had hung from the rocks. The photographers had a field day. She was very cooperative and when they asked for photos of her with the children and Lee, she even agreed to that.

Agent Rundle even got into the action and posed in his bathing suit next to Mrs. Kennedy, the children, Benno Graziani, and the caretaker of the beach cottage.

The next day, hoping the photographers were going to be less intrusive, Mrs. Kennedy decided to go water-skiing.

"It'll just be Caroline and me," she said.

Pointing to the water skis and motioning out to the water, I tried to explain to the Italian boat captain what we wanted to do. I spoke in English with my best Italian accent, hoping that perhaps some of the words might sound familiar. Mrs. Kennedy was doubled over with laughter as both of our hand motions got bigger and our voices louder in an effort to communicate. Finally, Mrs. Kennedy interpreted, and off we went.

The police had closed a stretch of water near the beach house so that other boats wouldn't be a nuisance, and we had Secret Service agents in another couple of boats, but this in itself created attention, and soon traffic was snarled on the hilly road overlooking the bay. I kept watch in the back of the *Pretexte* as Mrs. Kennedy, wearing a one-piece black bathing suit, easily popped up out of the water on a slalom ski. She skied back and forth across the wake, pulling tight on the rope, leaning back, in complete control, as the growing audience ashore whooped and hollered.

Not wanting to encourage the crowd, Mrs. Kennedy simply ignored them. We made a few loops around and then she gracefully let go of the rope and slid into the water. We raced around to pick her up, but instead of climbing into the boat, she looked at

Caroline and said, "Do you want to ski with me, Caroline?"

"Yes! Yes!" Caroline squealed.

Oh God.

"Mrs. Kennedy, I'm not so sure this is a good idea. How are you going to do this?"

"Oh, Mr. Hill, don't worry. She can stand on top of the skis. Toss me the other ski."

I knew there was no way I was going to talk her out of this, so I motioned to the agents in the other boat that Caroline was getting in the water.

Little Caroline was such a good swimmer that even though the water was a bit choppy, she had no problem treading water while the driver slowly pulled the boat around to get the rope taut. Mrs. Kennedy put Caroline in front of her on the skis, and, with bended knees, leaned slightly forward so Caroline could hold on to the wood handle of the towrope.

When the rope was taut and straight, I called out, "Are you ready?"

"Ready!" Mrs. Kennedy yelled.

The captain put the boat in gear, and as he accelerated, Mrs. Kennedy popped out of the water with Caroline balanced on the top of the two skis. It was a photo-perfect picture and the press who witnessed it were having the time of their lives.

The ski duo didn't last but a few seconds, though, as they hit a small wave and both of them toppled into the water. Caroline wasn't keen to try again, but she didn't want to get back in the boat, either.

"I'm going to swim all the way to shore, Mummy," she proclaimed.

Not wanting to squelch her daughter's enthusiasm, Mrs. Kennedy agreed to let her go, provided she have the inflatable ring, and of course a Secret Service agent.

I motioned to the other boat and yelled, "Caroline wants to swim back."

Agent Paul Landis immediately jumped into the water and swam with Caroline back to shore, while Mrs. Kennedy did a bit more water-skiing.

Sure enough, one of the press photographers with a very long telescopic lens on his camera had caught Mrs. Kennedy and Caroline together on water skis, and the next morning they were front-page news around the world. It ended up causing quite a controversy, especially in Great Britain, where one London newspaper ran the head-line:

PLEASE MRS. KENNEDY, DON'T DO IT AGAIN!

The article proclaimed that mothers everywhere were cringing at the picture, and "water skiing is hazardous for grown-ups. For a 4-year-old girl it's madness."

I knew what an accomplished water-skier Mrs. Kennedy was, and how strong a swimmer Caroline was, so I never felt they were in any danger. Just as the president wanted to pass along his love of sailing to his daughter, Mrs. Kennedy wanted to expose Caroline to the sport that she loved. Nonetheless, I got the feeling that Mrs. Kennedy may have received some strongly worded advice from her husband either by telegram or telephone shortly thereafter. Caroline did not water-ski with her mother again during our stay in Italy.

It became our routine to go to the beach house around ten o'clock each morning, and have a swim and then lunch, followed by an afternoon activity ashore or on the boat. When Mrs. Kennedy was at the beach house, the Italian caretaker and his wife handled everything. This middle-aged Italian couple adored the children and were eager to do anything for their famous guests. The wife cooked lunch every day while her husband hauled the beach toys, towels — and often the children — up and down the steps.

One day I was standing on the boat landing, when the husband came down the stone steps, carrying a big bowl.

"Buongiorno!" he said with a huge smile.

"Buongiorno!" I replied.

That was about the extent of our ability to converse with each other, so I just smiled and let him do whatever he needed to do. I watched as he knelt down on the concrete landing and peered into the water below. All of a sudden he thrust his right arm into the water and when his hand came out he had hold of a baby squid.

Mama mia! Did he really just do that?

He immediately put the squid's head into his mouth, bit it off and spit it out. I couldn't believe it. Never in my life had I seen such a thing.

He put the headless squid into the bowl and proceeded to repeat the procedure four or five times. He looked at me, and smiling broadly, said something in Italian, and then took the bowl of fresh squid and raced up the stairs.

A short while later, a wonderful aroma came wafting down the stairs. I looked up and saw the caretaker coming down the steps with a pasta bowl in his hands. He handed me the bowl, with a fork and big spoon, and indicated that I should eat it now. The homemade linguine was drenched in a flavorful garlic and olive oil sauce, all mixed together with a generous portion of fresh calamari. It was absolutely delicious. Just thinking about the slightly sweet, nutty flavor of the freshly caught baby squid in that garlic sauce still makes my mouth water.

The paparazzi were much less intrusive after Mrs. Kennedy posed for the bathing suit photos, but they never completely went away. They really resented the continued presence of Benno Graziani, and the situation became even more complicated when a man named Gianni Agnelli arrived.

We were up at the villa when a magnificent yacht sailed into the Bay of Salerno. The eighty-two-foot-long, two-masted yawl glided in like a prima ballerina making her grand entrance onstage, with its spinnaker flying. It was unlike any other sailboat I had ever seen. The mainsail, spinnaker, and smaller mizzen sail were all a deep red color, like a fine Chianti, and as the yacht cut through the water, its sails stood out against the blue sea like beautiful scarves, flying in the wind.

I soon learned that this was the *Agneta,* and she belonged to the chairman of Fiat corporation, Gianni Agnelli. Agnelli and his wife, Marella, ran in the same circles as the Kennedys, and had known them for several years, but I had no previous knowledge that the Agnellis were meeting up with Mrs. Kennedy in Ravello. The yacht was anchored quite a ways from the shore, and it was then that Mrs. Kennedy came to tell me her plans.

"My friends the Agnellis have arrived on their yacht, and Lee and Stash and I are going to go aboard. They're sending a small boat to the dock to take us out to it."

"Okay, Mrs. Kennedy," I said. "I'll alert the police and let them know." I tried to play it cool, but I was really looking forward to getting on that beautiful yacht.

I had never met Gianni Agnelli before, but he had a reputation for being a man with great charisma and impeccable style, a trendsetter. The *Agneta* with her long, lean lines, teak decks, and magnificent, richly varnished mahogany hull was every bit as sleek and classy as her owner.

Gianni Agnelli was standing on the deck of his yacht as we approached. Once we boarded, he gave Mrs. Kennedy and Lee each warm hugs. He was gracious and kind, and immediately introduced me to the three crew members, who gave me a tour of the yacht so that I could familiarize myself with the layout of the boat. They treated me like a guest as they showed me the master suite with a small marble fireplace, the two twin cabins and a Pullman berth, the main salon, galley, and several heads. The interior was as elegant as the exterior. When I returned to the deck, Mrs. Kennedy was so relaxed, laughing with her sister, Stash, Gianni, and his wife, Marella. It seemed her entire demeanor changed as soon as she boarded the yacht. It was so peaceful being out on the water, so far from the crowds and the

Mrs. Kennedy and Gianni Agnelli followed by Clint Hill

constant flashes from the ever-present cameras. I had the feeling we were going to be spending considerable time aboard the *Agneta*.

As it turned out, Agnelli offered Mrs. Kennedy the use of the *Agneta* for the rest of her stay in Italy, and while he and his wife would join Mrs. Kennedy on occasion, much of the time he wasn't there at all. The Italian police organizations — the Questura and Carabinieri — provided security coverage in addition to providing a chase boat and crew for our agents. To give Mrs. Kennedy and her guests as much privacy as possible, I was the only agent that stayed aboard the yacht.

One day Mrs. Kennedy decided she wanted to go to Paestum, an ancient Greco-Roman city about forty miles down the coast from Ravello, so we sailed down the coast on the *Agneta,* her red sails flying, creating a dramatic sight for the people ashore. When we got to Paestum, the captain had to anchor the yacht a hundred yards or more from the rocky shore. The only way to get ashore was by rowboat. I was somewhat concerned because the boat they hauled into the water was not much bigger than a bathtub. I didn't see how we were going to get Mrs. Kennedy, Lee, a female friend who had joined us, me, and the oarsman all into that tiny boat, but rather than make two trips, we all crowded in, and the crewman rowed us to shore.

Founded in about 600 B.C., Paestum was originally called Poseidonia, in honor of Poseidon, the Greek god of the sea. In 273 B.C., the Romans, after taking control of the area from the Greeks, changed the name to Paestum. The area is known for its well-preserved temples, which rival the Parthenon in size and beauty, and this is what Mrs. Kennedy wanted to see and explore. She had read the history of the area and was regaling the rest of us with stories about the ancient civilizations as we walked through the temples and ruins. She took a deep interest in history and it never ceased to amaze me how much she knew about not only American history, but also the histories of so many other regions of the world.

After walking around the large site, we headed back to the coast, where the crewman was waiting for us with the rowboat.

There had been a few paparazzi following us around as we toured the ancient city, and they of course followed us as we made our way back to the shore. The sea was a little bit rougher than when we had arrived and in order to get into the boat, we had to take our shoes off, roll up our trousers, and wade into the water.

The oarsman was seated in the middle of the boat and I tried to hold the boat steady

so Mrs. Kennedy and the two other women could get in gracefully.

"Do you need me to give you a hand, Mrs. Kennedy?" I asked. I was worried she might slip and the photographers would have a field day.

"No, thank you, Mr. Hill. I can do it just fine," she said as she hoisted herself into a seated position on the edge of the boat and then swung her legs around. She was laughing, completely ignoring the photographers, just having a great time. By the time we all got into the boat, it was sitting quite low in the water, and as the oarsman struggled to get the boat in motion against the surf, it felt like we were going to flip over. A few of the photographers had waded into the water, and were snapping away.

"For Christsake!" I yelled. "Put down your goddamn cameras and somebody give us a push before we swamp!"

Meanwhile, Mrs. Kennedy was laughing just as hard as she could. I don't know if she was laughing at me or whether she thought it would be hilarious if we actually did flip over.

Finally someone gave us a push and we got out beyond where the waves were breaking so we could get some momentum.

"Oh, Mr. Hill," she said. She was laughing so hard she could barely speak. "If you could have seen the look on your face when you thought we were going to tip over! I hope one of the photographers caught it. I would pay to have that shot!"

As it turned out, one of the photographers did get a shot of that look on my face and he gave both Mrs. Kennedy and me a copy of the picture. It was such a great snapshot of a moment in time, a photo that captures the mischievous, adventure-loving woman I had come to know so well, to care for so very much. It was a moment when she was carefree, enjoying life to its fullest.

We used the *Agneta* more and more as a mode of transportation to get to the places Mrs. Kennedy wanted to see because it was a respite from the prying eyes of the press and the gawking public. On the yacht, her privacy could be maintained. Mrs. Kennedy would read, or write, or sketch at her leisure, and simply enjoy the company of her sister and friends. Most of the time Gianni Agnelli was not on the yacht, but on one of the first evenings that he was, he introduced everyone to a new drink.

"What is that?" I asked Mr. Agnelli the first time he served the cherry-colored drink to Mrs. Kennedy.

"It's an *aperitivo*. We call it Negroni," he said.

"Here, try it," he said as he handed me a glass.

I took a sip and handed the glass back to him.

"Not bad," I said. It had a bitter, sort of sweet taste to it. "What's in it?"

"Campari — that's what makes it red — then it's mixed with sweet vermouth, and garnished with a slice of orange." He took a sip from his glass and then added, "Oh yes, and just a dash of gin for a bit of an extra kick."

I laughed. There was definitely more than "just a dash" of gin in that drink.

"It's very refreshing," Mrs. Kennedy said. "I rather like it. I'll have to remember to have Campari on hand at the White House for our Italian guests." She laughed.

Aperitivo time was a way to wind down after a day out on the water, and as the sun went down, when the bottle of Campari came out, it signaled the evening's activities were about to begin.

One evening, we took the *Agneta* to Capri, a stunning island that rises dramatically out of the Tyrrhenian Sea. It was a beautiful sail, and after anchoring at the port, we transferred to the Riva motorboat, the *Pretexte,* because Mrs. Kennedy wanted to cruise along the shoreline. She had been invited to dinner at the villa of Silvio Medici De' Menezes and his fashion designer wife, Princess Irene Galitzine, who were friends of the Agnellis. They had a lively al fresco dinner served at midnight, and it wasn't until after two o'clock in the morning that we returned to the *Agneta* and sailed back to Ravello.

A couple of days later, Mrs. Kennedy came to me and said, "Mr. Hill, I need you to do something for me like you did in Palm Beach. You know the problems we had with people when I wanted to go shopping on Worth Avenue? Well, I would really like to go shopping at the boutiques in Capri, but

I'm sure the same thing would happen."

"Yes, you're absolutely right, Mrs. Kennedy. I have no doubt you would be hounded by not only tourists, but also those damn paparazzi. I'm afraid it would be much worse than what we experienced in Palm Beach."

She sighed. "I agree. So, I came up with an idea."

As she said that, she looked at me and I could see the mischief in her eyes, like a little girl asking her daddy for something she knew Mummy wouldn't approve of.

"Would you go to Capri for me, Mr. Hill?"

"What exactly is it you want me to do?" I asked.

"Well, Irene Galitzine offered to go shopping for me. I'd like you to take the motorboat there and accompany her — you know the kinds of things I like — and then you can bring back the clothes to me here."

This is way outside my job description, and you know that, I thought to myself. But just like in Palm Beach, I would be keeping her out of exposure to large numbers of people. It seemed like a good protective move.

"Oh, Mrs. Kennedy," I said, shaking my head. I tried to look serious but I couldn't keep from smiling. "Yes, I will go to Capri for you. But don't you dare tell anyone that

I've done this."

She laughed and said, "Oh, I won't tell anyone, Mr. Hill. It will be our secret."

I explained to Agent Paul Rundle, the advance agent, what I was about to do, and he assured me he would take care of everything until I returned. The bigger problem was trying to explain to the driver of the *Pretexte* what I needed, but somehow he seemed to understand, and the next day we took off for Capri.

We hugged the coastline until reaching a point where we had to cross a considerable distance of open water in the Tyrrhenian Sea to get to the island. It was a windy day, and the water was filled with whitecaps and very choppy, and every time we went up over a wave and crashed down hard, it felt like we were being punched over and over again. I had never felt seasick before, but this time I was very close. It seemed to take forever but finally we reached the marina, and fortunately I managed to avoid being sick. I disembarked and proceeded to the villa to meet Princess Irene Galatzine — I was a bit windblown and sunburned, but no worse for the wear.

The princess was a strikingly beautiful woman, very tall and elegant, and I felt somewhat like the hired help, literally just off the boat, but she was extremely gracious, and eager to go shopping for Mrs. Kennedy. I had never heard of her before the previous night's dinner, but Mrs. Kennedy had informed me that she was famous for designing trousers for evening wear, known as "palazzo pants." Apparently she was quite well known in the fashion world. So, there we were, Princess Irene Galatzine and me, shopping together in the upscale boutiques on the Isle of Capri.

We selected an assortment of dresses, trousers, gauzy blouses, jewelry, shoes — you name it. We had a whole damn wardrobe for Mrs. Kennedy. By the time we finished and returned to the villa, it was getting dark, so going back to Amalfi across that rough body of water was out of the question.

"You'll have to stay here at the villa," the princess said. "I'll make sure the boat driver is informed and have him available for you first thing in the morning."

"Well, thank you very much," I said.

She showed me to a guest bedroom and told me to make myself at home. "And you must have dinner with me, Mr. Hill."

"Oh, no," I protested. "I don't want to be any trouble."

"I insist," she said. "Truly, it will be a

pleasure."

I hadn't intended on staying overnight and I had no clothes to change into for dinner, so I just went into the bathroom and washed up as best as I could.

When it came time for dinner, I was surprised to find that it would just be the princess and me dining alone. It was a simple meal of seafood and pasta with a salad and excellent Italian bread. Princess Irene made me feel comfortable, but being a participant — rather than an observer waiting in the wings — was something I wasn't used to.

So, that's how I ended up spending the night at the home of Princess Irene Galitzine. My life had been one adventure after another. It sure was a long way from the North Dakota Children's Home to the residence of a princess on the Isle of Capri. I felt like the luckiest man in the world.

In the morning, after some juice, extremely dark coffee, and a biscotti I was ready to leave. I now had in my possession a large trunk filled with purchases the princess had made on Mrs. Kennedy's behalf. We loaded it on the boat and off to Amalfi I went. The trip back was smoother than the one to Capri, no whitecaps, and we made good time. Arriving at the beach house, we were met by the caretaker, who carried the trunk up to the house. Mrs. Kennedy and Lee were there and very glad to see me, and especially the trunk full of goodies. It was as if Christmas had arrived in August.

Mrs. Kennedy insisted I stay as she and Lee went through the various items of clothing. When I began to tell them about the wild boat ride across the choppy waters, they started laughing hysterically.

"I want you to tell me everything, Mr. Hill," Mrs. Kennedy said with childlike delight in her voice. "From the moment you left here. Every detail. What Irene said, where you shopped, what you ate for dinner. Don't leave anything out."

So, as Mrs. Kennedy and her sister gave me an impromptu fashion show, I regaled them with details of my adventure on the high seas, and the night with the princess on the Isle of Capri.

Thus far, I had managed to protect Mrs. Kennedy while also keeping things in line with the president's instructions. Then one evening Mrs. Kennedy informed me that she, along with Lee, Stash, and their guests, was going to go to Positano — to a nightclub.

Clint Hill and Mrs. Kennedy in Italy

The president's words immediately popped into my head. *And above all, no nightclub pictures.*

"Okay, Mrs. Kennedy, whatever you want. I'll handle it," I said.

We left Ravello and traveled down the coast to Positano, yet another picturesque town on the Amalfi coast. We had alerted the police and advised them to provide a contingent of officers dressed in plainclothes, to make our large group, which included Mrs. Kennedy, several friends, and several Secret Service agents, as inconspicu-

*Paul Landis escorts Mrs. Kennedy
in Positano*

ous as possible. The nightclub was crowded, and while Mrs. Kennedy did not go unnoticed, we managed to keep the paparazzi outside. Everyone was dancing and laughing, having a great time, into the wee hours of the morning. I remember watching Mrs. Kennedy enjoying herself so much with her friends. Oh how I wished I could be out there on the dance floor with them, a participant rather than a bystander.

■ ■ ■ ■

As the days went by, everybody fell more in love with Ravello. It was so picturesque, so charming, the people so warm and friendly. Finally, on August 31, we bid farewell to Italy. The three weeks on the Amalfi coast had been nothing less than enchanting, and all of us, especially Mrs. Kennedy, were sad to leave. When I think back and remember those special times, one of the things that stands out is the memory of the view in the evening, looking down the coastline. Anchored in the harbor at Amalfi, a thousand feet below Ravello, the fishing boats and private yachts were decorated with strands of tiny white lights throughout the rigging, so that it looked like a hundred thousand candles dancing in the water. It was magical.

15
OCTOBER CRISIS

After a month in Hyannis Port and three weeks in Italy, I assumed we would return to Washington, but we ended up flying straight from Rome to New York to Quonset Point, Rhode Island, where the president met us, along with an enormous crowd and full press coverage. It was a wonderful, happy family reunion, and from there we were off to Hammersmith Farm for the next several weeks.

While Mrs. Kennedy typically spent September weekends at Hammersmith Farm, the president was particularly interested in being there in September 1962 because the America's Cup yacht races were being held off the coast of Newport in Narragansett Bay. The America's Cup is the oldest active trophy in international sport, a series of races between the defender — the yacht club that last won the title — and the challenger. This year, America's team from the New York Yacht Club was defending its title against Australia — the first time the challenger was from a country other than Great Britain or Canada. There were plenty of social events surrounding the races, including a reception for crew members at Hammersmith Farm and a black-tie dinner in honor of the Australian and American competitors, which created plenty of work for the Secret Service.

After spending so much time on the *Agneta,* Mrs. Kennedy appeared to take a real interest in the races, which seemed to please the president. It was an entirely new sport for me to watch and I found it interesting — especially the days we were aboard the

USS *Joseph P. Kennedy, Jr.,* a U.S. Navy destroyer named after the president's older brother, who was killed during World War II. Some of the races were very close, and in the end the New York Yacht Club's *Weatherly* defeated Australia's *Gretel* 4–1 in the best-of-seven race series.

Also around this time, a new yacht joined the mix of boats the president had at his disposal. The USS *Manitou* was a beautiful sixty-two-foot yawl, a Coast Guard vessel, brought to Newport as an addition to the presidential fleet specifically because of the president's love of the sea and sailing. The president was excited about the opportunity to have a large sailing yacht available, and the *Manitou* had everything he wanted. She was sleek, fast, and maneuverable, and capable of taking overnight trips with sleeping accommodations for nine people.

The last two weeks of September were a blur as we traveled between Newport and Hyannis Port — to visit the president's father and so the president and Mrs. Kennedy could vote for Teddy Kennedy in his first senatorial primary — and then back to Newport, followed by a one-night stop in New York City, where I accompanied Mrs. Kennedy to the brand-new Philharmonic Hall for a performance of the New York

Clint Hill's favorite photo of JFK at the helm of the Manitou

Philharmonic Orchestra, led by Leonard Bernstein, then back to Newport again for the finish of the America's Cup races. While the president returned to Washington during the weekdays, Mrs. Kennedy intended to stay at Hammersmith Farm with the children until October 9, 1962. We did have a brief return to Washington — to Middleburg, actually — because President Ayub Khan of Pakistan happened to be visiting the United States.

Mrs. Kennedy was eager to show Ayub

Mrs. Kennedy and Ayub Khan riding together at Glen Ora

Khan how delighted she was with Sardar, and she insisted on him coming to Glen Ora, so that they could ride together. There was nothing romantic between Mrs. Kennedy and Ayub Khan but their mutual love of horses was the bond they shared, and Sardar was the emblem of that bond. President Kennedy also realized that the first lady's trip to India and Pakistan earlier in the year had been immensely successful in the Cold War campaign to promote the interests and ideology of the United States around the world.

The long summer and early fall away from Washington was about to come to an end, and I must admit I was a little bit sad about it. I thoroughly enjoyed being "on the road" where there was no routine, and while at times it was more challenging to protect Mrs. Kennedy, I thrived on the constant activity. The time spent in Hyannis Port, Ravello, Amalfi, Capri, New York City, and Newport had been wonderful. And because I had shared all these adventures with Mrs. Kennedy, she and I were closer than ever before. We enjoyed each other's company, I knew how she liked to have things done, and we trusted each other implicitly.

Finally, on October 9, 1962, we were headed back to the White House. The *Caroline* was unavailable, so Mrs. Kennedy, Caroline, John, and I, along with the Kiddie Detail agents and several staff members, boarded a U.S. Air Force plane and flew to National Airport in Washington, D.C.

At one point during the flight Mrs. Kennedy came to me and asked, "Mr. Hill, will there be any press at the airport when we arrive in Washington?"

"I honestly don't know, Mrs. Kennedy," I said, "but let me see what I can find out about the situation before we land."

"I really do not want any photos taken."

I understood her concern because this would be the first time in more than three months that she and the two children would be seen in public together. In all likelihood there would be a swarm of photographers waiting to get the shot of the three of them getting off the plane. It was also somewhat unusual for us to be flying on a military aircraft without the president aboard, and I certainly didn't want that to stir up any controversy, either.

"Okay. I understand. I'll make the appropriate arrangements."

I contacted the U.S. Secret Service office at the White House and requested a restricted area be established for our arrival. Secret Service personnel would be there with a car for Mrs. Kennedy and the children, White House cars for staff, and a baggage truck. When we landed, the pilot taxied the plane to the spot we had agreed on, and I could see that all the necessary vehicles were standing by, just as I had arranged, behind a gate waiting for the all-clear to proceed toward the plane.

I was standing behind Mrs. Kennedy as she began going down the steps to the tarmac, with Caroline and John in front of her, when I noticed a motorcycle following our vehicles through the gate and toward the plane. There were two people on the motorcycle — a courier driving and a photographer I recognized, holding his camera up and shooting one shot after another.

Goddamnit.

This particular photographer had been overly aggressive and intrusive in the past, and I had had it with him.

As I got to the bottom of the steps, I ran toward him, grabbed hold of him, pulled the camera out of his hands, and ripped the film out of the camera.

"What the hell are you doing?!" he screamed at me.

"You're in a restricted area and I'm confiscating your film," I said.

I saw two more canisters of film in his chest pocket, and without saying anything, I grabbed those and shoved them in my own jacket pocket.

He was really putting up a fuss and by this time the airport police had come over.

"He's all yours," I said.

By this time Mrs. Kennedy, John, and Caroline were in the car, so I took my place in the front passenger seat. I turned around and said, "Sorry about that, Mrs. Kennedy. That was Roddy Mims from UPI. We've had trouble with him in the past."

I pulled out the canisters of film from my pocket and showed them to her. "But I got the film, which, as you could tell, he wasn't happy about."

She smiled and said, "Well I'm happy about it. Thank you so much, Mr. Hill. I really appreciate the fact that you went after him."

I hated that the children had to see that confrontation, but it didn't seem to faze them. The matter was forgotten, as Caroline chattered away to her mother on the ride back to the White House.

Shortly after arriving at the White House, I was notified that the president wanted to see me in the Oval Office *immediately.*

Geez. Word travels fast.

When I walked into the Oval Office, President Kennedy and Press Secretary Pierre Salinger were standing there, waiting for me.

The president had his arms folded and got right to the point.

"What happened at National Airport, Clint?" he asked.

I explained Mrs. Kennedy's concerns, and what I had done to arrange a private arrival.

"Then, Mr. President, photographer Roddy Mims came riding into the area we had restricted, on the back of a motorcycle driven by a courier. I stopped him, confiscated his film, and turned him over to the airport police."

"Look, Clint, I know your intentions were honorable, but the press are making an issue out of it and we have to make a decision as to how to handle it."

"I know Roddy can be pushy and obnoxious," Salinger interjected, "but we have to resolve the issue before it gets blown way out of proportion."

President Kennedy had unfolded his arms and had an apologetic look on his face.

"Clint," the president said, "I'm sorry, but I'm afraid you are going to be the scapegoat in this case. You'll have to take the blame."

"I understand," I said. "I didn't mean to cause a problem for you, Mr. President."

"It's all right. Pierre will take care of it," President Kennedy said. "And thank you for always looking after the best interests of Mrs. Kennedy and the children, Clint. I honestly do appreciate it."

"Thank you, Mr. President," I said.

Pierre Salinger told the press that there had been a "misunderstanding." The film would be returned to the company the photographer worked for, and the matter would be considered closed.

I didn't like the decision, but I accepted it knowing that the president knew my intentions were good, and that for public relations reasons, the finger had to be pointed somewhere. They didn't want the Office of the President or the White House press office blamed for denying the press access.

It was one of those situations in which I learned that my obligations and loyalty to Mrs. Kennedy would have to be weighed against how willing I was to risk being chastised for my actions by her husband.

I also had to explain the situation to the assistant chief of the Secret Service and the Special Agent in Charge of the White House Detail, but the two of them agreed that I had acted appropriately, and I was advised to continue doing my job as I had in the past. My name appeared in the newspapers along with the story, and while the photographer claimed I told him he was under arrest, that simply wasn't true. The furor died down after a couple of days and was never mentioned again.

It was around this time that I felt I had finally found the right person to be my assistant — Paul "Debut" Landis from the Kiddie Detail. During our three weeks in Italy, I had had the chance to evaluate how he worked in a foreign environment and because Caroline was with us so much, I got to see how he and Mrs. Kennedy interacted as well.

Nobody ever explained to me why Agent Jeffries was removed from Mrs. Kennedy's detail, but I had a sense that personality conflict had something to do with it, and I wanted to make sure that I chose someone in whom Mrs. Kennedy had confidence. Even though he was the youngest agent on the detail, Paul was extremely conscientious, easily able to adapt to changing situations — a necessity if you were going to be protecting Mrs. Kennedy — and, perhaps just as important, we worked well together as a team. He happily accepted the position and it was like a breath of fresh air to have someone working with me after having only temporary assistance for the previous seven months. We brought in an agent named Tom Wells from the Miami office to replace Paul on the Kiddie Detail, and once we were back at full strength — two agents with Mrs. Kennedy and three with the children — I had a renewed sense of confidence in our ability to do the job properly and effectively.

On Monday, October 15, Prime Minister Ahmed Ben Bella of Algeria came to the White House and was given an official arrival ceremony on the south grounds, complete with military review and herald trumpets. Mrs. Kennedy was not scheduled to participate, but she wanted John to witness the ceremony, and all the pageantry, with his father performing his duties as the President of the United States — and she wanted to do so in a very low-key, unobtrusive way. John, now nearly two years old, was fascinated by the military. He loved the uniforms, the marching, and the weapons. So Mrs. Kennedy called Miss Shaw and asked her to bring John down to the area of the Rose Garden near the president's office.

"Come, John," she said as she lifted him up into her arms. "Let's go watch the ceremony. You can see all the military men in their uniforms."

John's eyes were wide as he saw the procession gathering, the row of colorful flags representing the various military units, and the two countries. I walked alongside Mrs. Kennedy as she carried him to a spot just behind a hedge. She was holding him up high enough so he could see, while keeping the two of them somewhat hidden from plain view, and John was filled with questions.

"What's that? Why are they doing that? What are all those flags? Put me down."

Mrs. Kennedy set him down and squatted next to him. When she couldn't answer the

Mrs. Kennedy, John, and Clint Hill watch ceremony from behind bushes

questions, she turned to me and said, "Mr. Hill surely knows, don't you Mr. Hill?"

So I squatted down and tried to explain to young John what all the pageantry was about.

Mrs. Kennedy understood that their time in the White House was a privilege, and even though John and Caroline were so young, she made every effort to include them in these types of historic events so they would have a better understanding of what their father did.

■ ■ ■ ■

Also at this time, President Kennedy's father came for a rare visit to the White House. Mrs. Kennedy had arranged for him to sleep in the Lincoln Bedroom and had set aside most of Tuesday, October 16, to spend with him, so I had anticipated a quiet day in which I could catch up on things in my office, a small corner of the Map Room on the ground floor of the White House, directly across from the elevator that went to the residence. On the morning of October 16, National Security Advisor McGeorge Bundy showed up before the president had come down from the residence. A Secret Service agent escorted Bundy to the elevator and up he went.

Later, I would learn the reason for Bundy's unusual early morning visit to the president's bedroom: A U-2 spy plane had taken aerial photographs of Cuba's military bases, which showed that nuclear missiles were installed on launchpads. The intermediate-range missiles were being brought to Cuba on Soviet ships, and now there was photographic evidence that Khrushchev's claim of only having defensive weapons was nothing less than a lie. The

Soviets had just turned up the heat in the Cold War, eighty miles from the coast of Florida, and the ramifications were terrifying.

The Secret Service had well-established plans to protect the president, his family, and key members of the government in the event of an emergency or a major catastrophe. Whether we would go to the bomb shelter on-site at the White House or relocate to an undisclosed site outside the metropolitan area would be determined by the threat and the actual situation. This was not something I had ever discussed with Mrs. Kennedy, however. I decided I needed to have a frank talk with her about our procedures, in case the unthinkable were to happen. When Mrs. Kennedy emerged from the private residence on Wednesday, October 17, I asked her to come into my office, and shut the door behind us.

"Mrs. Kennedy, I'm sure you are aware of the situation that has developed regarding the Soviet Union, Cuba, and the United States, right?"

"Yes, Mr. Hill. The president has discussed it with me."

"Well, I know this is a terrible thing to have to talk about, but I think it's important that I let you know what the Secret Service plans are in the event of an emergency."

Standing there in front of me, she looked so beautiful — a young wife and mother with the world at her feet.

I reached out my hand and touched her elbow.

"You know about the bomb shelter here, under the White House. I know that J. B. West gave you a brief tour of the facility a few months ago . . ."

I just had to state the facts.

"In the event . . . a situation develops . . . where we don't have time to leave the area, we would take you and the children into the shelter for protection."

Before I could explain any further, she pulled away from me, in what can only be described as defiance, and said, "Mr. Hill, if the situation develops that requires the children and me to go to the shelter, let me tell you what you can expect."

She was looking me straight in the eyes. She lowered her voice, into a deep whisper, and with complete and utter conviction said, "If the situation develops," she repeated, "I will take Caroline and John, and we will walk hand in hand out onto the south grounds. We will stand there like brave soldiers, and face the fate of every other American."

I was not completely surprised by her response, but hearing her say it out loud made me realize what I would have to do, should we get to the point that moving her and the children into the bomb shelter was the directive.

I knew then and there that, should that occasion arise, she may or may not have forgiven me, but I would have picked her up, wherever we were, and into the shelter we would have gone. As long as I was responsible for her protection, nothing else mattered.

But instead I said, "Well, Mrs. Kennedy, let's just pray to God that we will never be in that situation."

During the next few days the situation was very tense. The president and Mrs. Kennedy tried to maintain a regular schedule to make everything appear normal. The president traveled to Bridgeport, Waterbury, and New Haven, Connecticut, returning the same day. At the White House, he would pop in and out of the Cabinet Room, where the National Security Council's Executive Committee, or ExComm, was secretly meeting, and at one point he had a meeting with Foreign Minister Andrei Gromyko and Ambassador Anatoly Dobrynin of the USSR.

On Friday, October 19, I took Mrs. Kennedy, John, and Caroline to Glen Ora — as was our normal weekend routine when we were in Washington — while the president traveled to Cleveland; Springfield, Illinois; and Chicago.

On Saturday morning, October 20, 1962, Mrs. Kennedy came to me and said, "Mr. Hill, the president just called and he is on his way back from Chicago. He wants the children and me to return to the White House. Will you arrange for a helicopter?"

This was highly unusual, so I knew something must have happened with the negotiations. *Why would the president be leaving Chicago early? And why the urgent need for a helicopter when we could easily drive back?*

"Of course, Mrs. Kennedy."

When I called for the helicopter, I found out that indeed the president had left Chicago early — due to a "bad cold."

I knew damn well the president didn't have a cold, and never before had he requested Mrs. Kennedy to return to the White House from Glen Ora.

Additional photos and analysis had concluded that the Soviets were readying fighter jets and bombers and were assembling cruise missile launchers. Additionally, there was evidence that SS-5 missiles were being assembled, which were capable of reaching anywhere in the continental United States. President Kennedy decided it was time to alert the American public that we were facing a chilling crisis. There was no more time for discussion. He had to make a final decision on military options. On Monday evening, October 22, from his desk at the Oval Office, the president appeared on live television and radio and somberly laid out the indisputable evidence that had been gathered over the past six days. In the seventeen-minute address he gave Khrushchev an ultimatum to "halt and eliminate this clandestine, reckless and provocative threat to world peace and to stable relations between our two nations" or else the United States would, justifiably, take military action.

Looking into the cameras, the president stated, "I have directed the armed forces to prepare for any eventualities; and I trust that in the interest of both the Cuban people and the Soviet technicians at the sites, the hazards to all concerned in continuing this threat will be recognized."

He outlined the immediate steps the United States was taking, including a strict "quarantine" — essentially a blockade — on all ships containing cargoes of offensive weapons, as well as a request for an emergency meeting of the Security Council of the United Nations.

He ended the solemn address with this: "My fellow citizens, let no one doubt that this is a difficult and dangerous effort on which we have set out . . . but the greatest danger of all would be to do nothing.

"The path we have chosen for the present is full of hazards, as all paths are — but it is the one most consistent with our character and courage as a nation and our commitments around the world. The cost of freedom is always high — and Americans have always paid it. And one path we shall never choose, and that is the path of surrender or submission.

"Our goal is not the victory of might, but the vindication of right — not peace at the expense of freedom, but both peace and freedom, here in this hemisphere, and, we hope, around the world. God willing, that goal will be achieved.

"Thank you and good night."

The readiness of the defense establishment, a state commonly referred to as DEFCON, for "Defense Condition," is noted by a numbering system that indicates the severity of the situation. DEFCON 5 is the least severe condition, while DEFCON 1 means a nuclear war is imminent. On October 22, a DEFCON 3 was ordered for the entire military establishment, meaning an increase in readiness from that which is normal. The Strategic Air Command, however, was placed on DEFCON 2, meaning they were prepared for war. Never before had we reached the stage of DEFCON 2. Secretary of Defense Robert McNamara put it best when he said, "We are staring down the gun barrel of nuclear war."

The ExComm was meeting daily, sometimes twice a day, and the president was in and out of the Situation Room for immediate updates. Mrs. Kennedy was calm, but extremely concerned, and she remained close to the children at all times. She stayed mostly in the private quarters so that she could be available whenever the president needed her.

At the same time, the Secret Service was on heightened alert for whatever might happen. We were braced for an evacuation of key personnel by helicopter and knew exactly who would go in which helicopters. We all knew that in the event that a nuclear attack was imminent, there would be people scrambling to get on the helicopters. If people tried to get on who were not authorized, as a last resort we would have no choice but to shoot them. It was a sickening thought, but this was the reality of the situation we faced.

The following Friday, October 26, there seemed to be a breather in the negotiations. Word came that Khrushchev had agreed to keep his ships out of the quarantine zone for forty-eight hours. That morning, Mrs. Kennedy called me in my office and said, "Mr. Hill, I'm going to go to Glen Ora with Caroline and John. The president will be joining us tomorrow."

"Okay, Mrs. Kennedy," I said. "I'll make the arrangements. I think some time in Glen Ora would be very beneficial to you right now."

I tried to put Mrs. Kennedy at ease, but I knew that there would be no relaxing for the Secret Service agents. We had to remain vigilant, fully expecting that at any moment the word would come for us to evacuate immediately.

As it turned out, the president didn't come to Glen Ora on Saturday, and I was about as tense as I'd ever been. All of us were. You didn't want to think about what might happen, but you had to go over every possible scenario in your mind to be prepared. It was excruciating.

On Sunday morning, after a sleepless night, we got word that the president was coming to Glen Ora. When he got off the helicopter with a smile on his face, I knew that everything was going to be all right.

Khrushchev had agreed to dismantle the missiles in Cuba, and the Russian ships carrying nuclear materials had turned around. President Kennedy had redeemed himself after the Bay of Pigs disaster, and was in high spirits. But most important, he had won Khrushchev's respect, and the two of them had averted nuclear war.

I thought to myself, *Thank God, I won't have to carry Mrs. Kennedy kicking and screaming into a bomb shelter.*

16
THE THIRD PALM BEACH CHRISTMAS

Around the time of the Cuban Missile Crisis, there was another crisis that Mrs. Kennedy had to deal with on a personal level.

"Mr. Hill," she said, "I just got word that Mrs. Tartiere is not going to renew our lease for Glen Ora, and she wants to move back in as soon as possible."

She was visibly upset and I could understand why. Middleburg was the one place she really felt comfortable and could completely relax.

"Oh, I'm sorry to hear that, Mrs. Kennedy. I know how much you enjoy being here."

"Yes, this really came as a surprise and I just don't know what to do. I love this area so much. I so enjoy being able to ride with the hunts, and it's such a wonderful place for the children, and for the president to come and relax."

"Well, you know Camp David is always available for you. I know it doesn't have the ambience of Middleburg, but it certainly affords you privacy."

"Yes, I know we have Camp David," she said. Then she got that look on her face, that sort of mischievous look, as if a bright idea had just popped into her head. Her eyes widened, and she said, "Let's just see what we can come up with."

Over the past year and a half, as Mrs. Kennedy and I drove through the Virginia countryside, she had often commented about how much she liked the area and how wonderful it would be to have a place of their own someday. She had in fact looked at some property that was for sale, and I figured this was what she had in mind.

It wasn't too long after this that we were at Glen Ora for the weekend, when she told me she had found out about some land that she wanted to go look at.

"It's quite close to Bunny Mellon's and it's called Rattlesnake Mountain. Isn't that a great name?"

"I suppose," I said, "if you are partial to rattlesnakes in your backyard."

She laughed and said, "I've made arrangements to go look at the property. It's owned by Hubert Phipps, and I told him we'd meet him there this afternoon."

"Okay. That sounds great. What's the address?"

"There's no address per se, but I told Mr. Phipps you would be able to find it."

I checked with the state police and determined that Rattlesnake Mountain was not far from Middleburg, and near a little general store called the Atoka Store. So we got in the station wagon and drove out to meet Mr. Hubert Phipps at Rattlesnake Mountain.

I soon learned that Phipps was a gentleman farmer who owned about a thousand acres and was willing to sell about forty of them to the Kennedys. When we got there, I couldn't believe we were in the right place because there was no mountain in sight. It turned out Rattlesnake Mountain was just an undeveloped piece of land slightly more elevated than the surrounding area.

As we traipsed around the brush and grass, I kept my eyes peeled for rattlesnakes, my hand on my revolver, just in case. The property was far enough off the road and somewhat shielded by trees so that it had the secluded atmosphere Mrs. Kennedy wanted. Its best selling point was a beautiful view of the Blue Ridge Mountains in the distance, which Mrs. Kennedy loved.

A week or so later, the president and Mrs. Kennedy's sister, Lee, came out to tour the property. Mrs. Kennedy was already planning the house, how it would sit, where the man-made lake stocked with fish would go, and I thought, *Mr. President, whether you like it or not, you are about to own property on Rattlesnake Mountain.*

Sure enough, the property was purchased, architectural plans based upon Mrs. Kennedy's own sketches were decided upon, and construction began. The house would not be finished until the spring of 1963, but fortunately, in all the trips I made with Mrs. Kennedy to view Rattlesnake

Mountain, we never came across a snake of any kind.

Thanksgiving Day, November 22, 1962, was spent, as usual, in Hyannis Port, and by mid-December we were back in Palm Beach. This was my third Christmas in Palm Beach and by this time I was very comfortable with the Kennedys' traditions and routine. Once again the president and Mrs. Kennedy rented the Paul residence, and this year Lee and Stash and their two children came to spend the holidays with them, while the rest of the extended Kennedy family congregated at the ambassador's residence. Provi brought her son Gustavo down, and he played with John and Caroline, just like another cousin. Stockings were hung from the mantel of the fireplace in the living room, and the children were eager with anticipation for Santa Claus to come.

Mrs. Kennedy wanted to find a place to take the children to see Santa, so Agent Landis located a Santa Claus at Burdines department store in West Palm Beach, and off we went for a visit. Both Caroline and John sat on Santa's lap, telling him their gift requests.

"I want a talking doll," Caroline said.

"And I want a toy helicopter!" John piped

in. It was a priceless scene, but Mrs. Kennedy insisted no photographs be taken, and the store complied with our requests.

The next week was typical Palm Beach activity. The children would go with the agents and Miss Shaw to the Lake Trail to play, while Mrs. Kennedy would swim in the saltwater pool at the ambassador's residence, or remain at the Paul residence sketching, reading, or writing notes about future projects.

Meanwhile, the president had been to New York City and to Nassau, Bahamas, for a four-day conference with Prime Minister Macmillan of the United Kingdom to discuss the complex Cold War issues. It wasn't until December 21 that he was able to join the family in Palm Beach, and Mrs. Kennedy decided she wanted to surprise him.

Air Force One landed and while a group of local politicians greeted the president, I waited with Mrs. Kennedy, John, and Caroline off to the side of the arrival area, hidden from view. John and Caroline thought this was great fun and could hardly contain themselves.

Just as the president was about to get into the official car that was waiting for him, Mrs. Kennedy said, "Okay, John and Caroline, now go surprise your daddy."

The two children ran to greet their father with hugs and kisses. It was a charming family reunion after the trauma of the Cuban Missile Crisis and having been apart for much of the pre-holiday season.

Even though Christmas carols played on the radio and garland and lights were strung all over town, it never really felt like Christmas to me in Palm Beach. This was the tradition for the Kennedys, however, and they so enjoyed being together during these great big family gatherings. There were definitely times when it was difficult to be on the outside looking in, looking at this happy, beautiful family as they laughed and played. I can still see the joy on President Kennedy's face as he played with John and Caroline and their new toys on Christmas Day, 1962.

It would be the last Christmas John and Caroline would spend with their father. The last Christmas Mrs. Kennedy would spend with her husband. I was thirty years old. And for me, too, Christmas would never be the same again.

One important piece of the Cuban Missile Crisis was the quiet negotiations for the release of the Bay of Pigs prisoners. President Kennedy had vowed that the United

States would not invade the island of Cuba and in return Fidel Castro had agreed to release the 1,113 men who had been held captive in Cuba since the failed invasion twenty months earlier, for the ransom of $53 million in food and medical supplies.

On December 27, 1962, President Kennedy invited five leaders of the Cuban brigade who had just landed on U.S. soil to meet with him privately at the Paul residence in Palm Beach.

After the president had spoken with the men for about an hour, he told me to bring Mrs. Kennedy, John, and Caroline down to the patio to say hello.

I could tell that Mrs. Kennedy had briefed the children on who these men were, and when their father introduced them, they shook hands with the men with wide-eyed curiosity. Mrs. Kennedy spoke to the Cuban brigade leaders in Spanish and while I couldn't understand a word that was being said, the pride and appreciation in the men's eyes was evident.

"They are such brave men," she told me. "I wanted John and Caroline to meet them so that when they are old enough to understand, they will remember them, and the sacrifices they made."

As the group left, President Kennedy

thanked them once again for their valor and added, "I hope someday to visit a free Cuba."

Two days later, we flew to Miami on the presidential helicopter to the Orange Bowl so that President and Mrs. Kennedy could publicly honor all the 1,113 Bay of Pigs survivors who had just been freed. I was surprised when Mrs. Kennedy told me she would be joining the president to this very public event, making an appearance before a mass audience, and it was a clear indication of how close the two had become during and after the Cuban Missile Crisis. Additionally, she knew that her ability to speak Spanish to the crowd could only help her husband in overcoming what remained the biggest regret of his presidency.

Some forty thousand people jammed the Orange Bowl stadium to welcome home the brave freedom fighters, all of whom were dressed in their khaki uniforms — many of them missing arms and/or legs. The ceremony was wrought with emotion as President Kennedy was presented with the brigade's war-torn flag, which had flown during the three-day battle at the Bay of Pigs, and which had been carefully saved as "their most treasured possession."

As he graciously accepted the flag, President Kennedy stepped up to the microphone and boldly proclaimed, "I can assure you that this flag will be returned to this brigade in a free Havana."

The stadium erupted into a thunderous roar.

Then Mrs. Kennedy stepped to the microphone and spoke, without notes, in fluent Spanish.

There was barely a dry eye in the audience as she concluded her brief remarks, and again the audience roared with applause. Then the president and Mrs. Kennedy got into a white convertible and as the car slowly drove out of the stadium, they stood and waved to the exuberant crowd.

I and the other agents jogged alongside the car, constantly scanning the crowd for any sign of disturbance or disruption, as we headed toward the waiting helicopter outside the arena. I helped Mrs. Kennedy out of the car, and as we walked toward the helicopter, the president came alongside her.

"You were wonderful, Jackie," he said with a beaming smile on his face. "They loved you. Your remarks were just perfect."

Under normal circumstances, I would never interject myself into a conversation like this, but I had to quell my curiosity.

"Mrs. Kennedy," I said, "you got such an

At Orange Bowl, Agents Jerry Blaine, Ken Giannoules, Clint Hill, and Paul Landis work left side of
car

ovation that I have to ask . . . what exactly did you say?"

She and the president laughed and before she could answer, President Kennedy said, "Great question, Clint. I'd like to know myself."

I knew that, more than likely, Mrs. Kennedy had shown her husband her intended remarks prior to the speech, so he was just ribbing her, and she knew it.

We reached the helicopter and as soon as we got aboard, Mrs. Kennedy pulled out the piece of lined yellow paper on which she had handwritten her remarks, and read them, in English: "It is an honor to stand here today with some of the bravest men in the world — and to share in the joy of their families who have hoped and prayed and waited so long. I am proud that my son could meet your officers. He is too young to realize what you did — but I will tell him your story as he grows up. My hope for him is that he will be a man a fraction as brave as the members of Brigade 2506."

It was a lovely and heartfelt sentiment. Brief, but extremely meaningful and personal. Finally, it seemed, the president could put the failed invasion behind him, and move forward with a renewed sense of purpose and pride.

On New Year's Eve, President and Mrs. Kennedy attended a lavish party, for the second year in a row, at the residence of Charles and Jayne Wrightsman. It was the social event of the season. The Dom Pérignon was flowing, and the party lasted until three o'clock in the morning. As we entered 1963, it seemed there was much to celebrate.

There was something different about Mrs. Kennedy, though. I wasn't exactly sure what it was, but there was a sparkle in her eyes, like she was keeping a secret.

■ ■ ■ ■

PART FOUR:
1963

■ ■ ■ ■

17
MONA LISA
AND NEW YORK CITY

On January 8, 1963, we returned to Washington on Air Force One, and arrived back at the White House by helicopter just a few hours before President and Mrs. Kennedy were due at the French Embassy for an eight o'clock dinner in honor of the unveiling of the *Mona Lisa* at the National Gallery. I barely had time to go home, shower, and change into my tuxedo before returning to the White House.

When Mrs. Kennedy came out of the elevator from the residence on the arm of the president, she looked more stunning than I had ever seen her before. She wore a flowing, pale pink gown and no jewelry but for a pair of exquisite diamond earrings that hung like sparkling raindrops from her ear to her jaw. The dinner at the French Embassy was an elegant affair for about one hundred people, hosted by Ambassador Herve Alphand and his wife. The guests included France's minister of culture, André Malraux, and his wife, as well as many members of the Kennedy family, among them the president's mother, Rose. After the dinner, the schedule called for everyone to be transported to the National Gallery of Art, where more than one thousand other invited guests were waiting to see the unveiling of the most famous smile in the world.

Everything was going like clockwork until we got into the elevator at the gallery. The poor elevator operator took one glance at Mrs. Kennedy, and I could tell he was really flustered. He pushed the wrong button and then got even more flustered and somehow the elevator wouldn't budge. We were on a tight time schedule, and the president said, "Well, I guess we'll just have to walk up the stairs."

Mrs. Kennedy's dress was designed so that it hung nearly touching the floor in the front, and actually had a short train in the back that dragged along the ground. She had on high heels, and I was worried that she was going to trip.

"Mrs. Kennedy," I said as we approached the narrow stairwell, "I'm going to hold your dress up in the back to make sure you don't step on it, okay?"

I could tell that she was a bit put out by having to climb the stairs, but as soon as I said this, she seemed to relax.

Smiling, she said, "Oh, thank you Mr. Hill," and we proceeded up the stairs, with me behind her, uncomfortably holding her dress like an attendant at a wedding.

Mona Lisa's visit to the United States was an enormous success, both politically and culturally. After three weeks in Washington, she was transferred to the Metropolitan Museum of Art in New York City, and by the time she returned to France, more than one and a half million Americans had personally viewed Leonardo da Vinci's masterpiece. Mrs. Kennedy was absolutely delighted with the outpouring of interest in this important work of art. Her lobbying efforts with President de Gaulle and Minister Malraux had paid off, and the result was that there was a renewed appreciation of culture and fine arts in America.

A few weeks after the *Mona Lisa*'s arrival, I was walking with Mrs. Kennedy at Glen Ora when she shared some exciting news with me.

"Mr. Hill, I suppose you have noticed that I haven't been horseback riding like I normally do."

"Yes, Mrs. Kennedy, I had noticed that." I looked at her and smiled. "And also that you didn't water-ski when we were in Palm Beach."

She broke into a big grin and said, "I can't keep any secrets from you, Mr. Hill, can I?"

"I'm afraid not, Mrs. Kennedy. I know you too well. I'm so happy for you. When will the blessed event occur?"

"Doctor Walsh says sometime in mid-September."

"That's wonderful news, Mrs. Kennedy."

And that's how I found out that the president and Mrs. Kennedy were expecting their third child.

Nineteen-sixty-two had been an amazing

year — filled with wonderful memories and historic events which I had the privilege of witnessing. With the political successes of the previous months, and now the news of the impending birth of the Kennedys' third child, it seemed that 1963 was only going to be even better.

Mrs. Kennedy had informed me that she wanted to keep the news of her pregnancy quiet for the time being, so few people outside the close family knew about it beyond Paul Landis and myself. She did make it clear, however, that she was planning to curtail her activities quite a bit.

"Sorry, Mr. Hill," she told me one day, "but I don't foresee any trips to Ravello or Greece in the near future." Then, smiling, she added, "You'll just have to suffer with me in Palm Beach and Hyannis Port."

I laughed. "That will be just fine, Mrs. Kennedy."

The trips we had taken over the past two years had been wonderful, but I was glad to hear that she planned to take it easier now that she was pregnant. What I did notice, however, was that she was walking more than she ever had before. Any time she could find an opportunity to walk, she would walk. I didn't ask her directly, but I assumed that since she could no longer water-ski, ride horses, or play tennis, she was concerned about keeping fit, and not gaining excess weight. Thus, she walked. And when she walked, I walked.

Being physically fit was something that was important to President Kennedy as well. Shortly after he was elected, he published an article in *Sports Illustrated* titled "The Soft American," in which he noted how the television set, the use of cars to travel everywhere, and a myriad of other modern conveniences had resulted in a generation of people who were not used to strenuous physical activity. He ended the article noting that parents must be responsible for instilling this in their children. "We do not want our children to become a generation of spectators. Rather, we want each of them to be a participant in the vigorous life."

President Kennedy and Mrs. Kennedy, and indeed every member of the Kennedy family, lived by this philosophy. Whether it was swimming, playing tennis or touch football, horseback riding, waterskiing, or taking a vigorous walk, exercise was part of their daily lives.

In those early months of her pregnancy, when Mrs. Kennedy and I walked together, we talked about all sorts of things, and this was frequently when I found out about her upcoming plans. A few days after telling me she was going to curtail her activities, and that we weren't going to travel much this year, she informed me that she planned to take Caroline to New York City the first week of February.

"We'll just visit friends and do some shopping. I think Caroline is old enough now that she will really enjoy it," she said. The one thing she insisted on, however, was that the trip be kept as quiet as possible. She had always been private, but now that she was pregnant, I sensed a vulnerability in her that I hadn't seen in the past two years. It went unsaid, but I knew that there was always the underlying fear that she might lose the baby she now carried. And if God forbid it did happen, she certainly didn't want to have to deal with it in the public eye.

The night before we were to leave for New York City, I was at home, packing for the trip, when I got a phone call from the agent on duty at the White House.

"Clint," he said, "we just had some unusual activity here that I thought you should know about."

Unusual activity?

"What happened?" I asked.

"Well, the President and Mrs. Kennedy decided to take a spur-of-the-moment walk outside the White House grounds."

"Spur of the moment?"

"Yes, that's right. It was completely unannounced. They just came down the elevator, and walked out the Southwest Gate. We had to scramble all the agents from their posts to provide protection."

This *was* highly unusual. In the two years President and Mrs. Kennedy had been in the White House, I'd never known them to walk outside the White House grounds without informing the agent in charge — especially at night.

"Were there any incidents?" I asked.

"No. Everything was fine, and we got them covered by the time they left the Southwest Gate. They simply took a leisurely stroll around the perimeter fence to the Northwest Gate and came back inside. They were only gone about twenty minutes."

"Thanks for letting me know," I said. I wasn't sure what was going on, but this little spontaneous walk proved to be a predecessor of things to come.

In New York, Mrs. Kennedy stayed at their suite at the Carlyle Hotel, while Caroline stayed at the Smith residence. The presi-

dent's sister Jean Kennedy Smith and her husband, Steve Smith, had two young sons, Stephen Jr. and William. Stephen, or "Stevie" as he was called, was about Caroline's age, and the two were close. The Smiths' luxurious apartment was located across the street from Central Park, just a couple of blocks from the Carlyle.

The week in New York City was filled with activity — Mrs. Kennedy met friends for lunches at Giovanni's and Le Pavillon, and one evening at Le Club, the European style nightclub Oleg and Igor Cassini started — but she also spent a lot of time showing Caroline around the city, sharing with her daughter the things she loved about New York. Walks in Central Park, visits to museums, and even a visit to the United Nations. They were having such a wonderful time, and toward the end of the week Mrs. Kennedy informed me that the president would be joining them on the weekend.

"We want to keep it private," Mrs. Kennedy said. "No police escorts, no motorcades, no official functions. We just want to enjoy the city like we used to."

When it was just Mrs. Kennedy and Caroline, we were able to come and go without attracting too much attention. But when the president arrived, keeping a low profile was a much bigger challenge. There would always be at least five or six Secret Service agents around the president, and trailing closely behind the president's limousine was the not so unobtrusive follow-up car.

As soon as the president arrived in New York, he came straight to the Carlyle to see Mrs. Kennedy, and then, surrounded by his Secret Service detail, walked the two blocks to his sister's apartment to see Caroline. Of course he was instantly recognized, and while he made it to Jean's place without incident, the word was out that the president was in town, on the Upper East Side of Manhattan.

That evening, the president and Mrs. Kennedy had dinner with friends at Le Pavillon, before going to the theater to see *Beyond the Fringe,* a satirical British comedy featuring Peter Cook and Dudley Moore. The night was capped off by an after-theater party at the Earl E. T. Smith's residence, a friend from Palm Beach who had been U.S. ambassador to Cuba.

I could see that after two years in the White House, they were yearning for a sense of "normalcy." It was a real challenge for the Secret Service agents to keep these presidential movements private yet still maintain an adequate amount of protection, without police escorts or the blocking of streets, but we managed. Both the president and Mrs. Kennedy appreciated the effort and they thanked each of the agents personally.

The next morning, the president wanted to take Caroline to Central Park before church. Once again he walked from the Carlyle to the Smith residence, and picked up Caroline and her cousin Stephen. Agents were posted outside the door of the apartment building, which caused some attention, and by the time the president came out with the two children, a crowd had gathered.

This was exactly what the president had hoped to avoid. Not wanting to ruin the children's outing, he left Caroline and her cousin with Agents Bob Foster and Tommy Wells, and returned to the Carlyle, where he went in the main entrance at Seventy-sixth Street. He was really distraught about not being able to do something so simple as take a walk with his five-year-old daughter in Central Park, so the agents came up with an idea. We took him through the hotel and snuck him out a little-used back door on Seventy-seventh Street, where we had an unmarked car waiting. We drove the short distance to the park, and got the president out without anyone noticing, then met up with Caroline, Stephen, and the Kiddie Detail agents. The president walked around the park with the children for about twenty minutes in complete anonymity. No public interference and no press. President Kennedy loved it.

It was wonderful to see the president able to have this special time — just a father spending time with his daughter in Central Park.

The next item on the agenda was Mass, and the president got back to the Carlyle just in time to pick up Mrs. Kennedy and her sister, Princess Radziwill, to drive to St. Ignatius of Loyola Church. I took my place in a pew directly behind Mrs. Kennedy, while Agent Art Godfrey sat next to me, behind the president. The other agents were scattered around the church.

When it came time for the collection plate to be passed around, we all knew what to expect. The president would reach his hand behind him, holding it out, palm up. Neither he nor Mrs. Kennedy ever carried cash, so one of the agents would put a twenty-dollar bill in the president's hand for the collection.

Sure enough, the president's hand came back toward Art Godfrey. Godfrey looked at me, then rolled his eyes, and it was all I could do not to laugh. He pulled out his wallet and put a twenty in the president's hand. The president took the bill, looked at it, and then, without saying anything, stuck his hand back again. Godfrey turned to me and opened his wallet to show me it was empty. So I pulled out my wallet, and placed another twenty-dollar bill in the president's hand. Once again he looked at it and then stuck his hand back. Now Godfrey was cracking up. All I had left was a ten, so I placed that in the president's hand and hoped he didn't reach back again. Fortunately, fifty dollars was sufficient on this particular Sunday.

We would always get reimbursed by the president's secretary, Evelyn Lincoln, but providing cash to the President of the United States for the collection plate was one of those things we all joked about.

After the services, the president, Mrs. Kennedy, and Mrs. Radziwill got into the unmarked Secret Service car we were using, and we proceeded to the restaurant Voisin, where they were going to meet Prince Radziwill and Chuck Spalding for lunch. I was in the follow-up car, and suddenly, at Sixty-seventh Street and Park Avenue, the president's car stopped.

Agent Roy Kellerman jumped out of the front passenger seat of the president's car and said, "The president and Mrs. Kennedy would like to walk the rest of the way to the restaurant."

Walk? In New York City? In broad daylight?

I knew Kellerman didn't think this was a good idea, either, but I guessed that this was at Mrs. Kennedy's urging. It was a beautiful day in New York City, and I knew how she hated being driven anywhere when there was the possibility of walking. So we got out and walked with the president and Mrs. Kennedy to Voisin. It was just four and a half blocks, but it was rather unnerving to have the president and first lady so exposed, without any advance preparations.

I had a feeling the same thing would happen on the way back to the Carlyle after lunch, and sure enough it did. The president and Mrs. Kennedy walked partway back to the Carlyle, talking and laughing as they walked briskly down Park Avenue. It was challenging for the agents to cover this extemporaneous activity, but it was wonderful to see them thoroughly enjoying themselves — like they were just an ordinary couple — thrilled to be expecting a child, with so much to look forward to.

On the flight back to Washington later that afternoon, I thought about the spontaneous activity that had taken place in New York City and outside the grounds of the White House. This was inevitably going to be the new standard.

Our jobs just became a little more difficult.

18
THE SUNSHINE HIGHWAY

Mrs. Kennedy, Chuck Spalding, Lee, Clint Hill, and Prince Radziwill

The next weekend it was back to Middleburg, where the new home was under construction on Rattlesnake Mountain, then back to Washington by helicopter for a couple of days. I had just enough time to get my laundry done, retrieve clothes from the cleaners, and repack. Now we were off to Palm Beach for a few days in the sun.

Once again, President and Mrs. Kennedy returned to the C. Michael Paul residence, which they had rented for the winter of 1962–63. By the time we got to the Paul residence it was after eleven o'clock, and when my head hit the pillow in my room at Woody's Motel, it was after midnight.

Fortunately, Mrs. Kennedy took the next morning easy, while the president played with John on the beach and took Caroline and some friends out on the *Honey Fitz.* That evening they had a dinner invitation at the Wrightsman residence. Paul Landis had relieved me, and I was comfortable that Mrs. Kennedy was in a secure environment. I was looking forward to getting to bed early for once, and getting a full night's sleep.

A White House phone had been installed in my room so that I had a direct line to the Palm Beach White House switchboard in case of an emergency. I had barely gotten out of my clothes, and was sitting on the bed in boxers and a T-shirt when the White House phone rang.

I picked up the phone.

"This is Clint."

"Oh, Mr. Hill," the breathy familiar voice said, "the president and I would like you to do something for us."

I looked at my watch. It was eight o'clock. Paul Landis was there, as well as the President's Detail agents. *What could they possibly need me to do?* I didn't have a good feeling about this.

The previous month, President Kennedy had unwittingly started a fad that had by this time spread from coast to coast, and of which I was about to become a spontaneous participant. It all began when the president came upon a 1908 executive order in which President Theodore Roosevelt set forth rules for Marine officers to be able to complete a fifty-mile hike. President Kennedy sent a memo to Marine Corps commandant David Shoup suggesting that a similar fifty-mile challenge would be a good test to see how the present-day officers could perform the task.

Concerned that the average American was becoming more and more unfit, President Kennedy announced that he would put his White House staff to the fifty-mile test as well. It was meant to be a publicity stunt to kick-start a national fitness campaign, and the press ate it up. Poor Pierre Salinger, who was himself a poster child for the "soft American," declined the challenge but publicly vowed to increase his daily dose of exercise. Meanwhile, the president's brother, Attorney General Robert Kennedy, readily accepted the challenge and completed his own fifty-mile hike in just seventeen hours.

Now, two weeks later, Mrs. Kennedy was calling me at eight o'clock in the evening with a special request — not just from her but from the president as well.

"Yes, Mrs. Kennedy," I said. "What can I do for you?"

"You know Stash and Chuck Spalding are here with us, and they are going to go on a fifty-mile hike."

"Oh really?" This was news to me.

"Yes, they're going to walk on the new Sunshine Parkway, and the president and I plan to go out and check on them from time to time, so we would like for you to be there to make sure everything is okay. The president wants to make sure nothing happens to them."

"Sure, Mrs. Kennedy. Whatever you need me to do."

"Oh, Mr. Hill, you are so wonderful."

"When do they want to start?" I asked.

"At twelve midnight, tonight. Will you be ready?"

"I'll be ready, Mrs. Kennedy."

As I hung up the phone, I thought, *What*

have I gotten myself into now? What will I wear? What about shoes?

The only shoes I had were my Florsheim wingtip dress shoes. They were well made and stood up well to the long hours spent standing, but I wasn't sure how comfortable they'd be on a fifty-mile hike. I had no choice. They would have to suffice.

I didn't have workout clothes. The most comfortable things I had with me were a pair of casual slacks and a sweatshirt. I got dressed, jumped in my car, and drove to the Paul residence.

The president and Mrs. Kennedy had gone to the Wrightsmans' for dinner, so I telephoned their residence and informed Paul Landis what was going on. His response was a hearty laugh.

The Secret Service Command Center, when I notified them, had a similar reaction. Everybody was glad it was me, and not them, going through this ordeal. While they were laughing hysterically, at my expense, I was trying to think ahead to everything we might need.

I contacted the Army sergeant who was assigned to me to drive Mrs. Kennedy, and told him I needed him, the station wagon, and a big cooler with ice. Our station wagon had radio equipment so I could stay in touch with Palm Beach base and the Secret Service Command Center, and I figured the ice would come in handy one way or another.

I soon found out that Prince Radziwill and Chuck Spalding had been practicing for this hike for months. They had the best hiking boots money could buy. I also learned this whole escapade was the result of a bet. The president had challenged his buddies that they were not in good enough physical shape to do what Americans were doing all across the country. Me? I had only my Florsheims and my pride to do better than they did.

When we got together around 11:30, I also learned there would be a few important observers on this adventure: Professional photographer Mark Shaw, who had been with *Life* magazine, would be photographing the hike for posterity; and New York City doctor Max Jacobson and a Navy medical corpsman from the White House physician's office would be on hand for medical assistance.

The newly completed Sunshine State Parkway was a north-south highway that ran from Miami to Fort Pierce, along the east side of Florida. It was not yet fully operational, which made it an ideal place to walk without having to worry about traffic.

So there we were, Prince "Stash" Radziwill, Chuck Spalding, and me, with our entourage, at midnight on the Sunshine State Parkway. We began shortly after midnight on February 22. We were all competitive, and knowing the attorney general had finished in seventeen hours, we were determined to beat his time. Fortunately the weather cooperated, with comfortable, cool air as we began the walk. After a few miles, we all realized we were working up quite an appetite.

"Can you have some food sent out to us, Clint?" Stash asked.

"Sure," I said. "What do you want?"

"We need some protein," Chuck said. "How about some steaks?"

Steaks?

"Come morning a glass of champagne with some orange juice would be nice," added Stash.

This was obviously not your average fifty-mile hike. So, periodically, we would stop for a short rest, a cigarette — the three of us were all smokers — and I would radio back to the house and request certain things be sent out to us.

Steaks, orange juice, bottled water, champagne. When I asked, people responded.

Everyone seemed to be in on this little jaunt and was eager to help.

We walked through the night, and shortly after the sun came up, Paul Landis brought Mrs. Kennedy and Lee out to see how we were doing. They walked with us for a while, verbally challenging Stash and Chuck Spalding to go faster. I was determined to stay ahead of the pack, and that just led to more jokes, more laughter. After about thirty minutes, they got back into their car to return to Palm Beach.

"We'll be back to check on you!" Mrs. Kennedy called out. "Don't give up!"

Every so often we would stop to eat, relieve ourselves, and rest. Chuck and the prince had come prepared with foldout mats to spread out on the grass, and a few hours later, they happened to be resting when Mrs. Kennedy and Lee returned, along with President Kennedy. Everybody was in good spirits, and the visit by the president gave us all renewed determination to finish what we had started.

By this time, the word had spread and soon the Florida State Police stopped by to encourage us. On and on we walked down the Sunshine State Parkway. Mile after mile after mile. Prince Radziwill and Chuck started to have problems with their feet, and

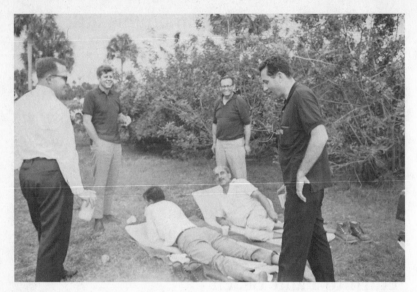

President Kennedy jokes with Clint Hill during fifty-mile hike

when they took off their boots, big blisters were forming. I could feel the same thing happening to me, but I didn't dare mention it. All of us were bound and determined to carry on.

At one point, Dr. Jacobson administered oxygen to Stash and Chuck to give them a boost. I declined the oxygen, but made the mistake of sitting down in the front seat of the station wagon during one of our breaks, and fell sound asleep. It lasted just long enough for Mark Shaw to take a photo, and then they woke me up and we were back to the walk.

Throughout the journey, I would radio

back to the command post to advise of our progress. Somewhere around the forty-five-mile point, President and Mrs. Kennedy returned again to encourage us.

Finally, at about eight o'clock on the evening of February 23, we reached the fifty-mile point, and I breathed a sigh of relief. The adrenaline that had been flowing for the past twenty hours now stopped and I could feel the effects. Aches and pains in my back and legs, blisters on my feet. But, by God, we had finished.

On the drive back to the Paul residence, all I could think about was getting in a hot shower and going straight to bed. But when we pulled up, I was informed that the president and Mrs. Kennedy wanted me to come inside.

They were entertaining a small group of friends, and as soon as I walked in, President Kennedy handed me a tall glass filled with champagne.

"Congratulations, Clint!" he said.

Then he pulled out a handmade medallion made of purple construction paper that was attached to a ribbon of yellow crepe paper. As President Kennedy placed the mock medal around my neck, he read the inscription he had handwritten on the front:

"For Dazzle. February 23, 1963. The Order of the Pace Maker, He whom the Secret Service will follow into the Battle of the Sunshine Highway. John F. Kennedy."

He looked at me and with a twinkle in his eyes, he added, "I even drew the presidential seal on there to make it official."

Everybody laughed, and I was beaming. I was so impressed that the President of the United States had taken the time to prepare a handmade, personally inscribed medallion to me. It had been an arduous — some might say frivolous — task, but this simple, sincere gesture by President Kennedy made every step worth it.

The kid from the North Dakota Children's Home has come a long way.

A few weeks later, a package arrived for

me at my office in the White House. Inside
was a leather-bound photo album. Engraved
on the front in simple gold letters, it read:

FOR C.H. FROM M.S.

And on the spine:

THAT PALM BEACH 50

Inside were thirty original photos by Mark
Shaw, all printed on heavy card stock,
chronicling the fifty-mile hike.

It's been fifty years since that momentous
hike, and still that leather-bound book, and

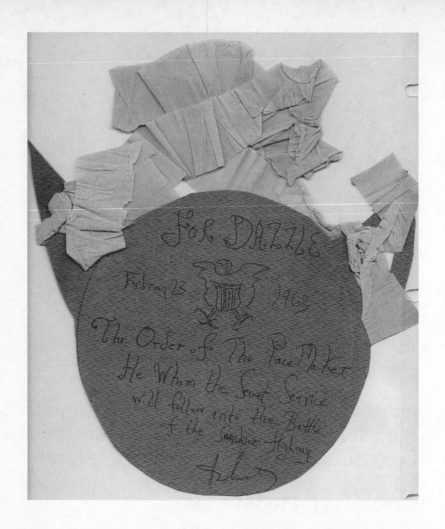

the handmade paper medal presented to me
by President John F. Kennedy, are two of
the most precious mementoes I have.

19
CAMP DAVID AND THE *KAMA SUTRA*

One day, we were walking alone together in Palm Beach along the beautiful Lake Trail, which overlooks the Lake Worth Lagoon, when Mrs. Kennedy told me her plans for the upcoming months.

"When we get back to Washington, I told the president I plan on attending as few events as possible," she said. "You know, only if there's a state dinner or a reception or something for somebody important."

"I understand, Mrs. Kennedy."

I realized that she still wanted to keep the news of her pregnancy quiet, and at the same time, she was concerned about overexerting herself. I got the sense that the fear of losing this baby was always in the back of her mind.

"We have to move everything out of Glen Ora, you know," she said, "but the new house at Rattlesnake Mountain isn't finished yet."

She paused, and turned to me with a questioning look on her face. "The president suggested we spend weekends at Camp David."

"I think that's a great idea, Mrs. Kennedy." Truly, I was so glad to hear that she was considering Camp David. I had no doubt she would love it.

As we walked, with the smell of the ocean and the balmy breeze surrounding us, I tried to explain what it was about Camp David that was so unique. She had a keen sense of history, and I figured that she might be more excited about the prospect of spending time there once she understood how the retreat had been utilized by previous presidents.

The heavily wooded property is about 125 acres and sits on one of the highest elevations in the Catoctin Mountains in Maryland. Originally developed in the 1930s by the Works Progress Administration as a camp for federal government employees and their families, President Franklin Delano Roosevelt requested it be converted to a presidential retreat in 1942 and named it "Shangri-La."

Roosevelt brought Winston Churchill there, and it was in this secluded environment that they planned the Allied invasion of Europe during World War II. When Eisenhower became president, he changed the name from Shangri-La to Camp David, after his firstborn grandson.

"The reason I think you will enjoy it, Mrs. Kennedy," I said, "is because it is so private — much more so than Glen Ora."

"Really?"

"Absolutely. It's operated by the U.S. Navy and the entire property is surrounded by a high wire fence that's closely patrolled by armed Marine guards, as well as constant electronic surveillance. It is so secure and so private that President Eisenhower thought it the best place to confer with

Premier Khrushchev about the Cold War. They spent two days at Camp David."

"Yes, I knew that," she said. "But I guess I never really thought about the reason why Eisenhower chose to entertain him there."

"Believe me, Mrs. Kennedy, it is a unique place that very few people in the world have ever had the opportunity to experience. There are paths and trails throughout the woods — you can literally walk for miles and miles without seeing another human being. It's really the only place where you and the children and the president can roam freely without Secret Service agents hovering over you."

She broke into a smile and with a glimmer in her eye, she quipped, "Oh, Mr. Hill, if you had told me that from the beginning, I probably would have gone there right after the Inauguration and never left!"

We laughed and continued walking and talking, and I got the feeling we would soon be spending a lot of time at Camp David.

On Sunday, March 3, I flew with Mrs. Kennedy, Caroline, and John on the *Caroline* back to Washington. When we landed in the section of the terminal for private planes, I was surprised to see President Kennedy waiting there to greet his family. It was somewhat unusual for him to make the effort to come to the airport, when we could easily make it back to the White House in less than ten minutes, but the president had clearly missed his family and was eager to see them.

The very next weekend, we were off to Camp David.

The president's schedule didn't allow him to come up until Sunday, but Mrs. Kennedy was eager to get out of Washington, so we drove her and the children up on Saturday.

Once you are on the grounds of Camp David, it is so secluded, so private, that you feel as if no one could ever find you, even if they tried. The views are spectacular, and the accommodations are elegantly rustic, with all the comforts befitting the President of the United States.

The centerpiece of the property is the large and luxurious presidential residence called Aspen Lodge, which has stunning views of the surrounding countryside. There is ample room for guests in well-appointed cabins that have names like Rosebud, Dogwood, and Holly, and the activities on the property are endless. There is a beautiful heated outdoor swimming pool, a putting green, driving range, a bowling alley, and even facilities for skeet shooting. Plus there are miles and miles of well-tended trails for walking and horseback riding. Brand-new stables had been built — complete with nameplates for Sardar and Macaroni — so that the horses could be boarded there when the president and Mrs. Kennedy were in residence. Meanwhile, Charlie the Welsh terrier came up in the car with the kids.

Everybody loved being at Camp David, just as I had anticipated. John loved tromping through the woods, finding sticks that immediately became imaginary swords or rifles, while Caroline would ride Macaroni around the athletic field or through the trails, as Mrs. Kennedy walked along.

From then on, Camp David became the regular weekend retreat for the entire spring of 1963. President Kennedy would arrive sometime Saturday and leave Sunday afternoon or Monday morning, while Mrs. Kennedy and the children would normally arrive prior to the president. Both the president and Mrs. Kennedy were huge history buffs, and the location of Camp David allowed them to take Caroline and John to the nearby historic sites of Gettysburg and Antietam.

As it turned out, during the months of April, May, and June 1963, Mrs. Kennedy spent far more time at Camp David than at the White House. Frequently, the children would return with the president on Sunday, since Caroline had school, and Mrs. Kennedy would stay at Camp David a day or two longer.

The first time she decided to stay on after the president had left, I couldn't help but tease her about it.

"So, Mrs. Kennedy, I guess Camp David isn't as bad as you thought it would be."

She smiled and said, "Oh, Mr. Hill, I just couldn't have imagined that it would be so wonderful. It has everything one could want or need, and so beautiful, too. It's strange, isn't it? But I feel like I have a sense of freedom here more than anywhere else."

She was the most idolized woman in the world, and she could have anything she wanted, but what she craved most was privacy.

Soon it was Easter, and we were back to Palm Beach, back to the C. Michael Paul residence. Mrs. Kennedy remained secluded, venturing out only for our frequent walks, and the daily cruise on the *Honey Fitz* with the president and other guests. She decorated Easter eggs with the children, and spent time almost every day visiting her father-in-law, Ambassador Kennedy. She was consumed with final preparations for the house at Rattlesnake Mountain, and would sit by the pool, her ever-present yellow legal pad in hand, writing instructions and notes as to how she wanted things done. No longer appreciating the implications of "rattlesnake," she began calling the house Atoka in reference to the area in which it was located.

When we were in Palm Beach, Mrs. Kennedy didn't have her normal social and secretarial staff with her, so often Paul Landis and I would act as the go-betweens, whether it be with staff, friends, family, or even the president on occasion. The truth was, Mrs. Kennedy was very hard to resist. We adored her. Our job was to protect her, and as long as nothing interfered with that mission, we would walk on water if she asked. And she knew it.

President Kennedy attended pre-Easter services at St. Ann's and St. Edward catholic churches, but on Easter Sunday the family celebrated the holy day with a private Mass at Ambassador Kennedy's residence, as they had done the previous year. It was a sign of the tremendous respect the president had for his father to make these special arrangements — so that the elder Kennedy, wheelchair-bound and unable to communicate, could worship with his son, the President of the United States, in privacy.

By this point, Mrs. Kennedy was well into her pregnancy, and much as she would have liked to simply remain in hiding until the birth, she acquiesced that it was time to go public. On Monday, April 15, Pierre Salinger held a press conference in which he read a statement that said, "The White House announced today that Mrs. Kennedy is expecting a baby in the latter half of August. Mrs. Kennedy has maintained her full schedule for the past few months. Because of this active schedule, her physicians have now advised her to cancel all her official activities."

Within minutes, newspapers around the country reprinted their headlines for the evening editions.

JACKIE'S EXPECTING 3RD CHILD
KENNEDYS ARE ELATED: CHILD DUE IN AUGUST

Telegrams and congratulatory presents and cards came pouring in from around the world. The public's excitement over Mrs. Kennedy's pregnancy was enormous. Of course the publicity and interest were exactly what Mrs. Kennedy didn't want, but as I explained to her, this would be only the second baby born to a sitting U.S. president, the last being when Grover Cleveland's wife had a baby girl in 1893. Mrs. Kennedy's "condition" — as we referred to it in those days — was big news.

After the announcement, Mrs. Kennedy's public appearances were rare. She attended a play at the National Theater, and participated as hostess at the state dinner for the president of India, who had so graciously hosted her the previous year. When His Majesty Hassan II, King of Morocco, came to Washington, Mrs. Kennedy accompanied the president to greet him, and rode in the motorcade from the airport to Blair House, the official guest residence across the street from the White House. This was very unusual for her, but I soon learned why. After the king's visit, Mrs. Kennedy told me that Morocco was one of the places she had always dreamed of visiting someday, and after meeting Hassan II, she was even more intrigued.

Mrs. Kennedy would visit Morocco much sooner than she ever imagined.

The month of April meant the end of Glen

Ora and the movement of things into the almost-ready new residence. Finally, on May 6, 1963, Paul Landis and I took Mrs. Kennedy to Atoka for a one-night stay. Mary Gallagher and a few of the White House domestic staff came along to help get the interior of the house in shape. There were pages and pages of notes on what was to go where. No detail had been overlooked.

Furniture was being moved, plants positioned, and paintings hung. Among the paintings were some I recognized from Mrs. Kennedy's 1962 trip to India. They were very small in size, very colorful, and very erotic. The paintings depicted couples in various positions while making love. She and Mary spent a great deal of time trying to determine how best to arrange the paintings, which were going on a prominent wall, *in the dining room.*

Once they were hung, Mrs. Kennedy looked at me with a mischievous look in her eyes. She was starting to "show" a bit by this time — she was still very slim, but there were the telltale signs — and her face had that beautiful glow a woman has when she is expecting a child.

"What do you think of these Kama Sutra paintings, Mr. Hill?" she asked.

I don't think I had ever blushed before in

my life. But damn if I didn't feel my face get hot.

"I think they're fine, Mrs. Kennedy," I said, trying not to smile. "At least they'll be a great conversation starter. They'll have tremendous shock value."

She just laughed and said, "Oh, Mr. Hill."

I thought the paintings seemed more appropriate for a private area like the master bedroom, but I wasn't about to tell her that. I was certain she hung them there for the exact reason I had stated. Shock value. Pure and simple.

The next day it was back to the White House and then on to Camp David. With all the time and effort Mrs. Kennedy had put into building this house, and trying to make everything perfect, I was surprised to learn that Atoka would not be the residence of choice — at least for the near future. President and Mrs. Kennedy decided to rent out the house for the summer of 1963, which caused some consternation to the Secret Service and the White House Communications Agency because of the extensive security and communications equipment that had been installed as the house was being built.

Mrs. Kennedy's original intent was to go to Hyannis Port for the entire summer, beginning around the president's birthday or shortly thereafter, but she enjoyed Camp David so much that the date to go to Hyannis Port kept getting pushed back.

In early 1963, Letitia Baldridge had informed Mrs. Kennedy that she was resigning from her job as social secretary. Like so many White House staffers, she worked long hours, typically six or seven days a week, with no time for a personal life. I knew the past year had been tough on Tish — she thought Mrs. Kennedy should have attended more White House social functions, and hosted more ladies' luncheons and teas. But that wasn't Mrs. Kennedy's style. And there had been plenty of times in which Tish was thrown into a frenzied search for a replacement when Mrs. Kennedy declined to attend a function at the last minute. They both knew it was time for Tish to move on, and as far as I knew, there were no bad feelings about her resignation.

Tish gave a generous four months' notice, and in that time, Mrs. Kennedy decided to hire an old friend of hers from Miss Porter's school, Nancy Tuckerman. Like Tish, Nancy had exquisite taste and style, but her calmer personality was much more compatible with Mrs. Kennedy.

On Tish's last day, Mrs. Kennedy and the

staff threw her a going-away party in the China Room — the room on the ground floor of the mansion where all the china from previous administrations is displayed in glass cases. There was champagne and beautiful, thoughtful parting gifts, including a small round table made by the White House carpenters, on top of which was an inlaid piece of paper that had been signed by the senior staff, as well as President and Mrs. Kennedy, Caroline, and a scribble by John. But perhaps one of the most memorable moments was when Mrs. Kennedy ushered in the Marine Band, and they sang a tongue-in-cheek tribute to Tish that Mrs. Kennedy herself had written. That was typical of Mrs. Kennedy — always taking the time to write or draw something personal and befitting to the recipient.

As it happened, Tish's last day, May 29, 1963, was also President Kennedy's forty-sixth birthday. He had a typically full schedule with back-to-back meetings, but the staff managed to throw him a surprise birthday party late that afternoon in the Navy Mess.

Located on the lower level of the White House, the Navy Mess is a simple dining hall where the staff eats meals — prepared and served by Navy stewards. It's not a

Clint Hill, Pam Turnure, Tish Baldridge, and Mrs. Kennedy

place the president normally went, but around 5:45 that afternoon, somebody escorted him down there. Mrs. Kennedy and I were there waiting, along with Nancy Tuckerman — her first day on the job — and most of the president's staff.

As soon as the president walked in, somebody handed him a glass of champagne, and we all started singing "Happy Birthday." He broke into a big smile and acted as though he were surprised. In reality, I think he must have known what was going on. It is very difficult to surprise the president — any president. The last thing a president wants is to be surprised. He relies on his top staff

441

to keep him well informed, and if they don't, they are soon out of a job.

But the president played along, as he was presented with an array of gag gifts. There was a miniature rocking chair, boxing gloves to deal with Congress, "Debate Rules" from Richard M. Nixon. But the biggest laugh came when Mrs. Kennedy presented her gift — a basket of dead grass.

"Mr. President," she deadpanned, "on behalf of the White House Historical Society, it is with great honor and with the utmost respect, that I present to you genuine antique grass from the antique rose garden."

The president loved it. That too was typical of Mrs. Kennedy's self-deprecating sense of humor. In giving the gift to her husband, she was simultaneously mocking herself, as well as the staff members and others who adulate the president.

That evening, Mrs. Kennedy had planned a truly special event for her husband's birthday — a cruise on the Potomac aboard the beautiful presidential yacht, the USS *Sequoia*.

A classic teak and mahogany 104-foot motor yacht built around 1925, the *Sequoia* was operated by the U.S. Navy and had been made available to every president since Herbert Hoover. Due to her shallow draft

Surprise party at White House for President Kennedy's 46th birthday

of less than four and a half feet, the *Sequoia* wasn't an oceangoing vessel, but she was ideal for cruises along the usually calm waters of the Potomac.

President Kennedy was happiest when he was on the water, and this night was no exception. Mrs. Kennedy had invited about twenty-four guests, who were told to arrive promptly for an 8:01 departure. We had

Secret Service agents on a couple of security boats, but there were just three agents aboard the *Sequoia* — Floyd Boring and Ron Pontius from the President's Detail, and myself.

None of President Kennedy's political advisors had been invited — the guest list included only family members and his closest friends: Bobby and Ethel, Sarge and Eunice, Teddy, the Bartletts, Ben and Tony Bradlee, the Fays, British actor David Niven and his wife, Florida senator George Smathers and his wife, Bill Walton, Lem Billings, and a few others.

It was a dreary, rainy evening, making the open-air top deck unusable, so everybody was crammed inside the main and aft salons. The interior of this classic yacht feels like a cozy gentleman's library with low ceilings, varnished mahogany paneling and cabinetry, and fine fabric for the drapes and furnishings. The captain steers the boat with a large, classic wood and brass wheel, from the windowed pilothouse on the main deck. Behind the pilothouse there is the galley, the large main salon, which is connected to the smaller, cozier aft salon by a narrow hallway and bar area. At the rear is the fantail — sort of an outdoor covered porch.

Agents Ron Pontius, Floyd Boring, and Clint Hill on U.S.S. Sequoia

The yacht is elegant and spacious, but with about twenty-four guests, three agents, the crew, and the three-piece band Mrs. Kennedy had arranged, on this night it was close quarters.

To accommodate all the guests for dinner, the mahogany Chippendale dining table was extended to fill the entire main salon, so drinks and hors d'oeuvres were served on the aft deck and covered fantail. While Agents Boring and Pontius and I stood post on the exterior walkways, the guests inside dined on roast filet of beef and 1955 Dom Pérignon champagne. People were in lively spirits to begin with, and as the night wore on, and the champagne flowed, the party got louder and livelier. There were plenty of toasts, and after birthday cake at the dining table, the president opened presents in the aft salon. Then the dancing started. They were doing the twist, the cha-cha, and everything in between. It was wild. I don't think I had ever seen the president and Mrs. Kennedy having more fun. Nobody wanted the night to end, but the captain docked the *Sequoia* around 1:20 A.M., and finally, everybody went home.

Mrs. Kennedy was thrilled that the party had gone off so well.

It's been a long time since I've thought about that night, that wonderful raucous

President Kennedy opens gifts on U.S.S. Sequoia

night. I can still see the president's surprise
and amusement while opening his gifts. I
can still hear the music, the guests singing
along, and the president having such a
wonderful time surrounded by his closest
family and friends. What a privilege it was
for me to have been there, to witness the
joy and laughter. But always, when I remember that special birthday celebration on the
Sequoia, I can't help but think that it

shouldn't have been his last.

At forty-six, it shouldn't have been his last.

20
LOSING BABY PATRICK

JFK conducts business during family photo session on Squaw Island, August 1963

On June 22 1963, President Kennedy departed on a two-week trip to Europe, with stops in England, Ireland, Italy, and Germany. It was history in the making and I have to admit that I was disappointed not to be able to join my colleagues on what I knew would be a challenging and significant trip.

When I saw the news reports about President Kennedy delivering what would forever be known as his "Ich bin ein Berliner" speech, all I could think about was the complex challenge faced by the Secret Service agents assigned to protect him. The photos showed hundreds of thousands of unscreened people — many watching from balconies and rooftops — as President Kennedy spoke, all alone at a podium on an open stage. He was a sitting duck.

How do you protect someone in that environment? All it takes is one lucky shot — and that first shot is free. You never know it's coming. After that, all you can do is react.

This scene played itself over and over as the president traveled to Rome, Naples, and Dublin. I knew the guys on the detail had to have been living on pure adrenaline.

Once again this summer, the president and Mrs. Kennedy had rented a house on Squaw Island — very close to the house they'd rented the year before — still less than a mile from the Kennedy compound. The large, rambling, gray-shingled house was at the end of the narrow, one-lane gravel road on Squaw Island, set back on a heavily wooded piece of property so that you could barely see it from the road. A simple wooden sign hung over the front door with the moniker: BRAMBLETYDE. The home had ample space for the children to play outdoors, a stunning view of the Atlantic Ocean from the entire backside of the house, and a private beach. Plenty of privacy, and close enough — but not too close — to the rest of the family.

This was now the seventh house the Kennedys had occupied on a regular basis, outside the White House, in the two and a half years since Kennedy was elected. So once again the Secret Service and the White House Communications Agency had installed the extensive communications and surveillance equipment to ensure the security of the president and his family while in residence. A semipermanent trailer was placed at the base of the driveway to serve as the Secret Service Command Center and secretarial office. It had everything we needed — radios, telephones, and a typewriter to write up our daily reports — but unfortunately, not even a hint of an ocean view.

Once President Kennedy returned from Europe, he began the usual summer schedule in which he arrived at Hyannis Port on Friday afternoons, and left Monday mornings. There was always such a hubbub of activity during the weekends that when the president and his entourage left, the atmosphere during the week would return to a much slower, relaxed pace. Mrs. Kennedy continued to walk regularly, and often we would walk together from Brambletyde to the ambassador's residence, where she would visit with her father-in-law on the porch — sometimes for hours at a time. He couldn't speak, but you could see the joy in his eyes as she chatted away, or read aloud from magazines and newspapers.

She didn't want to be seen in public at this time, so she would frequently send me to Lorania's Toy & Book Shop in Hyannis to buy candy or inexpensive toys for the children. She'd give me a list of things and then, as I was walking out the door, she would add, "Oh, and Mr. Hill, why don't you pick up a few magazines for me while you're there, too."

I knew what she meant. She loved to read the tabloids — especially if there were articles or photos of her in them — but she certainly didn't want anyone to see her buying them.

Other than quiet outings, Mrs. Kennedy

spent a great deal of time secluded in her upstairs bedroom and adjoining office, from which she could hear the sound of the waves, and look out to the vastness of the Atlantic Ocean. She was spending a lot of time doing early planning of events for fall entertaining at the White House, and was consumed with preparations for the baby. Chief Usher J. B. West had been given instructions on transforming a small room in the private residence into the new nursery, using John's white crib, and adding some new drapes and a new rug.

This was the first year her personal secretary, Mary Gallagher, had come up to the Cape for the entire summer, and Mrs. Kennedy kept her busy with dictation, correspondence, and detailed requests to J. B. West, Oleg Cassini, and Nancy Tuckerman, who was now handling the social side of things. Provi was there, of course, and Paul Landis and I worked closely with both her and Mary to ensure that the things Mrs. Kennedy requested were accomplished. We, along with the White House switchboard operators, became experts in locating people with whom Mrs. Kennedy wanted to speak, wherever they were. Everybody's joint mission was to keep the first lady happy, and to keep anxiety levels to a minimum.

■ ■ ■ ■

The baby was due in September, and while Mrs. Kennedy planned to return to Washington to deliver the baby by Caesarean section at Walter Reed Army Hospital, we had to have an alternate plan in case of an emergency while we were at the Cape. A representative from the Boston Secret Service office and I accompanied Drs. John Walsh and Janet Travell to visit the various hospitals in the Hyannis Port area, and we determined that Otis Air Force Base Hospital, which was less than twenty miles from Hyannis Port, was the best option in terms of proximity, security, and facilities. As one final precaution, Dr. Walsh agreed to stay in Hyannis Port for the duration of the summer so that he could assist Mrs. Kennedy with any problems.

July 28, 1963, was Mrs. Kennedy's thirty-fourth birthday, and she was adamant that it be celebrated in a low-key way. There was the standard noontime cruise on the *Honey Fitz,* and then a quiet family dinner that evening at Brambletyde. Quite different from the wild celebration on the *Sequoia* for President Kennedy's birthday in May, but that's what she wanted.

Mrs. Kennedy on the Honey Fitz, *Hyannis Port, July 1963*

During this extended period of time at Squaw Island, Agent Landis and I managed to arrange our schedule so that we could each have a day off every week. The weekends were filled with a flurry of activities when the president was in residence, but during the week, as long as one agent on duty worked a sixteen-hour day, the other could have the day off. It was a real treat to have an entire day completely to ourselves.

Wednesday, August 7, 1963, happened to be my designated day off.

Caroline, who was now five years old, had a riding lesson scheduled that morning, and Mrs. Kennedy decided to go along and watch, as she often did. So Paul Landis drove Mrs. Kennedy and Caroline to the stables, while Agent Lynn Meredith from the Kiddie Detail followed in a separate car.

Shortly after they arrived at the farm, Mrs. Kennedy was standing by the fence outside the riding ring. Suddenly, she turned to Paul.

"Mr. Landis, I don't feel well. I think you better take me back to the house."

"Of course, Mrs. Kennedy," Paul said.

Agent Meredith was standing nearby, but before Paul could tell him what was going on, Mrs. Kennedy said, "*Right now,* Mr. Landis."

There was no doubting her sense of urgency so Paul got Meredith's attention and said, "I'm taking Mrs. Kennedy back to Squaw Island. You stay here and take care of Caroline."

As Paul helped Mrs. Kennedy into the backseat of the car, she got a worried look on her face, and repeated, "We better hurry, Mr. Landis."

As soon as they pulled away, Paul radioed the command center.

George Dalton, an assistant to the president's naval aide, who worked closely with us at Hyannis Port, was on duty in the Secret Service trailer.

"George," Paul said. "I'm bringing Mrs. Kennedy back to the house. Get Dr. Walsh to come immediately, and put a helicopter on standby." He looked over at Mrs. Kennedy and added, "And call Clint. Tell him we've got an emergency."

The two-lane country road back to Hyannis Port was filled with dips and bumps, and Paul was driving as fast as he felt he could without causing Mrs. Kennedy any discomfort, but she kept urging him to go faster.

"Mr. Landis, please go a little faster. *Please* go faster!"

As Paul sped up to eighty miles per hour

on the windy, bumpy road, he thought, *Please God, don't let her have this baby in the car. Please let me get to the house in time.*

Fortunately, as Paul pulled into the driveway at Brambletyde, Dr. Walsh was just arriving. They helped Mrs. Kennedy inside and after a brief examination, Dr. Walsh said, "We need to get her to the hospital right away."

I had rented a tiny cottage on the other side of Hyannis Port for the summer and was sound asleep when the phone rang. It was George Dalton.

"Clint," George said, "Mrs. Kennedy is going into labor. You better get over here."

Oh God. The baby isn't due for another five weeks. She can't have the baby now, it's too early.

I got dressed as fast as I could, grabbed my commission book and my revolver, and just as I was walking out the door, the phone rang again.

"Clint, they're taking the helicopter to Otis."

Oh God.

"Okay. I'll meet them there."

As I raced to Otis, I radioed the Secret Service Command Center and told them to contact SAIC Behn's office at the White

House. The president needed to know his wife was about to have the baby.

It was about a ten-minute flight to Otis Air Force Base, and normally a twenty-five-minute drive. I arrived just as the helicopter was landing.

As soon as I saw Mrs. Kennedy, I could tell she was deeply worried.

"It's going to be okay, Mrs. Kennedy," I said, as we rushed her into the special wing that had been prepared just for such an emergency. I placed my hand on her arm and tried to reassure her with my eyes, but we both knew what the other was thinking.

Please God, I prayed, *please let the baby be all right.*

As Mrs. Kennedy went into emergency surgery, Agent Landis immediately took control of the security around the hospital wing, while I waited outside the operating room.

I tried to keep my mind occupied by thinking about everything that needed to be arranged in the aftermath of the delivery: *Who needs to be contacted? What will she need and want from the house? How do we keep the damn press away?*

I found myself pacing back and forth, as if I were the expectant father, just as I had done when John was born two and a half years earlier.

So much had changed in those two and a half years. At that time, I had just met her a few weeks earlier. Now we were so close, and had spent so much time together, we could practically read each other's minds. I knew how much this baby meant to her, and I couldn't bear the thought of something happening to her, or to the child.

At some point, Paul Landis told me that President Kennedy was airborne from Andrews Air Force Base.

"But he's not on Air Force One," he said.

"What do you mean?" I asked.

"Apparently none of the planes were available. He and some staff and the agents are coming in on two JetStars."

The Air Force had a group of four-engine jet aircraft in its VIP fleet that could be used as Air Force One. A JetStar, which only holds about six or eight passengers, and couldn't travel at nearly the same rate of speed, would only have been used as a last resort. As it turned out, because the president didn't have any travel plans on his schedule that day, one of the Air Force planes was in the air on a check flight, and the others were having routine maintenance done. It was bad luck, and damn bad timing. Once again the president was going to miss the birth of his child.

Shortly before one o'clock in the afternoon, while the president was still airborne, Dr. Walsh came out of the surgery room.

"Clint, you can breathe easy. Mrs. Kennedy has delivered a baby boy, and she is doing fine."

"How is the baby?" I asked.

"Well," he said, "he's small. He weighs just four pounds, ten and a half ounces." With a worried look in his eyes, he added, "We have some concern about his breathing."

"What do you mean?"

"We've put him in the incubator and we'll know more in a little while."

"Okay, thank you, Dr. Walsh. I'll make sure the president gets the news immediately. He's on his way, and should be here soon."

The president arrived at Otis about forty minutes later.

"Congratulations, Mr. President," I said.

"Thanks, Clint. How is Mrs. Kennedy?"

"I believe she's still under sedation, but you should talk to Dr. Walsh." I didn't know how much he knew at that time, and I didn't want to be the one to tell him there might be a problem with his newborn son.

461

The president went in to see his wife, and then spent time conferring privately with Dr. Walsh.

President Kennedy walked over to me and said, "Clint, find the base chaplain. We need to baptize the baby right away."

"Yes, sir, Mr. President."

A short while later, the president and Mrs. Kennedy's son was baptized Patrick Bouvier Kennedy. The name had been decided in advance — Patrick after President Kennedy's paternal grandfather and Bouvier for Mrs. Kennedy's father.

After the baptism, Mrs. Kennedy was moved into the recovery suite that had been prepared for her, and baby Patrick was taken into a separate area where he could be monitored.

This was my first glimpse of the baby. As soon as I saw him, tears welled in my eyes. He had a perfectly shaped head, and the tiniest hands and feet. He was beautiful. But he was clearly fighting for each breath, as his poor little chest struggled to get the oxygen he needed to survive.

He looked so alone in the sterile incubator, with tubes going every which way. Oh, how I wanted to pick him up and hold him close. He was so fragile, and more than anything, I wanted to protect him. But all I could do was hope and pray.

Please, do anything to me, God. But please don't let Patrick die.

As the doctors continued their tests, it became increasingly clear that Patrick's respiratory problems were serious. He had a condition known as hyaline membrane disease — a common affliction in premature babies due to incomplete lung development. They didn't have the capability of treating him at Otis — he needed to get to Children's Hospital in Boston, where they were better equipped to handle the problem. Time was of the essence, but it was too risky to transport him by helicopter. He had to go by ambulance, and he had to have a Secret Service agent with him. This was the son of the President of the United States.

I wanted to stay with him, to try to protect him, but I needed to be with Mrs. Kennedy when she awoke. I had to be there for her.

"Paul," I said to Agent Landis, "Mrs. Kennedy would want one of us to be with him."

He nodded.

"You go with the baby in the ambulance, Paul."

So Paul got in the ambulance with tiny baby Patrick and the medical crew, and at 5:55 P.M., with a full police escort, they raced to Boston.

I had rushed to Otis that morning without showering or shaving, and by this time, I knew I looked awful. I sent someone to the PX to get me a razor and some shaving cream, and snuck into a bathroom so I could at least splash some water on my face and have a quick shave. I had a feeling it was going to be a long night.

After visiting with Mrs. Kennedy once more, President Kennedy flew to Hyannis Port to check on Caroline and John. I stayed outside Mrs. Kennedy's door as nurses went in and out. I was relieved when Louella Hennessey, the wonderful nurse who had helped care for all the Kennedy babies, arrived, because I knew what a comfort she would be to Mrs. Kennedy. President Kennedy returned an hour or so later, and went in again to visit with Mrs. Kennedy.

When he came out, he said, "Clint, I'm going to Boston to be with Patrick. I know you'll make sure Mrs. Kennedy is well taken care of. Just make sure I'm kept informed."

"Yes, sir, Mr. President. I will make sure you are fully aware, should anything change."

All the activity — the constant coming and going of people and staff — was a blessing for me. As long as I was busy, I could keep my emotions in check. Every time I thought about baby Patrick, so small and alone inside the incubator, it nearly tore me apart. Throughout this time, Mrs. Kennedy seldom woke up, but continued to remain in a stable condition.

President Kennedy had brought two of Mrs. Kennedy's staff with him — Pamela Turnure and Nancy Tuckerman — which was a great relief for me. Now I could focus strictly on security and privacy. My emotions, however, kept taking me back to that incubator leaving Otis Air Force Base with the tiny boy inside, gasping for air, fighting for life. I thought of my own two sons and how much they meant to me. How much I wished I could spend more time with them. How fortunate I was that they were healthy and growing rapidly like youngsters their age do.

If only Patrick can survive this threatening ordeal, he too will be growing and developing before my eyes — just as I've watched John and Caroline. Something I have been unable to witness with my own sons.

Mrs. Kennedy was still in and out of consciousness, and had not been told of the seriousness of Patrick's condition — only that he had a lung problem similar to what John had been born with. Taking the baby to Boston was just a precaution.

Once President Kennedy and his Secret Service detail arrived at Children's Hospital, with the added assistance from the Boston Secret Service Field Office, it was decided that Agent Landis should return to Otis to assist me. He arranged for an official car and got back to Hyannis at 2:20 A.M.

The president remained overnight in Boston with Patrick. I stayed with Mrs. Kennedy.

The next day, August 8, there was nonstop activity. Both Paul and I were at Otis doing whatever we could to ensure Mrs. Kennedy was all right; the president was flying back and forth between Boston and Otis and Hyannis Port; Mary Gallagher, Pam, and Nancy were handling the onslaught of phone calls and messages from friends, relatives, world leaders, and the general public. Everybody was concerned about Patrick. Meanwhile, Mrs. Kennedy was still sleeping most of the time. She had no idea that her son's life was hanging in the balance.

We were getting limited information from Boston because no one seemed to know Patrick's exact condition. But it apparently had not improved. We all went to bed that night hoping and praying he would pull through.

By this time, field office agents had been brought in to supplement Paul Landis and me, so we didn't have to work twenty-four hours a day.

I had not left Otis since we arrived the morning of August 7, and had taken over one of the bedrooms in the suite so I could at least try to get some sleep. I wanted to make sure that if Mrs. Kennedy needed anything in the middle of the night, though, that there was a familiar agent there to help her, so I asked Tommy Wells from the children's detail to stand outside her door throughout the night.

I lay in bed, rarely sleeping, my mind going over and over the possibilities should Patrick not make it. At 4:15 A.M. on Friday, August 9, I was awakened by the sound of the phone ringing.

"Clint Hill," I answered.

"Clint . . ." It was Jerry Behn, the Special Agent in Charge of the White House Detail. "We have just been informed that Patrick has passed away."

Tears welled in my eyes as I tried to keep my voice steady.

"He died at four-oh-four this morning. The president wants Dr. Walsh to tell Mrs. Kennedy. Fortunately, you don't have to do that. But I wanted you to be the first to know."

"Thanks for letting me know, Jerry."

Before I could even digest what had happened, I heard the phone ringing outside my room in the area we had set up as the Secret Service Command Post. I could hear Tom Wells on the phone, getting the same awful news I had just received. A few minutes later, I heard Agent Wells call Dr. Walsh. There was no going back to sleep, so I got up and walked into the hallway.

I looked at Tom and could tell that he too was having a tough time holding it together.

"I guess you heard the news," he said to me.

"Yeah. Behn called to tell me."

"You know, Clint," Tom said, "Nurse Lumsden — the night duty nurse — was going in and out of Mrs. Kennedy's room all night. And each time she came out I'd ask, 'How is she doing?' And every time the answer was the same. She'd say, 'Mrs. Kennedy is really having a tough time tonight. She's been so restless all night, just tossing and turning. She just can't seem to get to sleep.' It happened all night long."

Tom paused. He looked down, and gulped as he fought the emotions.

"Then, at four o'clock, Nurse Lumsden

came out and said, 'She's finally gone to sleep. Just now. She just fell asleep.' "

He looked up at me to see if I understood what he was saying.

I nodded.

"And then," Tom said, "it wasn't but a few minutes later that I got the call."

"Thank you, Tom. I'm so glad you were out here. I know she appreciated it, too."

My heart ached. My whole body ached. I wanted to go in and hold Mrs. Kennedy, to tell her how sorry I was. How much I felt her loss. But she needed to sleep. She had been fighting all night, just as her baby son was fighting for his life.

I went back to my room, closed the door, and put my head in my hands.

This was the third child she had lost. It was far more than any woman should ever have to bear.

At 6:30 A.M., Dr. Walsh arrived and broke the tragic news to Mrs. Kennedy.

She was devastated. It was heartbreaking to see her in such emotional pain, and I felt so helpless. I was supposed to protect her. But there was nothing I could do, nothing anyone could do to protect her from the pain of losing a child. I was thankful that Nancy Tuckerman and Pam and Mary and

Louella Hennessey were there to comfort her. It was all I could do to stand outside the door, and hold my feelings inside.

When President Kennedy arrived later that morning, he looked like he had been to hell and back. The doctors had called him, knowing death was imminent. They had released Patrick from the lines and tubes, and President Kennedy was able to hold his son in his arms, for the first and last time.

I looked at the president and said, simply, "My condolences, Mr. President."

"Thank you, Clint," he said.

I turned the knob and opened the door to Mrs. Kennedy's room. He walked in and I quietly closed the door again. My heart wrenched with anguish as I stood outside the room, knowing the pain the president and Mrs. Kennedy were sharing inside.

The funeral services for Patrick Bouvier Kennedy were held on Saturday, August 10, in Boston, with Cardinal Cushing presiding. Paul Landis and I stayed with Mrs. Kennedy at Otis for, still weak from the Caesarian operation, she was unable to attend. *She couldn't attend the funeral of her baby son.*

On Sunday, August 11, the president brought Caroline in the morning, and John

Clint Hill with President Kennedy and children as they exit Otis AFB Hospital

in the evening, which seemed to boost Mrs. Kennedy's spirits more than anything. The next day he brought the two of them together, before he had to return to Washington to get on with his job as President of the United States.

My heart ached for her as she continuously tried to maintain her composure. Nancy, Pam, and Mary, all close friends, attempted to support her as best they could. Her sister, Lee, finally arrived from Europe, and she seemed to help Mrs. Kennedy more than anyone did.

The president continued to come and visit as often as possible, while juggling his own grief, visiting Caroline and John, and dealing with world issues, which didn't stop for the death of a president's son.

I had been with Mrs. Kennedy through the births of two sons and the death of one. I couldn't imagine anything more difficult.

21
ONASSIS AND THE *CHRISTINA*

Sue Roosevelt, Mrs. Kennedy, Aristotle Onassis, and Franklin D. Roosevelt, Jr. aboard Christina

After the death of Patrick, the other agents and I noticed a distinctly closer relationship, openly expressed, between the president and Mrs. Kennedy. I first observed it in the hospital suite at Otis Air Force Base but it became publicly visible when Mrs. Kennedy was released from the hospital, a week after the birth. With press photographers snapping away, President and Mrs. Kennedy emerged from the hospital suite hand in hand. It was a small gesture, but quite significant to those of us who were around them all the time. Prior to this, they were much more restrained and less willing to express their close, loving relationship while out in public. The loss of Patrick seemed to be the catalyst to change all that.

The president had to return to Washington, but Mrs. Kennedy and the children elected to stay for the rest of the summer — as they had planned — at the Cape. It was the best place for her to recuperate and day by day, her physical strength began to return. Emotionally, however, she was drowning in sorrow. The loss of her son was constantly on her mind, and she seemed to become more and more depressed.

She continued to write notes and request information be passed on to various individuals, but you could tell her heart wasn't in it. She spent time with the children, but for the most part remained alone and secluded in her room in Brambletyde. There was nothing anybody could say or do to ease her pain. We simply hoped that time would heal this tragic wound.

The president came as often as possible to Hyannis Port, midweek for one night in one case and for an extended stay over Labor Day weekend. Not only was he taking great pains to be supportive to Mrs. Kennedy, but I noticed that he was paying more and more attention to the children than ever before. He started taking John with him to visit Ambassador Kennedy or out to the Allen Farm to watch Caroline ride. He would go swimming with John and Caroline in the ocean — watching with delight as they jumped to him from the decks of the *Honey Fitz*. Taking Caroline to Sunday church services with him became a regular occurrence. Having Caroline and John ride on the helicopter from the Kennedy compound to Otis Air Force Base with him as he was departing for Washington on Air Force One became more common. This was all new.

One day — it must have been at the end of August or the beginning of September — Mrs. Kennedy called me at the command post to say she wanted to go for a walk. When she came out of the house, she seemed to have a brighter look on her face than I had seen in weeks.

We began walking, and she turned to me,

with a glint in her eye.

"How would you like to go back to Greece, Mr. Hill?"

I looked at her with surprise. "I would *love* to go back to Greece."

She smiled and said, "Well, I have arranged to join Lee and Stash on a cruise through the Greek islands on a private yacht."

"That sounds wonderful, Mrs. Kennedy. When will you be leaving?"

"We haven't decided for sure, but we're hoping to go in a few weeks."

A few weeks? I tried to be nonchalant, but I needed to find out as much information as possible. Mrs. Kennedy still didn't truly understand how much effort it required for us to ensure her security outside the country.

"Do you know the name of the yacht?" I asked.

"Yes, actually I do. It's called the *Christina.* It's Mr. Onassis's yacht."

I lost my breath and was unable to speak for a few seconds. President Kennedy's words — the request he had made before Mrs. Kennedy's first trip to Greece back in 1961 — came rushing into my mind: *Whatever you do in Greece, do not let Mrs. Kennedy cross paths with Aristotle Onassis.*

I was stunned to think that now, for some reason, it was all right for Mrs. Kennedy to associate with this man.

This trip to Greece had apparently been a topic of conversation between Mrs. Kennedy and her sister, Lee, when Lee came to be with her immediately after Patrick's death. Lee and her husband, Prince Radziwill, were friends of Onassis and had been on his yacht. It seemed that Lee had contacted Onassis and the invitation had been extended. A trip to the Greek isles, on what was reputed to be the most luxurious private yacht in the world, was too good of an opportunity to turn down.

I knew Mrs. Kennedy would not go on a trip like this without her husband's concurrence. But why now, after the loss of their son, would the president be willing to let her go on Onassis's yacht, where, I assumed, the owner himself would be aboard? I could only surmise that it was because she had been so depressed, and perhaps the president thought a trip might give her something to look forward to.

"I don't want a lot of publicity," she said, "but I suppose everyone will find out."

"Yes, I'm sure the word will get out, and," I added, "there will be a great deal of interest."

I asked her a few questions about who else would be aboard, any other stops she might make, but it seemed the trip was still in the planning stages.

"Please let me know as soon as possible of any additional details, okay?" I requested.

"Oh, Mr. Hill, you always want to have so much information about these little trips I take."

Mrs. Kennedy's "little trip" was going to involve the ambassadors of two countries, a contingent of Secret Service agents and State Department personnel, and the navies of Greece, Turkey, and the United States. My job was to make sure she didn't have to worry about any of that.

As soon as we returned from the walk, I called my supervisor, Jerry Behn, the SAIC of the White House Detail, to let him know Mrs. Kennedy's plans. We had to notify the Paris Secret Service Field Office, which handled operations in Europe, and get Agent Ken Giannoules — our Greek-speaking agent — to start setting things up as soon as I received the schedule.

A few days later, Mrs. Kennedy informed me that the dates were set. We were leaving October 1 and would be gone two weeks. Mrs. Kennedy was only bringing Provi with her — no other staff — and it was to be kept as private as possible.

As we began to make the plans for the trip, information was flowing back to me that a great many people were very upset about Mrs. Kennedy going to Greece. Members of Mrs. Kennedy's staff as well as the president's were expressing concern about this proposed trip and how it would appear to the public — not just that she was choosing to vacation abroad, but specifically that she would be associating with Aristotle Onassis. Not only did he have some long-standing legal issues with the United States government, but his reputation was that of a womanizer and opportunist. There had always been concern about Mrs. Kennedy's sister Lee's friendship with Onassis, but to have Mrs. Kennedy herself spending time on his private yacht? This took on a whole new set of problems. There was grave concern that once Onassis got his foot in the door, he would take advantage of the situation to the detriment of everyone but himself. The general theme was that he could not be trusted.

The president had been made aware of the potential political fallout, but he insisted that Mrs. Kennedy would be permitted to go as planned. That was the end of that.

We remained at Squaw Island for the

seventy-fifth birthday party for the president's father on September 6, and then it was on to Hammersmith Farm in Newport, for most of the rest of September. On September 12, the president flew in from Washington to celebrate their tenth wedding anniversary. Good friends Ben and Tony Bradlee came as weekend guests, and the next few days were spent swimming at Bailey's Beach, cruising on the *Honey Fitz,* and playing golf at the Newport Country Club. Mrs. Kennedy seemed to be slowly coming out of the depressed state she had been in and began enjoying activities again. It was wonderful to see her renewed spirit and happy expression return.

Mrs. Kennedy and the children finally returned to the White House with the president on Monday, September 23. It was the beginning of the school year for Caroline in the school established by Mrs. Kennedy within the White House. To get the school year off to a rousing start, Mrs. Kennedy had arranged a surprise for all the children on Wednesday, September 25. Mrs. Kennedy, Caroline, and John met the students at the entrance to the White House and announced they were going on a field trip. To Dulles Airport. For a ride on the Goodyear blimp.

You've never seen a group of students more excited in your life.

I was up to my eyeballs trying to make arrangements for the trip to Greece, so I sent Paul Landis and the Kiddie Detail agents with Mrs. Kennedy and the twenty youngsters for the adventure of a lifetime.

Later, Mrs. Kennedy told me what a wonderful time they all had, especially John.

"You know how much John loves airplanes and flying, Mr. Hill. I think someday he is going to be a pilot."

We were scheduled to take a commercial flight from New York City to Rome, and then on to Athens, the evening of October 1. It so happened that the Imperial Majesty Haile Selassie, Emperor of Ethiopa, was arriving in Washington the same day. In her first public appearance since the death of Patrick, Mrs. Kennedy joined the president for the welcoming ceremonies at Union Station, and rode in the short motorcade to the Blair House, where the emperor was staying. The seventy-one-year-old Selassie was small in physical stature, but he was held in high regard around the world, having been the respected leader of his country for more than four decades. He came bearing personal gifts — an exotic leopard-skin coat for Mrs. Kennedy, a carved ivory doll for Caroline, and a carved ivory soldier with sword for John — and Mrs. Kennedy found him charming. They spoke in French together, and I could tell she wished she could have spent more time with him, but because of our departure that evening, she wasn't able to attend the state dinner that was planned in his honor.

Ever since Mrs. Kennedy's trip to Greece had been announced, I kept waiting for the president to call me into his office to give me some sort of instructions concerning Mr. Onassis. But I never got the call. Nothing was ever said.

There were quick good-byes to the children and the president and then we were off — Provi, Paul Landis, Mrs. Kennedy, and me — on our way to National Airport, where the *Caroline* was waiting to take us to New York for the scheduled TWA flight.

The New York Secret Service Field Office had arranged for the *Caroline* to taxi and be nose-to-nose with the big 707 to facilitate our transfer from one plane to the other. No press, and no crowds. Just the way she liked it.

We boarded the aircraft and settled into the first-class section. All except Agent Landis, that is. We had reserved a seat in the section behind first class next to the bulkhead for one agent to occupy. Poor Paul was given that assignment. His job was to preclude anyone from the rear coming into the first-class section. We had reserved six seats for Mrs. Kennedy — four in the center to be made into a bed, with an additional two seats by the window for her to sit in. Two additional seats in first class were for Provi and myself. It would be a long, sleepless night for Paul and me as we crossed the Atlantic.

Mrs. Kennedy slept almost the entire way, and after graciously signing photographs for the crew — I always kept a stash of her photos in my briefcase for such occasions — we transferred to the plane that would take us to Athens.

The weather was hot and sunny when we arrived in Athens, under a beautiful clear blue sky. As we were about to deplane, Mrs. Kennedy turned to me with a smile on her face and a gleam in her eye.

"Mr. Hill, are you ready to have some fun? I sure am."

It was so nice to see her smiling again. It was obvious she was looking forward to the next two weeks.

"Yes, Mrs. Kennedy," I said, returning the

smile. "I think all of us will have a good time."

But, believe me, I thought, *I am going to know everything that is going on.*

Prince "Stash" Radziwill and Mrs. Kennedy's sister, Lee, were there to greet us, along with U.S. ambassador Henry Labouisse. Agent Giannoules had done a great job of handling everything for our arrival, assisted once again by Nick Damigos from the State Department, who knew all the local officials and was keyed into anything that might affect Mrs. Kennedy's visit.

We spent the first few days of the trip in Athens, where once again the beautiful seaside villa owned by Markos Nomikos had been made available for Mrs. Kennedy and her guests. There was a courtesy visit to King Paul and Queen Frederika at the Tatoi Palace one afternoon, and as we drove down the long driveway, Mrs. Kennedy got a big grin on her face.

"Mr. Hill, you look so worried," she said.

"Yes, Mrs. Kennedy, I'm thinking about the last time we were here."

She laughed and said, "Don't worry. I promise I won't sneak off for a high-speed ride with Prince Constantine again. And remember? You did catch us."

"Oh, I remember only too well," I said

with a smile. "I'll be paying very close attention to your every move this time."

"I thought you always did that, Mr. Hill," she said, laughing.

Her teasing and playfulness was back, it was good to see, and true to her word, she didn't try to pull a fast one on me. At least not at the Tatoi Palace. The next day, we were to begin our cruise on the *Christina*.

In the nearly three years that I had been with Mrs. Kennedy, I had had the opportunity to sail aboard some fabulous yachts. Nomikos's *Northwind,* Gianni Agnelli's *Agneta,* and of course the yachts in the presidential fleet — the *Honey Fitz,* the *Manitou,* the *Sequoia.* But nothing could have prepared me for the *Christina.*

Anchored in the bay at Glyfada, the 325-foot *Christina* made the other yachts in the harbor look like bathtub toys. We were met at the dock by a few members of the crew, and two sleek mahogany-hulled Hacker speedboats — the tenders for the *Christina.* Our bags were loaded, and off we sped to the massive white yacht in the distance.

There were a great many staff to greet us and yes, Aristotle Onassis himself was standing on deck as we boarded. Gray-haired, with black bushy eyebrows, he was

shorter than I had expected, and had a stocky frame. He had a very large nose, an oily, olive complexion, and dark circles surrounding rather small eyes.

"Welcome, welcome," he said. "Welcome aboard the *Christina*." He greeted Lee with a kiss on each cheek — as Europeans do — and then proceeded to do the same to Mrs. Kennedy. I cringed as I watched him place his hands on her arms and lean in to graze her cheek with his lips.

This is the man President Kennedy had told me — in no uncertain terms — to make sure Mrs. Kennedy did not meet in 1961. Now, here she is being greeted by him on his yacht as his guest. Did I misunderstand something?

All these thoughts ran through my mind

as the other guests appeared on deck. There was Franklin D. Roosevelt Jr. and his wife, Suzanne; Onassis's sisters Artemis Garofalides and Mrs. Calliroë Patronicola; Greek actor Alexis Minotis; Silvio Medici De' Menezes and his wife, Princess Irene Galitzine. Many of these people I had met previously — and of course Princess Irene and I had shopped and dined together in Capri — but under these conditions, I felt like an intruder, completely out of place.

A steward escorted Mrs. Kennedy to her cabin, as I followed along, with Provi not far behind to make sure all was well with her mistress. The stateroom Mrs. Kennedy had been assigned was furnished as royally as any palace she had stayed in, while the en suite bathroom had solid gold fixtures, with faucets in the shape of dolphins. I had no idea splendor of this extreme existed. It was only the tip of the iceberg.

As Paul and I explored the yacht we encountered extravagance upon extravagance. A spiral staircase with pillars of onyx soaring three levels above a mosaic floor bearing the image of the Greek letter omega. A lounge with a stunning lapis lazuli fireplace surrounded by bookshelves containing rare volumes. A seawater swimming pool on the aft deck inlaid with an exquisite mosaic copied from the Palace of Knossos in Crete. If you want to dance, push a button and the floor of the pool rises, the water drains, and the mosaic tile floor of the pool is now at room level, ready to accommodate your every move.

Want a drink? Go to Ari's bar on the main deck. A wooden circular bar made from the timbers of a Spanish galleon with heavy sailing rope as the facing. You are sitting on bar stools covered in whale foreskin. Your arms and feet are resting on footrests and handholds of ornately carved whales' teeth accented in gold. Under the glass top to the bar itself are tiny ship models, which, at the flick of a switch, move on a lighted relief of the sea.

There is a library, and more lounge area, complete with a grand piano. Need to leave in a hurry? Lower the helicopter to the proper position and have a pleasant flight. And just to make sure you have absolutely everything you need or want, a seaplane is available to act as a courier bringing the latest newspapers, mail, and any provisions needed for the cruise. It also acts as a taxi, ferrying people leaving or joining the cruise. But beware, the standard trick is to fly over the *Christina* upside down after taking off, leaving the passenger somewhat ill, as

Prince Radziwill would find out upon his early departure.

Paul and I were led to the cabin he and I would share. Located in the bowels of the yacht, as part of the crew area, it was small and somewhat cramped, but we each had a bunk and our own head. Not bad for two government employees.

"What do you think, Paul?" I asked as we stood on deck looking back at the shore. "Think you can handle this for the next two weeks?"

"It is unreal," he said. "I think you could live on this yacht and never have to get off."

It was true. The *Christina* even had its own laundry and dry cleaning facility. I had been given a copy of the manifest, which listed the names, nationalities, and passport numbers for everybody aboard the ship. Thirteen passengers, and a crew of forty-eight, which included hairdressers, chefs, electricians, and engineers. From a security standpoint, it was ideal — a self-contained city with very few people to deal with.

The crew weighed anchor and the *Christina* began to move away from the Greek mainland toward the coast of Turkey, slicing through the water with hardly an indication on deck that we were moving. Paul remained in proximity to Mrs. Kennedy while

I went to the bridge to check with the captain and obtain as much information as possible about the immediate itinerary.

We were on our way to Istanbul, Turkey. But the captain didn't know what, if any, activities were planned upon arrival.

I found Mrs. Kennedy coming out of her stateroom. She had changed into a pair of lightweight trousers and a thin blouse. Her hair was pulled back with a scarf, and she had a pair of oversized sunglasses propped on top of her head.

"So, Mr. Hill, what do you think of the *Christina*?"

"It's a very nice yacht," I said as my mouth curled into a smile. "Not bad."

She laughed. It was wonderful to see her laughing again.

"Mrs. Kennedy, can you tell me what your plans are for the rest of the day, and what you think you might do tomorrow?"

"Oh Mr. Hill," she said as she grabbed my hands. "Will you please stop worrying about me and just try to enjoy yourself? This is so pleasant." She gave my hands a quick squeeze and added, "I want you and Mr. Landis to have a good time."

"Thank you Mrs. Kennedy, I appreciate that, but I do need to know your plans. I know we are on the way to Istanbul, but can you give me some more specific information?"

"I want to see the Blue Mosque in Istanbul and one of the national museums. You'll have to check with Mr. Onassis — he knows where I want to go."

"Okay. Thank you, Mrs. Kennedy, I'll do that."

I guess Mr. Onassis and I are going to get to know each other.

I went back to the bridge and told the captain I needed to talk with Mr. Onassis. He used the intercom system to connect with Mr. Onassis.

"Tell Mr. Hill to come to my suite," Onassis said over the intercom.

The captain pointed me to Onassis's suite, which was located just behind the navigation bridge.

I knocked at the door, and he immediately opened it.

"What can I do for you, Mr. Hill?" he asked. He spoke fluent English, with just the slightest hint of an accent. I had been surprised to see that the manifest listed his nationality as Argentine.

"I need to understand the immediate plans, and Mrs. Kennedy suggested I talk to you regarding the specific details."

"Well, Mr. Hill, we are on the way to

Istanbul, as you know." He stared at me with his beady brown eyes, speaking slowly, in a somewhat condescending tone. "We will be going up through the Bosporus into the Black Sea and then come back out so Mrs. Kennedy can visit the Blue Mosque and the Topkapi Palace in Istanbul."

He stared at me with intensity as he spoke. *Was he trying to intimidate me?* It wasn't going to work.

"I see, Mr. Onassis. I'll have to go ashore ahead of Mrs. Kennedy to make sure it is safe for her and that everything is ready."

"Fine, I'll arrange for you to do that," he said. "I'll let you know as soon as I talk with my people onshore."

"Thank you, Mr. Onassis. And just so you are aware, this will be the case everywhere we go, so the more information you can provide me in advance, the better."

With that I left the suite and went back to the bridge. I scanned the horizon, looking for one of the U.S. Navy ships that I knew were surveilling us. I never did see one, but I knew they were there.

That evening Mr. Onassis approached me and said, "Mr. Hill, the local authorities will send a launch to pick you up tomorrow morning as we pass the area on our way to the Black Sea. They will take you ashore to meet with Mr. Brown, the U.S. consul general. Will that be satisfactory?"

"Yes, sir. That will be fine." I was certainly glad that he was cooperating, and even helping facilitate our security activities.

Paul and I kept a watchful eye on Mrs. Kennedy, but gave her plenty of space. She enjoyed dinner with the other guests and a relaxing time in conversation, while soft strains of music wafted throughout the yacht. Shortly before midnight, she retired to her stateroom. Alone.

The following morning, as the *Christina,* escorted by two Turkish gunboats, passed through the Dardanelles into the Sea of Marmara in the area off Istanbul, a launch pulled alongside. An external ladder had been lowered so that I could make the transfer between the two boats. It was a windy day, and there was a steady chop in the water, with such a strong current that the operator of the launch could not keep his craft very close to the bottom of the ladder. The gap between the two vessels was about five feet, and there was no choice but for me to jump.

The launch was bobbing up and down, a constantly moving target. I knew if I jumped and didn't make it, I would be sucked under the *Christina* and that would be the end.

I knew Onassis was watching from above, probably with sinister delight. It was my first test.

I gathered all the energy I could and hurled myself across the gap with one giant leap. The Turkish crew grabbed me as I plopped into the launch. It wasn't graceful, but I made it. All in one piece.

I heard a whistle from above, and there was Paul standing on the top deck, smiling, giving me two thumbs up.

The launch whisked me ashore, where I met with Turkish authorities and the U.S. consul general, Ben Brown. While the *Christina* cruised through the Bosporus into the Black Sea, across which are Ukraine and Russia, and turned around, I got a quick tour of the area.

A few hours later, Paul Landis accompanied Mrs. Kennedy and a few of the other guests as they came ashore on one of the *Christina*'s tenders. Consul Brown and I were there to meet them with several cars, and a low-key police escort. Meanwhile, scores of plainclothes and uniformed Turkish police scattered throughout the tourist areas we were about to visit.

As we approached the Blue Mosque, the wailing sound of the muezzin calling the Muslim faithful to prayer sounded from high up in the minaret. Mrs. Kennedy dutifully placed a pair of loose slippers over her shoes, as did everyone else, before entering the mosque. A guide had been arranged to explain the history of the mosque, and Mrs. Kennedy listened with rapt attention as she admired the intricately tiled walls. At one point, she sat cross-legged on the Persian carpeted floor, along with rows and rows of Muslims who were praying, as the guide explained the religious rituals.

Even though the trip was unannounced and so spontaneous I had only found out about it a few hours earlier, word spread fast, and soon there were mobs of people clamoring around our little entourage. I was surprised at the number of American tourists there, and they seemed to be the most aggressive in terms of trying to get close to her. The Turkish police didn't put up with any nonsense, though, and they did a great job of keeping the people from crowding us too much.

From the Blue Mosque, we went to the museums within the Topkapi Palace and the St. Sophia Byzantine church, the Hagia Sophia. Still more tourists swarmed around us, but Mrs. Kennedy largely ignored them, focusing instead on the exquisite pieces in the collections — emeralds and rubies the size of eggs, a two-foot solid gold elephant, and a throne of solid gold encrusted with emeralds. Needless to say, she was impressed.

The three-hour shore visit was capped off with Turkish coffee in a private reception room, and then we were back to the *Christina* via the Hacker tenders.

I was relieved this little sojourn was over, but I also realized this was probably how it was going to be wherever we went. *Too many people, too little time for preparation, too many of them, too few of us.* At least when we were aboard the *Christina,* there were no unknown outside influences.

We traveled through the night in heavy rain through the Dardanelles, down the coast of Turkey, and anchored off the coast of Lesbos. By morning the storm had passed, and Mrs. Kennedy went for a swim in the crystal clear sea. A short time later we were moving again, this time on the way to Crete, some three hundred miles away. Everybody was in a relaxed mood, and the daylight hours on board were spent sunbathing, reading, and enjoying lively conversation. Mrs. Kennedy spent most of the time chatting with her sister and Princess Irene.

Onassis kept largely to himself in his suite near the bridge. I spent a lot of time on the bridge with the captain, and it seemed that Onassis was constantly on the phone. I couldn't understand a word he said, but even through the closed door, you could tell that he was rattling off orders to somebody. He would emerge for lunch and then again at cocktail hour, and would intermittently be on the phone barking orders and spending time with his guests, paying no more attention to Mrs. Kennedy than to anyone else.

We arrived in Crete under a cloudless sky and blazing sun. Mrs. Kennedy wanted to tour the Palace of Knossos, so I quickly went ahead to make arrangements. Viewing the frescoes and exploring the ruins of this ancient Minoan civilization, Mrs. Kennedy listened intently to our personal tour guide, and barraged her with questions. It was clear that Mrs. Kennedy knew much about the history already.

About halfway through the cruise, Mrs. Kennedy said she needed to talk to me. We went to the top of the ship near the smokestack for absolute privacy.

"Mr. Hill, I know I told you that King Hassan of Morocco, when he was our guest last spring, had extended an invitation to me to visit Marrakech. I've decided to take him up on it. I have already cleared it with the president and we will be going directly there from Athens."

So now we were adding Morocco to the itinerary. One thing was for sure — Mrs. Kennedy made life interesting.

"That sounds wonderful, Mrs. Kennedy. Have any flights or other arrangements been made?"

"Oh, yes. You won't have to worry about that at all. King Hassan is sending his personal plane to pick us up in Athens and take us straight to Marrakech. So you see, it won't be any problem at all."

I laughed. "No, Mrs. Kennedy, it won't be any problem at all."

"I think Pierre is going to announce it to the press in a day or two but I wanted to make sure you knew so you can do the things you have to do — but I don't want anyone else to know. Only Lee knows and I'll tell Provi as we get closer to leaving."

"Thank you for telling me."

I understood that she didn't want anyone else on the boat to know where she was going once we got off the yacht in Athens. And there was good reason. There was an ongoing border clash between Algeria and Morocco that had escalated very recently. I knew that if she had cleared the trip with the president, he was monitoring the situation closely. But I needed to get Ken Giannoules on a plane to Marrakech as soon as possible.

"Are you enjoying the cruise so far?" I asked.

"It's been wonderful, really a dream come true. I hope you and Mr. Landis are enjoying yourselves."

"Yes, we are having a good time," I replied. "The *Christina* really is rather impressive," I said with a grin. "And you know, I am not easily impressed."

"Yes, Mr. Hill. I know," she said with a smile. She stood up and said, "Come, join us for hors d'oeuvres. We're not going off the yacht tonight, so you can relax. Tomorrow we're going to Levkas, and Mr. Onassis's private island, called Skorpios."

I had heard that Onassis owned his own island. *Who the hell owns their own island?* Located in the Ionian Islands, west of mainland Greece, Skorpios was about four and a half miles in circumference, and covered with lovely pine, cypress, and olive trees. It was extremely private, and offered absolute seclusion. We stopped for a swim and walked around the island, but Mrs. Kennedy was eager to return to the yacht and move on to see more historic sights.

We headed back to Glyfada near Athens, stopping at Delphi on the way to see the famous temple of the Oracle of Delphi. As we approached the point of anchorage in the Bay of Glyfada, Onassis decided he wanted to take Mrs. Kennedy and the rest of the party to one of his favorite places. Cars and security had to be arranged, so I contacted the Greek national at the State Department — a guy named Greg — who had been so helpful throughout the trip, and went ashore ahead of the party to get everything set.

Paul remained with Mrs. Kennedy, and once I had everything arranged, he got into one of the Hacker tenders with her, as Onassis took the helm. I had the cars and drivers waiting at our predetermined spot and watched as the boat headed toward me. Suddenly the boat turned sharply, increased speed, and started racing down the coast.

"Goddammit! What the hell is he doing?!" I yelled.

Greg was standing nearby, watching the same thing. He said something in Greek to the drivers, and said, "Clint, get in. Let's go!"

I jumped into one of the cars and we raced down the coast. He had a pretty good idea where Onassis was going. We arrived at a point and parked the cars, just as the tender came into sight.

Onassis pulled the boat to the dock where we were standing waiting, and glared at me. His normally tanned complexion had gone pale, and he looked like he had just lost the biggest battle of his life. We had outsmarted him and he did not like it one bit.

Paul had a big smile on his face. "Way to go, Clint," he whispered.

Without the help of Greg and the knowledge of the drivers, I would have been left standing at the seaside wondering where to go. They made me look good. I made sure they knew that and thanked them profusely.

Mrs. Kennedy approached the car and as she got in, she said in a low voice, "Nice save, Mr. Hill." That was all the thanks I needed. Outsmarting Onassis was a real pleasure.

We remained overnight on the *Christina,* preparing for our departure for Marrakech the following day.

The next morning, we bade our host a hearty thank-you and good-bye. Onassis gave Mrs. Kennedy and Lee some parting gifts of expensive jewelry to remember the trip, while Paul and I left with nothing but our memories of being on one of the most incredible yachts in the world, and the satisfaction of having helped Mrs. Kennedy have a trip of a lifetime, without incident.

We went straight to the Athens airport and boarded the Royal Moroccan aircraft King Hassan had sent for Mrs. Kennedy. The Caravelle jet, which could hold eighty to one hundred passengers, was all ours — just Lee, Provi, Paul Landis, Mrs. Kennedy, and me. We were on our way to the next adventure.

Ken Giannoules had gone to Marrakech several days earlier to advance Mrs. Kennedy's visit to Morocco. It was not an official visit and even though it had been announced to the press, there was no formal motorcade planned. Still, it was clear the people of Morocco were thrilled to have the first lady of the United States as a guest, and the reception was enthusiastic. Once again we witnessed Mrs. Kennedy's international popularity. Women in long black robes and veils called out with their unique shrill shriek of welcome.

Men dressed in the traditional djellaba and turban politely applauded as we drove to the Bahia Palace, inside the thirty-foot-high walls of the ancient city. Mrs. Kennedy loved it.

By sheer coincidence, Mrs. Kennedy's

visit occurred during the reverent celebration of King Hassan's firstborn son, Prince Mohammed, who had been born on August 21. It was a Moroccan and Muslim custom to celebrate when the baby was forty days old.

I was worried about how this would affect Mrs. Kennedy, since Patrick, had he lived, would have been nearly the same age. She handled the situation with grace and dignity. She said to me at one point, "Isn't it wonderful they are able to celebrate the life and hope for the future of their new son? The president and I had similar hopes and dreams for Patrick."

There was also a festival in which hundreds of Berber tribesmen had traveled to the city with their horses, guns, and tents. The event took place on a field about two football fields in length. Mrs. Kennedy, Lee, Agent Landis, and I were seated under a tent on the sidelines as the tribesmen began dancing and singing to the rhythmic sounds of their drums. Mrs. Kennedy loved this kind of stuff.

Agent Giannoules had warned us that there would be gunfire as the tribesmen charged each other on horseback, demonstrating their horsemanship and skill as fighters. When I explained this to Mrs. Kennedy, she said, "Oh, that sounds so exciting!"

She hadn't brought a camera, but Paul Landis had one that he had been taking pictures with all week.

She turned to Mr. Landis and said, "Mr. Landis, why don't you go down on the field and take some pictures?"

"That's a great idea, Mrs. Kennedy," he said.

He got up and walked down to the arena. The Berber tribesmen, all dressed in their traditional clothing, then began to line up on horseback at one end of the field.

All of a sudden, without warning, a gun fired into the air. *Crack!* The riders charged, creating a cloud of dust, amid the whoops and hollers and the sound of the horses' hooves trampling down the field, right toward Paul.

"Oh no!" Mrs. Kennedy exclaimed in horror as she threw her hands to her face.

When the dust cleared, there was Paul, his face white as a sheet, yet still snapping away with his camera, just inches from the tramping horsemen.

Mrs. Kennedy and I burst out laughing. We could hardly contain ourselves at the sight of Paul, visibly trembling, as the tribesmen circled around in mock battle.

When Paul was able to make his way back to where we were seated, I couldn't help myself.

"Paul," I said, "if you need to go to your room and change your shorts, feel free to do so."

"Oh, Mr. Hill! Poor Mr. Landis!" Mrs. Kennedy laughed and laughed and laughed. It was so wonderful to hear that laugh again.

It was music to my ears, and I knew everything was going to be okay.

The next day we left Marrakech on King Hassan's private plane and headed for Paris. On the Pan Am flight back to New York, Mrs. Kennedy couldn't stop talking about the trip. She was in great spirits.

"You know, Mr. Hill," she said, "the president is going on a trip to Texas next month, and he wants me to join him. I had told him I didn't want to go — I didn't think I was ready. But now I feel so much better and I really want to help him as much as I can.

"Maybe I will go after all."

22
Preparing for Texas

Mrs. Kennedy rides Sardar in Middleburg

As soon as we returned from Greece and Morocco, Mrs. Kennedy was eager to spend as much time as possible in Atoka. Beginning the weekend of October 25, 1963, it became the habit that every Friday, after Caroline's school let out at 1:00 P.M., Mrs. Kennedy, the children, Maud Shaw, and I would helicopter directly to the Atoka property, with Paul Landis and the children's agents driving the cars, filled with suitcases and things Mrs. Kennedy had decided to bring to the new house.

The sprawling ranch-style house at Atoka that Mrs. Kennedy had designed and decorated sat on a rise with tremendous views of the countryside. It was very secluded, with not another home in sight, and had acres and acres of rolling meadows for Mrs. Kennedy to ride her beloved horses. Sardar and Macaroni had been transported there, along with a new pony named Leprechaun — a gift for John from the people of Ireland. Beautiful stables had been built to accommodate the horses — and the Secret Service agents. An office with brand-new equipment had been designed into the stable building as the Secret Service Command Post, which really worked out well, but also served as a subtle reminder of where we stood in the pecking order.

That first Friday afternoon, the first thing Mrs. Kennedy wanted to do was ride Sardar. It was a glorious autumn day, and from the vantage point at the back of the house, I could see the entire thirty-nine-acre property. As I watched her gallop at full pace, the wind blowing in her hair, her body moving as one with her beloved Sardar, I thought, *This is what she needed more than anything.* The cruise on the *Christina* was magnificent, no doubt about it, but there was nothing that compared to the joy on her face when she was riding.

When she finished, I was waiting by the stables with the groom they had hired to care for the horses. After dismounting, Mrs. Kennedy handed the reins to the groom and said, "Mr. Hill, come walk with me to the house."

I always thought she looked so beautiful in her riding clothes — natural, no makeup, and after an exhilarating ride, her face was flushed from the exercise. But despite how much she seemed to have enjoyed being back on Sardar, I could tell something was wrong.

As we started walking, she said, "You know I told you I was going to go with the president to Texas . . ."

"Yes . . ." I had a feeling I knew what this was about.

"Well," she said, "I'm having second thoughts, after this incident with Adlai Stevenson."

Adlai Stevenson, the ambassador to the United Nations, was one of Mrs. Kennedy's friends. The day before, he had been heckled while giving a speech on world peace in Dallas. Then, when he emerged from the auditorium, a group of anti–United Nations protesters attacked him with placards, and someone reportedly spat on him. The police had to force back the protesters, and by all accounts, it was an ugly scene.

"Yes, I did hear about that," I answered.

"I had dinner with the Roosevelts last night, and they tried to talk me out of going — especially to Dallas. What do you think?"

She had been so excited about the trip just a couple of days earlier, and now it seemed she was rethinking everything. I wondered whether it really had to do with the Stevenson incident.

"Are you sure you're not just trying to get out of going to Johnson's ranch?" I asked with a smile.

The details of the trip were still being worked out by the political staff, but the word was that Vice President Johnson and his wife had extended an invitation for an overnight visit at their ranch near Austin.

She looked at me and laughed.

"Well, that is rather frightening in and of itself . . . but really," she said, turning serious, "I would like to know your opinion. Do you think the climate in Dallas is so . . . so hostile to the president that the people could mistreat us like they did Adlai?"

"Anything's possible, Mrs. Kennedy," I said. "But as far as I know, there are no more threats in Dallas or Houston or anywhere else in Texas than there would be in any other part of the South right now."

"I suppose it seems rather silly to be worried about going somewhere in your own country, when I've gone to places like India and Pakistan and Morocco, doesn't it?"

"It's not silly, Mrs. Kennedy. I don't want you to be uncomfortable for any reason. But right now, if you're asking my opinion, I don't see any reason why you shouldn't feel perfectly safe going to Texas with the president."

"Well, that makes me feel a lot better." She grabbed my hand and said, "Thank you, Mr. Hill. You always know exactly the right thing to say."

Over the next few days, I had a feeling she was still wavering, but on November 7, White House Press Secretary Pierre Salinger made the announcement to the press:

Mrs. Kennedy will accompany the president on the entire Texas trip. The trip is expected to include Houston and Austin and perhaps San Antonio, Fort Worth, and Dallas.

It was official. We were going to Texas.

■ ■ ■ ■

Caroline had become quite the equestrienne after her lessons during the summer in Hyannis Port, and it became almost a daily activity for Mrs. Kennedy and Caroline to go riding together. Meanwhile, John, who was nearly three years old, would tramp around the woods in cowboy boots and an army helmet. The agents had set up an army tent near the edge of the woods, and John would play for hours with his toy swords and guns, marching around, giving orders to his "army nurse," Miss Shaw.

Like clockwork, on Saturday, John would hear the telltale sound of the helicopter coming in — the impressive Army or Marine helicopter with the white top denoting the president was aboard — and he could hardly contain himself. There was nothing that boy loved more than helicopters. And he knew that when the chopper came in, that meant Daddy was coming.

We all got such a kick out of John and everybody would play along, saluting "General John" when he was in his military getup. He would salute back, giggling like crazy. The only problem was, he always saluted with his left hand. No matter how many times we told him to use his right hand, his instinct always seemed to be to use his left hand.

The weekend before Veterans Day, Mrs. Kennedy told John that Daddy was going to take him to a special ceremony on Monday, where he would get to see real soldiers, marching and saluting. She tried to explain that Daddy was the commander in chief of all the soldiers, and they would all salute him.

"Now John," she said, "when you see the other soldiers salute Daddy, you can salute him, too."

Agent Bob Foster was by little John's side when the president silently placed a floral wreath on the Tomb of the Unknown Soldier, at Arlington National Cemetery, and "wouldn't you know it," Bob told me later, "as soon as the uniformed military color guard saluted, John raised his hand — his right hand — and saluted his father, right on cue. I was proud of the little guy."

Two days later, on Wednesday, November 13, John got to see another military spectacle, when the Scottish Black Watch Regiment's Pipers and Band performed on the south grounds of the White House. Noteworthy because they were Britain's first kilted regiment, the famous military troupe was on tour in the United States and Mrs. Kennedy had invited them to perform on the White House lawn. Wanting to ensure an appreciative audience, she arranged for 1,700 underprivileged schoolchildren, along with the families of White House staff, to attend the four o'clock performance. Throngs of press people had come to the event as well — not so much because of their interest in the marching bagpipe band, but more for the opportunity to photograph the president, Mrs. Kennedy, and the children together.

It was a cold and dreary November afternoon, and while the Scotsmen in the regiment were wearing their traditional plaid kilts, everyone in the audience was bundled in winter coats, hats, and gloves. The president and Mrs. Kennedy walked onto the lawn, and after shaking hands with the commander, the president made a short speech acknowledging the brave and proud history of the Black Watch Royal Highlanders, and the fact that the colonel in chief of the regiment was the Queen Mother of Great Britain. Quipping that in one war — the War of Independence — they fought against us, he solemnly added that more important are the wars in which they have fought alongside us: World War I, World War II, and Korea.

"Personally," President Kennedy said, "the history of Scotland captured me at a very young age. The U.S., in fact all of us, love, I suppose in a sense, lost causes. And on occasion the history of Scotland has been a lost cause, but perhaps in some ways they have triumphed. Perhaps more today than ever before. We regard it as a great honor to have representatives of a great country to have as our guests here at the White House."

The audience cheered as the president and Mrs. Kennedy walked back across the lawn, then walked up the steps to the South Portico porch, where John and Caroline were patiently watching and waiting.

All eyes were on the balcony as President and Mrs. Kennedy took their seats, and when Caroline jumped into the lap of her father, cameras were snapping like crazy. It was rare for the public to see the family like this together in such a relaxed setting — something I witnessed regularly — and they loved it.

As soon as they were situated, the performance began. And what a performance it was. Dressed in the dark navy, green, and black plaid kilts for which they are noted, with white boots, and magnificent head-dresses made of black ostrich feathers, the regiment put on a spectacle like nothing that had ever been performed on the grounds of the White House. Trumpets, trombones, tubas, and drums harmonized together as a backdrop for the haunting sounds of the bagpipes. And as they played, the performers high-stepped and sword-danced in intricate maneuvers flawlessly timed to the tempo of the traditional Scottish tunes. For those of us who had the privilege of being there, it was something we will never forget. And in return, it was obvious that the Black Watch were incredibly honored to be able to perform in this prestigious setting, as the young American president sat on the balcony of the White House, surrounded by his family, tapping his hands on his knees to the rhythm of the drum.

On Wednesday, November 20, Mrs. Kennedy and I returned to the White House after another long weekend at Atoka. We were leaving the next morning for Texas, and while she was concerned with packing the proper wardrobe, I needed to get an update on the logistics and security arrangements.

I walked from my office in the Map Room, down the hall to the Secret Service office, and found Floyd Boring and Roy Kellerman, the two Assistants to the Special Agent in Charge of the White House Detail. Both of these men reported to Jerry Behn, the SAIC, and while Behn was taking a few well-deserved days off, they were the top men in charge.

"Hey, Clint," Floyd said as soon as I walked in the door. "We were just discussing the Texas trip."

"Great," I said. "That's what I wanted to talk about, too." I held up my copy of the schedule. "Looks ambitious."

They looked at each other and then Floyd said, "Clint, shut the door."

It wasn't unusual to close the door to the Secret Service room — there were lots of times our conversations needed to be confidential — but I wondered what was up.

"Listen, Clint," Floyd said. "You know we just came back from Florida, right?"

"Yeah. The president was in Cape Canaveral, Tampa, and Miami, is what I recall."

"That's right," Floyd said. "And something happened in Tampa you need to know about. I presume that since you've been at Atoka, you hadn't heard."

I shook my head. All I had heard was what

had been transmitted over the radio. I didn't recall anything out of the ordinary.

Floyd continued. "We had a long motorcade in Tampa, and it was decided that we should keep two guys on the back of the car for the entire route — just for added precaution."

I nodded. That wasn't all that unusual. There were steps and handholds built onto the back of the presidential limousine — the one we called "100X" — specifically for that purpose. Whenever there were heavy crowds, you wanted to have agents as close to the president as possible.

"So, we had Chuck Zboril and Don Lawton on the back of the car the entire way," Floyd said. "But partway through the motorcade, in an area where the crowds had thinned, the president requested we remove the agents from the back of the car."

"Really?" I asked. I had never heard the president ever question procedural recommendations by his Secret Service detail. "What was the reason?"

"He said now that we're heading into the campaign, he doesn't want it to look like we're crowding him. And the word is, from now on, you don't get on the back of the car unless the situation absolutely warrants it."

"Okay," I said. "Understood."

We then moved on to discussing the logistics for the trip ahead, how Mrs. Kennedy was feeling, and how I thought she would cope with the trip. We were all surprised that she was going, but Boring and Kellerman agreed that the president and Mrs. Kennedy seemed so much closer since Patrick died, and we thought it might actually be beneficial for her to get out in public. There was no doubt it would benefit the president — his poll numbers had dropped considerably in key southern states, and he needed all the help he could get if he were going to get reelected.

I returned to my office and sat down at my desk. I picked up the schedule and read through it again.

We were to depart the White House at 10:45 A.M. and arrive at San Antonio International Airport at 1:30 P.M. local time. Motorcade through the city to Brooks Air Force Base. President dedicates a new Aerospace Medical Center. Motorcade to Kelly Field. Fly to Houston. Arrive Houston at 5:00 P.M. Motorcade through Houston to the Rice Hotel downtown. Brief appearance by President and Mrs. Kennedy. Back in the cars. Motorcade to Sam Houston Coliseum for a banquet in honor of Texas congressman Albert Thomas. Depart the Coliseum 9:45 P.M. Cars to airport. Fly to Fort Worth. Arrive Fort Worth 10:45 P.M. Motorcade from Carswell Air Force Base into downtown Fort Worth. Arrive Texas Hotel 11:05 P.M.

Nine and a half hours on the ground. Five motorcades in three major cities. If the weather permitted, the president and Mrs. Kennedy would be in an open-top car. That was the norm. It was going to be a high-adrenaline day for everybody — the president, Mrs. Kennedy, and the agents. And that was just day one. The next day, we flew to Dallas and Austin for more of the same.

I suddenly wondered if I should have tried to talk Mrs. Kennedy out of the trip. She had such high expectations, and sincerely wanted to be involved in the campaign, but it was going to be exhausting. The last thing I wanted was for something like this to set her back. She had only just started laughing again.

23
THAT DAY IN DALLAS

Clint Hill walks beside car as President and Mrs. Kennedy depart Love Field

The White House was alive with activity when I arrived at 8:00 A.M. November 21. The fact that Mrs. Kennedy was going with the president added a whole different dimension to the trip. This would be her first domestic political trip since her husband had become president, and everybody wanted it to go well.

I immediately went to the lower level of the West Wing, where the White House Transportation Office was gathering baggage, and dropped off my suitcase. From this point on I wouldn't have to worry about my bags. When I arrived at my hotel room that night, all of my stuff would be there, waiting for me. There was no such thing as lost or misplaced luggage when you traveled on Air Force One.

At about 10:40 I heard the unmistakable sound of the helicopter landing on the South Lawn. I put out my cigarette, gathered the portfolio with all the details of the trip, and headed to the Diplomatic Reception Room to prepare to board the presidential helicopter.

It was always an impressive sight to see the Marine helicopter land right there on the lawn at the White House. And no one loved it more than John. As if on cue, the tousle-haired little boy came running in with Agent Bob Foster, as the president and Mrs. Kennedy followed closely behind.

"Hey John," I said. "Are you coming on the chopper?"

He looked up at me with the biggest grin you can imagine and said, "Yeah! Look!"

He pointed out the French doors. "There it is!"

His enthusiasm was contagious, and everybody laughed.

It had become habit now — almost every time the president left the White House, he would ask one of the children's agents to bring John for the short ride to Andrews Air Force Base. President Kennedy got such a kick out of seeing John's enthusiasm on the helicopter. I don't know who enjoyed it more — the president or his son.

As soon as the chopper touched down, the pilot powered down the rotors. When the Navy aide standing at the portico gave us the "okay" sign, we filed into the helicopter, which, as soon as the president boarded, became Marine One.

It was a short six-minute ride to Andrews, where pilot Colonel Jim Swindal had the presidential aircraft ready to go, engines running. It certainly was an impressive plane — with the blue, silver, and white theme that Mrs. Kennedy had had a hand in designing — and the proud UNITED STATES OF AMERICA boldly painted on the side. At times I still had to pinch myself that I was one of the privileged few who got to ride on Air Force One — on a regular basis. Only the presidential party and the shift agents assigned to the president and first lady would ride on Air Force One. Paul Landis was assigned to the backup plane with the afternoon shift agents. The president's midnight shift agents were already headed to Fort Worth to set up security for our arrival there later in the evening.

The entire day's itinerary was timed to the minute, and we had left the White House a few minutes late, so there was no time to delay.

"Okay, good-bye, John," the president said as he leaned over and gave his son a hug.

"I want to come," John whined. Tears welled in his eyes.

Mrs. Kennedy kissed him on the cheek and said, "It's just a few days, darling. And when we come back, it will be your birthday."

Wiping away a tear, she added brightly, "Maybe we'll have a surprise or two."

This didn't appease John in the slightest. He was really crying now. Oh, how he wanted to go on the big plane with Mummy and Daddy.

President Kennedy leaned over and gently patted his son on the leg. "John, like Mummy said, we'll be back in a few days."

Then the president stood up and looked at Agent Bob Foster, who had slid into the seat next to John.

"Take care of John for me, won't you, Mr. Foster?"

"Yes, sir, Mr. President," Foster replied. "I'll be glad to do that."

John continued to cry as the president and Mrs. Kennedy exited the helicopter. Before I got off, I gave a quick look around to make sure nobody had left anything.

"Bye-bye, John," I said. "You have fun with Mr. Foster now, okay? We'll be back in a few days."

We'll be back in a few days . . .

On the flight to San Antonio, I sat in the aft cabin next to Roy Kellerman, the Assistant Special Agent in Charge (ASAIC) of the White House Detail. Forty-eight-year-old Kellerman was the supervising Secret Service agent on the trip, and just as I would be with Mrs. Kennedy the entire time, so would Kellerman be with the president. Kellerman was in his twenty-third year with the Secret Service and was one of the agents we all really looked up to. Extremely detail-oriented and methodical, he had started as a shift agent with President Franklin D. Roosevelt, and had risen through the ranks while serving under presidents Truman, Eisenhower, and now Kennedy. At six foot four, with gray-streaked black hair, a leathered complexion, and steely eyes, he was an imposing figure — of all the agents, he probably had the most intimidating appearance of any of us. President Kennedy trusted him completely.

The Air Force One stewards served a light lunch to all on board. It was good to get something to eat because once the activity of the day began, we agents never knew when we'd get our next meal. When the opportunity presents itself, take advantage because it may be a long time until you have that chance again.

At 1:30 P.M. local time, we landed at San Antonio Airport. I looked out the window to see what awaited us.

"Take a look at that crowd," I said to Kellerman. "I bet there are five thousand people there."

"And that's just the airport," he said as he got up out of his seat. "Last word I got was that the police were expecting a hundred and twenty-five thousand along the motorcade route."

It wasn't anything we hadn't dealt with before. I just hoped Mrs. Kennedy had gotten some rest on the flight. It was going to be a long day. When Mrs. Kennedy emerged from the presidential cabin, she had changed into a short-sleeved white suit with a narrow black belt, and elbow-length white gloves. Knowing we would be riding in the open convertible, she had put on a black, beret-style hat to keep her hair from blowing in the wind.

When President and Mrs. Kennedy emerged from the rear door of the aircraft, the crowd went wild. Vice President and Mrs. Johnson and Governor John Connally and his wife, Nellie, were lined up at the bottom of the stairs to greet them in a formal procession. Everybody knew their places. It had all been planned down to the minute and arrivals like this were almost always the same.

The president and Mrs. Kennedy acknowledged the large crowd with waves and smiles, as the agents formed an envelope of protection around them. Not too close, but within an arm's length, at all times. The schedule called for them to proceed directly to the waiting limousine, but the people behind the fence line were screaming and waving signs that said KENNEDY IN '64. In typical fashion, President Kennedy couldn't resist going to the fence to shake some hands.

Mrs. Kennedy took me completely by surprise and followed the president toward the crowd. She had never done this before. This was the kind of thing she tried to avoid. I stayed close to her as she followed the president's lead, tentatively reaching her gloved hand into the crowd. Ladies were shrieking at the sight of the president and calling out "Jackie! Jackie!"

Mrs. Kennedy had indicated to me that she wanted to help her husband and I guess this was one way she was doing so. I thought back to our conversation at Atoka and her concerns.

Do you think the climate in Dallas is so hostile to the president that the people could mistreat us like they did Adlai?

No indication of that here in San Antonio, I thought. You couldn't ask for a friendlier or more exuberant crowd.

The motorcade vehicles were lined up ready to go, in a set procession, as outlined in the White House Advance Manual, which every White House Detail Secret Service agent carried. Two Secret Service vehicles had been flown to San Antonio ahead of time — the presidential limousine and the Secret Service follow-up car — while standard cars had been leased locally for the vice president and other members of the party.

After a few minutes, the president waved

good-bye, and he and Mrs. Kennedy took their seats in the limousine with Governor and Mrs. Connally.

The midnight-blue Secret Service parade limousine, SS-100-X, which we had been using since March 1961, was specifically designed for motorcades like this. SS-100-X was the most advanced presidential parade limousine of its time. The Ford Motor Company and Hess & Eisenhardt had taken a standard Lincoln Continental convertible and modified it, using specifications provided by the Secret Service. The original wheelbase of 133 inches was extended to 156 inches — with the extra room all being in the rear passenger compartment; built-in jump seats in front of the rear seat allowed for additional passengers; a hydraulic lift allowed the president to be raised nearly a foot higher if he so desired; a loudspeaker system could be used to address a crowd.

Then of course, there were the various roofs — the metal roof, a convertible top, and the Plexiglas "bubbletop." There was a roll bar that ran from one side of the car to the other, above and slightly to the rear of the front seat, which provided support and acted as the fastening device for the different tops. What we had come to realize, in the past two and a half years of using the car, however, was that while it made for a great handlebar for the president to hold on to while standing in the car during a motorcade, its presence made it extremely difficult, almost impossible, for the agent in the right front seat to be able to get into the rear compartment, in the case of an emergency.

One final drawback of this unique car was that, with the modifications, its weight had been increased from 5,215 lbs to 7,800 pounds, without passengers. And the specially designed 350-horsepower engine, although adequate for normal use, did not facilitate quick acceleration.

What was most useful, from the Secret Service standpoint, were the special handles on the trunk and the steps on the rear bumper area where two additional agents could ride, and have immediate access to the occupants, should the need arise. But, as I'd been told the day before, the president did not want us there, on the back of the car.

The Agent in Charge always rode in the right front passenger seat of the presidential vehicle, while the rest of the agents in the motorcade rode in the follow-up car — the large 1956 Cadillac convertible we called Halfback. Like SS-100-X, it had been modified with some special features. It could hold nine people in seats and had running boards along both sides, which, when you were standing on them, provided an elevated vantage point to observe the ever-present crowds. The running boards also served as launching platforms to get off and on the vehicle. Handholds attached to the edge of the windshield frame aided in our movement back onto the car.

Behind the front seat, built into the divider from the rear, was a cabinet that held additional armaments. On this day, the AR-15 rifle was there.

Normally President and Mrs. Kennedy would ride side-by-side alone on the rear bench seat, with guests occupying the jump seats. For some reason, Mrs. Connally joined the president and Mrs. Kennedy on the rear seat, while the governor sat in front of them, in the jump seat. It was a cloudless, sunny day, perfect weather for a political parade — and ideal for 100X to have no top on at all. Just the way President Kennedy liked it.

It seemed that half the city of San Antonio had come out to watch the president drive by. They lined the streets with WELCOME JACK AND JACKIE signs, screaming and hollering all along the motorcade route from the airport to Brooks Air Force Base.

I was riding on Halfback, immediately behind the presidential vehicle, with the agents on the 8:00–4:00 shift from the president's detail. Standing in the forward position on the left running board of the follow-up car, next to driver Agent Sam Kinney, this put me in close proximity to Mrs. Kennedy, who was seated on the left side of the presidential limousine, and gave me a somewhat elevated position from which to observe the crowd. There was an agent standing behind me, two others on the right running board, two agents in the backseat, and Emory Roberts, the 8:00–4:00 shift leader, was in the right front passenger seat.

As we traveled from San Antonio International Airport through the streets of the city, there were many places where the crowd was so dense that the people had spilled into the street. These were the situations in which I'd seen a mass of people surge toward the car, changing an otherwise peaceful motorcade into a swarm of chaos. It could happen in an instant. So, whenever I saw a particularly dense crowd alongside the road, I would jump off the running board, run to catch up with the presidential vehicle, and run alongside so that I was between Mrs. Kennedy and the people, until the crowds thinned. This could go on for a block, or a mile. Jump off, run, jog along for a while, fall back to the follow-up car, jump back on the running board. Off and on, on and off, for fifteen miles. The Florsheims were getting a good workout.

We arrived at Brooks Air Force Base, where another nine thousand people cheered as President and Mrs. Kennedy entered the stage area. The president made a speech to dedicate the Aerospace Medical Center, the program concluded, and we were back in the vehicles for another motorcade to Kelly Air Force Base where Air Force One, the vice president's plane, and the backup plane had been moved from the San Antonio airport.

At this point, the 4:00–midnight shift took over the president's protection, and the morning shift — Emory Roberts's 8:00–4:00 shift — headed to the venue in Houston to set up security in advance of the president's arrival. Paul Landis and I didn't have any replacement shift, so we carried on — me handling the motorcades and Paul moving ahead to our destination.

Everybody boarded their respective planes and flew to Houston — a thirty-five-minute flight. The first stop had been a success, and on board Air Force One, the president was thrilled. When we landed in Houston, we did the whole routine all over again — complete with Vice President and Mrs. Johnson and Governor and Mrs. Connally greeting the President and Mrs. Kennedy as they got off Air Force One.

There was a large, friendly, and enthusiastic crowd at the airport — nearly twice as many people as had been in San Antonio. And as before, President and Mrs. Kennedy willfully went to the fence line to greet the people who had come out to give them such a warm welcome.

I guess this is how you win votes and elections — shaking as many hands as possible, hoping that brief personal connection will turn into a vote.

I could tell Mrs. Kennedy was a bit tired, but she really seemed to be enjoying it.

After several minutes, it was time to pile into the cars again for the motorcade into the city to the Rice Hotel. There hadn't been time to securely transport SS-100-X and the follow-up car, so they were sent on to Dallas, to be used the following day. In Houston, the cars were standard Lincoln convertibles loaned to the Secret Service by the local dealer. The presidential vehicle was a bit tight as President and Mrs. Kennedy and the governor squeezed into the back-seat, while Mrs. Connally was jammed in the front seat between driver Agent Bill Greer and ASAIC Kellerman. Not much room to move.

The follow-up was also a standard Lincoln convertible, which was not very efficient for the agents working the motorcade. I sat on top of the car frame, with my legs straddling the door, one inside and one out. When the crowds were bigger, and I thought I might have to jump off quickly, I'd move to a sidesaddle position. It was awkward, and uncomfortable as hell. Running alongside the presidential vehicle was preferable, but it was impossible to run and keep up the entire way.

At the Rice Hotel another huge crowd was waiting to greet President and Mrs. Kennedy. More hand-shaking in the crowd, and then up to the suite that had been arranged for them to rest and relax for a few hours before the evening's activities.

Mrs. Kennedy's hair was windblown from having been in the open-top cars, and I could see in her eyes that she was somewhat drained.

"How are you doing, Mrs. Kennedy?" I asked. "Are you all right?"

"Oh, yes, Mr. Hill, I'm fine. It's been such

a wonderful day, hasn't it? I do need a rest, though, or I imagine I'll collapse later this evening."

"Well, just let me know if you need anything."

I waited outside the suite with ASAIC Roy Kellerman as various people came and went. Ken O'Donnell and Dave Powers, the special assistants to the president — and both longtime friends — conferred with President Kennedy, while Mary Gallagher assisted Mrs. Kennedy. They rested, ate dinner, and changed clothes. At one point the president called for Vice President and Mrs. Johnson to join them in the suite, and after a short visit the Johnsons left to attend the League of United Latin American Citizens (LULAC) dinner within the hotel.

The schedule called for the president and Mrs. Kennedy to drop by the LULAC reception at 8:20 P.M. On my copy, Mrs. Kennedy had written in red pencil: *Speech?*

At 8:40 P.M. the president and Mrs. Kennedy came out of the suite, smiling, and joking with Ken O'Donnell and Dave Powers.

Mrs. Kennedy had changed into an elegant black cut-velvet dress, with long sleeves and a neckline that accentuated her three-strand string of pearls. She had touched up her makeup and her hair was once again perfectly coiffed. She looked stunning.

Members of the hotel staff had lined the corridor, and as we walked past them to the elevators, the president smiled and said "Hello" as he guided Mrs. Kennedy, his hand gently on her elbow.

Kellerman and I escorted them to the LU-LAC dinner on the second floor of the hotel for a surprise visit. The president spoke briefly and then introduced Mrs. Kennedy, who proceeded to address the group in Spanish. They loved it. The crowd gave her a standing ovation and shouted "Viva Jackie!" and "Viva Kennedy!" as the president stood by, looking admiringly at his wife, and obviously elated by the response of the crowd.

We departed the Rice Hotel and drove to Sam Houston Coliseum to pay tribute to Congressman Albert Thomas. When the speech was finished we departed for Houston International Airport and once again boarded Air Force One. It was 10:15 P.M. when we departed Houston for Carswell Air Force Base, near Fort Worth.

Vice President and Mrs. Johnson were once again there to greet the Kennedys as they arrived at Carswell after the fifty-minute flight. It was now 11:05 P.M. and thousands of people were there to view the arrival, including a lot of young children. Considering the late hour, this was somewhat of a surprise to me. The crowd was boisterous, quite enthusiastic, and very pro-Kennedy. Once again President and Mrs. Kennedy willingly approached the crowd and expressed their thanks for the outpouring of affection. They entered the vehicles — again the standard Lincoln convertibles — but this time, because of the darkness, the top was up, making it feel that much more crowded.

There were some people standing alongside the road on the way into town, but when we pulled up to the Hotel Texas at 11:50 P.M., it was mobbed. There had to be four thousand people standing in the street and parking lot outside the hotel.

I couldn't believe it.

It's nearly midnight and here all these people are standing outside just to catch a glimpse of the president and the first lady? These people are crazy.

When President and Mrs. Kennedy got out of the car, the crowd went nuts.

Sure enough, the president dove into the crowd, Mrs. Kennedy followed, and I went right along beside her.

Finally, we escorted President and Mrs. Kennedy up to Suite 850. ASAIC Kellerman and I got them settled and made sure everything was all right before we turned their security over to the midnight shift.

It had been a long day for everybody.

I went down to the lobby to see if I could locate something to eat. The clock read almost 1:00 A.M., which meant by my body clock it was almost 2:00 A.M. East Coast time. I hadn't eaten for over thirteen hours. I had a craving for a nice big juicy burger and some fries. At the moment, I couldn't think of anything but food.

Paul Landis and a few of the other agents who had come in on the backup plane were in the lobby with some of the press corps. Everybody was famished. The Fort Worth Press Club was nearby and the newsies said the agents could join them.

Merriman Smith from the UPI was the senior member of the press corps, and I knew him quite well.

"Come on along, Clint," he said. "We'll get you fed."

We all walked over to the Press Club only to find the food was all gone.

They had some peanuts, so I had a scotch and soda and some nuts, bought a couple packs of cigarettes, and left. We heard there was a place called the Cellar Club nearby that served food. We went there only to find the only thing they were serving was some kind of homemade fruit drink. It was horrible. I went back to my hotel room, right next to the presidential suite — disappointed and hungry.

I called the Fort Worth White House switchboard and requested a wake-up call for 6:00 A.M., then called the hotel room service with an order for a nice big breakfast for 6:45. As soon as my head hit the pillow, I was sound asleep.

It had been a long day.

I awoke at 6:00 A.M. to the sound of the phone ringing. Those White House switchboard operators never failed. There was noise outside the hotel so I got up and looked out the window to see what was going on. It was drizzling rain, and a crowd was already gathering to hear President Kennedy speak. He wasn't scheduled to go out until about 8:30 A.M. and the people were already gathering — in the rain.

It never ceased to amaze me, the star power President Kennedy had. It was really an unquantifiable thing — and Mrs. Kennedy had it, too. People just went crazy over them.

I shaved and showered, and promptly at

6:45 A.M. breakfast arrived. The coffee was hot and black, and the eggs, bacon, and hash browns really hit the spot. This was one luxury I fully enjoyed.

I packed everything back in my suitcase so it was ready for the transportation guys to send over to the LBJ Ranch in Austin, where we were to spend the night, and got ready to go to the presidential suite.

I was standing in the hallway with Roy Kellerman and Emory Roberts when President Kennedy came out, flanked by Dave Powers and Ken O'Donnell.

"Good morning, gentlemen," President Kennedy said. "Did you have a good night?"

"Good morning, Mr. President," we responded.

"There's quite a crowd out there," Dave Powers said, gently urging the president. "Time to get moving."

A few minutes later, I heard women shrieking, and a thunderous applause. President Kennedy had just walked outside the hotel.

I remained at the security post, just outside the entrance to the suite, giving Mrs. Kennedy as much privacy as possible. Mary Gallagher was already inside packing Mrs. Kennedy's bags and helping her get ready.

At 9:10 A.M. the security phone at the entrance to the presidential suite rang. It was agent Bill Duncan, the advance agent, calling from the breakfast being held downstairs.

"Clint, the president wants you to bring Mrs. Kennedy down to the breakfast — *now!*"

"Okay," I said, "we'll be right there."

I checked Mrs. Kennedy's schedule and where it listed the breakfast there was a red check mark and a red-penciled footnote in her handwriting: *JBK won't attend.*

Oh well, I thought, *everything is subject to change.*

I walked into the suite and said, "Mrs. Kennedy, the president wants you down at the breakfast. Are you ready?"

"Come on in, Mr. Hill," she answered, not noting the urgency in my voice. I walked into her bedroom, where Mary was hurriedly packing Mrs. Kennedy's suitcase.

Mrs. Kennedy was dressed in her pink suit, the one with the navy collar. But I could tell she wasn't completely ready. She hadn't planned on going to the breakfast.

"Good morning, I hope you slept well," she said cheerfully.

"We've got another long day ahead," I said, trying to subdue my urgent attitude.

"Yes, I never realized how tiring campaigning could be," she said. "I guess I didn't do too much of it the last time."

"Mrs. Kennedy, did you know that the president is waiting for you at the breakfast?"

"I wasn't planning on going to the breakfast," she said.

"I know, Mrs. Kennedy, but the president wants you down at the breakfast right now."

She looked in the mirror and said, "Okay, I just need to put on my hat."

There was a matching pink pillbox hat laid out on the dresser next to some gloves. She put it on, looked in the mirror to adjust it, and then asked Mary to help her with the buttons on her wrist-length gloves.

Now she was ready. I opened the door and we walked out of the suite, toward the elevators.

Paul Landis had received the message and was waiting in the hall near the elevators.

"Good morning, Mr. Landis," she said with a smile.

"Good morning, Mrs. Kennedy, another busy day ahead for you."

"Yes, we will all be ready to relax tonight, won't we?"

The three of us got into the elevator and began the descent to the mezzanine level.

I led the way, walking briskly, with Mrs. Kennedy following, and Paul behind her. As we entered the Grand Ballroom, the place erupted with applause. The room was packed with people sitting at long tables. They had utilized every square foot of space available and about two thousand people were in attendance.

I could hear people commenting as she walked by: "Oh, isn't she lovely?" "Oh my goodness, she's even prettier in person!"

I led her to the dais and she was guided to her seat at the head table.

President Kennedy stepped up to the podium and said, "Two years ago, I introduced myself in Paris by saying that I was the man who had accompanied Mrs. Kennedy to Paris. I am getting somewhat that same sensation as I travel around Texas."

He paused, as the entire audience laughed.

Then, he added, glancing at Mrs. Kennedy, "Nobody wonders what Lyndon and I wear."

Mrs. Kennedy blushed and displayed that girlhood smile of innocence she had perfected. The president, in his inimitable way, had hidden what I knew was his displeasure with her lateness, turned the situation into a compliment of his wife, added a dose of humor, and the crowd loved it.

The breakfast concluded with gifts to both the president and Mrs. Kennedy, and we escorted them back to the suite. They had about a half an hour to relax before we headed to Dallas.

It had been raining lightly that morning in Fort Worth, so ASAIC Kellerman called Agent Win Lawson, the advance agent in Dallas, to check on the weather. It hadn't yet been determined whether SS-100-X would have the Plexiglas bubbletop on or off. It took some time to attach the bubbletop, and Sam Kinney, the driver agent in charge of the vehicles, would need to know as soon as possible.

Lawson reported it was clearing up and

should be nice.

ASAIC Kellerman said, "Tell Sam, top off."

That was the standard motorcade situation during the Kennedy administration. It was the same whether he was in Berlin, Dublin, Honolulu, Tampa, San Antonio, or San José, Costa Rica. Unless it was raining or there were other adverse weather conditions, the president wanted the top off during parade-type motorcades. He wanted maximum exposure with no evidence there was anything between him and the people. People felt a connection to President Kennedy when they saw him in person. That's what had gotten him elected, and now he needed to get reelected.

At 10:40 A.M. we left the Hotel Texas and headed for Carswell Air Force Base, where Air Force One, the vice president's plane, and the backup plane were ready to go. We used standard Lincoln convertibles again, but it had stopped raining, so the tops were off.

There were large crowds all along the thirty-minute route back to Carswell, and again a large crowd was waiting at the air force base. More shaking hands, and finally it was time to go.

The president's Secret Service detail had changed shifts at 8:00 A.M. I boarded Air Force One with ASAIC Kellerman and the 8:00–4:00 shift agents, while Paul Landis rode with the 4:00–midnight shift agents in the backup plane. The vice president's plane and the backup plane would arrive a few minutes before Air Force One, and we'd go through the same routine as we had the day before, with Vice President and Mrs. Johnson waiting at the bottom of the steps to greet President and Mrs. Kennedy as they came off Air Force One. Meanwhile, the midnight shift was already on its way to Austin to prepare for the arrival and overnight at LBJ's ranch.

With everyone on board, Air Force One was wheels up for Love Field in Dallas, and fifteen minutes later we were there.

There was a large crowd waiting behind a chain-link fence as Air Force One pulled up to its arrival point at Love Field. I checked my watch and noted the arrival time in the little black datebook I always carried: 11:40 A.M. Central Standard Time.

President and Mrs. Kennedy exited the plane, USAF 26000, through the rear doors and as they walked down the stairs, the crowd was delirious. Flags were waving, people were applauding and calling out —

it was another exuberant welcome in yet another Texas city. At the bottom of the steps, Vice President and Mrs. Johnson and Dallas mayor Earle Cabell and his wife were there to greet President and Mrs. Kennedy. I stood an arm's length away as Mrs. Cabell presented Mrs. Kennedy with a large bouquet of red roses.

It seemed strange to have the vice president and his wife continually greet the Kennedys at each arrival point in Texas. In this case they had just seen each other a few minutes earlier in Fort Worth. But this was the beginning of a campaign and strange things are done strictly for the photo opportunity. Our destination in Dallas was the Trade Mart, where 2,600 people had paid to have lunch with President and Mrs. Kennedy, and to hear him speak. It would have been much quicker to drive direct from Fort Worth to the Trade Mart in Dallas. Instead we drove from the Hotel Texas in Fort Worth to Carswell Air Force Base, boarded Air Force One, flew to Love Field in Dallas, then drove to the speech site. All of this to get a photo of President and Mrs. Kennedy coming off Air Force One in Dallas and to have a motorcade for maximum exposure. It seemed like a waste of time and money to me, but then politics and security really don't mix well. Kind of like oil and water.

As soon as they had gone through the receiving line, the president looked toward the crowd.

Without hesitating, the president headed straight for them. I waited for Mrs. Kennedy's reaction, and with her red roses in her arms, off she went behind him to greet the public. Paul and I stayed as close to Mrs. Kennedy as possible, looking into the crowd for any telltale sign of trouble. She and the president moved along the fence line shaking hands for about five minutes, much to the great delight of the people who had come to greet them.

Finally, they took their places in the presidential limousine — SS-100-X. Mrs. Kennedy sat in the left rear seat, the president in the right rear. After they were seated, Governor and Mrs. Connally folded down the jump seats — with Mrs. Connally directly in front of Mrs. Kennedy, and the governor directly in front of President Kennedy.

Agent Bill Greer was in the driver's seat. A native Irishman, and a Catholic, Greer and the president had become good friends in the past three years. Greer spoke with a bit of a brogue, and had a great sense of humor. But most important, he knew SS-

100-X better than anyone. He had driven it in motorcades all over the world, and knew how it handled in every type of situation. When Greer was driving, there was no question the president was in good hands.

ASAIC Roy Kellerman was the last one in the car, as he took his place in the right front passenger seat. I was standing next to Mrs. Kennedy, my right hand holding on to the door, scanning the crowd, as Bill Greer started driving forward.

ASAIC Kellerman radioed to base and all units, "Lancer and Lace departing."

It was 11:55 A.M. in Dallas.

Leading the motorcade, ahead of SS-100-X, was an unmarked sedan, driven by Dallas police chief Jesse Curry, with our advance agent Win Lawson in the front passenger seat. The only way Bill Greer knew where to go was to follow the lead car.

I jogged alongside 100X, next to Mrs. Kennedy, until Greer started picking up speed and the crowds had dissipated on our way out of Love Field. Then I dropped back and jumped onto the left running board of Halfback.

Driver Agent Sam Kinney was at the wheel of the Secret Service follow-up car. His job was to stay as close as possible to the presidential vehicle — keeping no more than five feet between the two cars — at all times. Both Kinney and Greer were highly experienced, and they had been working together as a team for a long time.

Assistant to the Special Agent in Charge Emory Roberts was the supervising agent sitting in the right front seat of the follow-up car. In the rear passenger compartment were George Hickey, responsible for the AR-15; Glen Bennett from the Protective Research Section, handling intelligence; and presidential assistants Ken O'Donnell and Dave Powers. Manning the running boards were Agents Jack Ready and Paul Landis on the right side, responsible for the right side of the presidential vehicle. On the left side were Tim McIntyre and myself, responsible for our side. Specifically, I was responsible for Mrs. Kennedy.

We traveled on Mockingbird Lane to Lemmon Avenue with four Dallas police motorcycle officers riding alongside the presidential vehicle, two on each side. The purpose is to create an extra barrier between the president and the crowd, but presidents generally do not like this arrangement because of the loud noise emanating from the motorcycles. It makes conversation within the vehicle very difficult.

The number of spectators was quite few

as the motorcade began its journey toward downtown Dallas, and Agent Lawson, in the lead car, had Chief Curry increase the speed. Bill Greer followed the lead, and as 100X increased speed, so did Halfback. Agent Kinney was keeping the two cars very close together. He kept his eyes on the back of the presidential vehicle and the gap between the two was never more than five feet.

Amazing, I thought. *I wonder how many times Sam has done this and never had an accident.*

The closer we got to downtown Dallas, the larger the number of spectators became. Groups formed along the way, some bearing signs, one of which read PLEASE MR. PRESIDENT STOP AND SHAKE OUR HANDS! President Kennedy could not turn down an opportunity like this, so he requested Bill Greer stop the car.

Suddenly the people with the sign charged toward the car. Roy Kellerman bolted out of the front seat of 100X, and those of us on the follow-up car jumped off and moved to our designated positions. It was our job to deny access to the presidential vehicle, but the president was standing up, smiling, shaking as many hands as he could. Loving every minute.

Mrs. Kennedy looked more uncomfortable when the people came at the car, but she went right along with it, smiling, waving, and shaking hands when we stopped.

It was always interesting to watch how different agents maneuvered themselves to get off or on the follow-up car while it was moving. Successfully going from a moving vehicle — the follow-up car — onto a fixed, stationary surface — the street — was a real challenge. The faster the vehicle speed, the more difficult it became. You had to have great balance and quick feet or you would end up going head over heels onto the street. To get from Halfback to the presidential vehicle while both were moving meant throwing yourself forward with your feet and legs going a similar speed as the vehicles. Not easy to do.

And when you dropped back to the follow-up car, you had to time it right, and jump with confidence, because if you fell, there was a damn good chance you were going to get run over.

The crowds became denser as we neared the center of town. People were yelling and clapping, waving banners and signs — it was an enthusiastic reception. Between the noise of the motorcycles, and the people, you could hardly hear yourself think. I

Crowds spill onto Main Street in Dallas on 11/22/63

didn't like being so far behind Mrs. Kennedy in this situation so I made a sudden decision and jumped off Halfback, ran to catch up to 100X, and leapt onto the rear step of the car. The president glanced back at me, but he didn't say anything. I knew he didn't want us on the back of the car, but I had a job to do. I would answer later if necessary.

When the crowds dissipated, I returned to Halfback.

As we turned onto Main Street, the spectators really increased. Both sides of the street were packed — ten to twenty people deep on each side, spilling into the street. Bill Greer, driving 100X, kept the car to the left to keep President Kennedy, who was in the right rear, as far away from the crowd as possible. Because of the crowds, the motorcycles were having a hard time staying alongside the president's car.

That put Mrs. Kennedy, seated in the left rear, right up next to the people. I immediately jumped from Halfback and got on the left rear of 100X to be near Mrs. Kennedy.

I crouched on the step, in an effort to be less conspicuous, yet still be in proximity should anything happen. I constantly scanned the crowd. People were everywhere — yelling, cheering, clapping. There were people on rooftops and balconies and fire escapes. People hanging out of windows. It was a beautiful sunny day, and warm. Windows were open all along the route.

Again I saw the president glance my way but not say anything. I stayed there, on the rear step of the limousine, all the way down Main Street.

Main Street came to an end, and the car turned right, onto Houston. At this point the number of spectators diminished considerably. I noticed on the right side of Houston that there were office buildings, and on the left was what appeared to be a plaza. Some concrete columns and a grassy

Clint Hill crouches on back of limousine on Main Street, Dallas, 11/22/63

area with a few people, but not many.

I looked back at Halfback, let go of the handhold, jumped off 100X onto the pavement, and in one fluid motion, jumped back to my position on the left running board.

Immediately in front of us as we traveled down Houston Street was a red brick building about seven floors high. Some windows were open in the building, but there was no indication of any problem. Windows had been open all along the route.

We turned left onto Elm Street. It was an unusually sharp turn, and because 100X was no ordinary vehicle, Greer had to slow down considerably. Halfback had similar problems and Kinney maneuvered slowly through the turn.

The vehicles straightened out and began to return to our normal parade pace of about ten miles per hour. I was scanning to the left at the grassy area when I heard a sudden explosive noise, over my right shoulder, from the back of the motorcade.

I turned my head toward the noise, and as my eyes moved across the president's car, I saw President Kennedy grab at this throat and lurch to his left.

I jumped off the running board and ran toward 100X. I wasn't thinking, only reacting. Somebody had fired a shot at the president, and I had to get there. I had to get on the car and get myself between the shooter and the president and Mrs. Kennedy.

I was running as fast as I could. Nothing else mattered.

I have been told there was a second shot, which occurred at this time. I did not hear it. My feet were hitting the pavement; the motorcycle engines were loud in my ears.

I'm almost there. Mrs. Kennedy is leaning toward the president. I'm almost there.

I was almost there. And then I heard the shot. The third shot. The impact was like the sound of something hard hitting something hollow — like the sound of a melon shattering onto cement. In the same instant, blood, brain matter, and bone fragments exploded from the back of the president's head. The president's blood, parts of his skull, bits of his brain were splattered all over me — on my face, my clothes, in my hair.

My legs were still moving. I assumed more shots were coming. I reached for the hand-hold and grabbed it.

Just as I grabbed it, the car lurched forward. Bill Greer had stepped on the gas, and the car reacted with a jolt. I slipped. I was gripping with all my strength, my feet now back on the pavement. My legs kept moving, as I held on, trying to keep up with the rapidly accelerating car. Somehow — I honestly don't know how — I lunged and pulled my body onto the car, and my foot found the step. In that same instant, Mrs. Kennedy rose up out of her seat and started climbing onto the trunk.

What is she doing? What is she doing?

The car was accelerating — we were really speeding up.

Good God, she's going to go flying off the back of the car! Her eyes were filled with terror. She didn't even know I was there. She was reaching for something. She was

reaching for a piece of the president's head.

I thrust myself onto the trunk, grabbed her arm, and pushed her back into the seat.

When I did this, the president's body fell to the left onto her lap.

As I peered into the backseat of the car, I saw the president's head, in her lap. His eyes were fixed, and I could see inside the back of his head. I could see inside the back of the president's head.

"My God! They have shot his head off!" Mrs. Kennedy screamed.

Blood was everywhere. The floor was covered in blood and brain tissue and skull fragments.

"Get us to a hospital! Get us to a hospital!" I screamed at Bill Greer.

I wedged myself between the left and right side of the vehicle, on top of the rear seat, trying to keep my body as high as possible to shield whatever shots might still be coming. I had my left hand on the top of the left door frame and my left foot wedged against the inside of the right frame, my right foot hanging over the top of the car frame on the right.

I twisted around to make eye contact with the follow-up car. They had to know how bad it was. With my one free hand, I gave them the thumbs-down sign and shook my head.

My head turned back to the gruesome scene in the car. Nellie Connally was hunched over the governor. And Mrs. Kennedy had her husband's head in her lap.

"Jack, Jack, what have they done to you?"

Thoughts swirled in my head. *Will we get there in time? Go faster, go faster! He's not breathing. Hang on Mr. President. Hang on. My God, what more can happen to her?*

And then came the thought that haunts me still: *How did I let this happen to her?*

Chief Curry, driving the lead car, had

slowed down to see what happened.

"Take me to the hospital, quick!" Bill Greer yelled.

Curry immediately sped up and got in front of us. We were now traveling on a multi-lane freeway going very fast. Sixty, seventy, eighty miles an hour. Still wedged up high, I was holding on with every ounce of strength in my arms and legs.

I turned my head and my sunglasses blew off.

Governor Connally lifted up and I realized for the first time that he also had been shot.

All time had stopped. It took an eternity to get to the hospital. Finally, we pulled up to the emergency section of a hospital. The sign said: PARKLAND MEMORIAL HOSPITAL.

It was 12:34, four minutes since the first

shot rang out in Dealey Plaza. An eternity.

Sam Kinney had stayed right behind us the entire way. When the cars stopped everyone raced to the presidential car. Emory Roberts took one look at the condition of President Kennedy and said, "I'm taking my men to Johnson."

Everyone knew it was the right thing to do. The agents in the follow-up car had seen the impact.

Agent Lawson had run into the emergency room to get help and gurneys because no one was outside to assist us. He came out with two gurneys and an orderly. The first thing we had to do was remove Governor Connally from the car. We couldn't move the president until the jump seat was folded up.

We got the governor on a gurney and he was taken inside. Mrs. Connally had remained amazingly composed, and went inside the hospital with her husband.

Mrs. Kennedy had not moved. She was holding on to the president, his head still in her lap.

"Mrs. Kennedy," I said. "Please let us help the president."

She would not let go.

"Please Mrs. Kennedy," I pleaded. "Please let us get him into the hospital."

She looked up at me. She was in shock. Her eyes were looking, but not seeing. And then I understood: *She doesn't want anyone to see him like this. Nobody should see the president like this. I understand, Mrs. Kennedy. You're right. Nobody should see the president like this.*

I took off my suit coat and placed it over his head and upper torso.

Now no one will see him, Mrs. Kennedy. It's okay now.

She still hadn't said a word, but as soon as my coat was covering the president, she released her grip.

Together, Agents Win Lawson, Roy Kellerman, Dave Powers, and I lifted the president's lifeless body onto the gurney.

Three shots had been fired in Dealey Plaza. And the world stopped for four days.

24
PARKLAND HOSPITAL

Doctors and nurses were everywhere — it was a blur of white coats — as we passed Trauma Room No. 2, where Governor Connally had been taken, and wheeled the president into Trauma Room No. 1. Mrs. Kennedy was holding on to the gurney, staring at her husband's body, my coat still over his head and torso.

As someone reached to pull my coat off, I grabbed her firmly by the arm and said, "Mrs. Kennedy, let's go wait outside."

"No," she said. "I'm staying in here with him."

"Clint," Roy Kellerman interrupted, "contact the White House. And keep the line open."

I looked at Mrs. Kennedy, not wanting to leave her, but Kellerman was right. We had to let the White House know what had happened.

Paul Landis stood outside the door of the trauma room, while I found a telephone and dialed the number for the special switchboard in Dallas that would get me straight to the White House.

"This is Clint Hill. Give me Jerry Behn's office in Washington and keep this line open."

Just as Jerry Behn, the Special Agent in Charge of the White House Detail, answered, Roy Kellerman came out of the trauma room and grabbed the phone.

As Kellerman began to explain the horror of what had happened less than ten minutes before, a medic rushed out of the trauma room.

"Does anybody know the president's

blood type?"

"O. R-H positive," Kellerman blurted out.

Just then, Mrs. Kennedy came out of the trauma room. Her face, still spattered with blood, was expressionless.

I strode over to her, afraid she might faint. Landis called out, "Somebody get a chair for Mrs. Kennedy."

There were agents and medical staff and policemen all over the place. People running around back and forth, in and out of the two trauma rooms. Somebody brought a chair and I said, "Mrs. Kennedy, sit down."

She sat down and looked at me. Our eyes met, and it nearly broke me. The light was gone, and all that was left in those beautiful brown eyes was pain. Sheer, unbearable pain.

A medic rushed out of the room and called out, "He's still breathing!"

Mrs. Kennedy stood up and asked, "Do you mean he may live?"

Oh God, I thought. *Please, nobody answer her. I saw what happened.*

Nobody answered, but as soon as Kellerman heard that the president was still breathing, he looked at me and said, "Clint, take the phone."

I left Mrs. Kennedy with Paul and took

the handset from Kellerman.

"Clint, what happened?" Jerry Behn asked.

"Shots fired during the motorcade. It all happened so fast," I said. I tried to remain as composed as possible, as I kept my eyes on Mrs. Kennedy. "The situation is critical, Jerry. Prepare for the worst."

Before Jerry could answer, the operator cut into the line. "The attorney general wants to talk to Agent Hill."

The attorney general. Robert Kennedy. The president's brother.

"Clint, what's going on down there?!"

Staring at Mrs. Kennedy, I repeated, "Shots fired during the motorcade. The president is very seriously injured. They're working on him now. Governor Connally was hit, too."

"What do you mean seriously injured? How bad is it?"

I swallowed hard, as the image of the president's head exploding replayed in my mind. The image of his lifeless body lying across Mrs. Kennedy's lap. His eyes fixed. His blood and brains all over her, all over me.

How do I tell him his brother is dead?

Looking away from Mrs. Kennedy, I closed my eyes, squeezed the phone hard, and said, "It's as bad as it can get."

The Secret Service agents from the President's Detail who had been stationed at the Trade Mart had raced to Parkland Hospital as soon as they heard the president had been hit. With them was Admiral George Burkley, the president's physician. Dr. Burkley had been in the VIP bus at the back of the motorcade. He had no idea how bad the situation was until he got into Trauma Room No. 1.

I knew the doctors at Parkland Hospital, along with Dr. Burkley, were doing everything they could to save the president, but I knew there was no hope.

Dr. Burkley walked out of the trauma room, his face contorted with pain.

Mrs. Kennedy stood up as soon as she saw him and said, "I'm going in there."

A nurse tried to stop her, but Dr. Burkley intervened and led Mrs. Kennedy back into the trauma room, so she could be with her husband when he took his last breath.

I was still on the line with Jerry Behn, when two priests arrived.

"Two priests just walked into the trauma room," I said.

Perhaps they will be of some comfort to Mrs. Kennedy, I thought. *At least they'll know the right things to say.*

A few moments later, Agent Roy Kellerman walked out of the room and came toward me. In a low voice, he said, "The priest has just administered Last Rites. This is not for release, and is not official, but the president is dead."

I had known it, of course. There was no way he could have survived. But still, to hear it said out loud. I could hardly breathe.

"What is it, Clint?" Jerry Behn asked on the other end of the phone. "What did Kellerman say?"

My chest tightened as I took a deep breath.

"The president is dead, Jerry. Roy said it's not to be released, but the president is dead."

There was silence on the other end of the phone. Jerry Behn had been the Special Agent in Charge since President Kennedy's Inauguration. He was with the president all the time, just like I was with Mrs. Kennedy. They had a great relationship. The president loved him, trusted him. With the campaign getting ready to get started, Jerry had decided to take a week off, to get some things done around the house. We all understood how that went. His first annual leave in three years. And now, *the president was dead.*

The world had stopped, but I had to keep going. Bobby's words echoed in my mind.

How bad is it?

"Jerry," I said, "I think you should advise the attorney general and the other members of the president's family immediately. They need to know before they hear it in the press."

The president is dead. Oh dear God. The president is dead.

Kenny O'Donnell, one of President Kennedy's closest friends and his chief of staff, had been riding in the follow-up car. He was beyond distraught.

"Clint," he said, "I need you to call a funeral home. We need a casket."

A casket. For the president. For Mrs. Kennedy's husband.

At least I had something to do. As long as I had something to do, the images would leave for a few minutes. When I stopped, or when I looked at her, still caked in blood, I couldn't see anything but the car moving away from me, the sudden explosion, and then Mrs. Kennedy, climbing onto the back of the car.

As long as I had something to do, that

slow-motion picture in my mind would pause for a while, and I could hold it together. Keeping busy was the only way I was going to get through this day.

I found one of the hospital administrators and said, "I need to contact a mortuary and obtain a casket."

"Yes, sir," the man said, as he led me to a small office. He found the number for the Oneal Funeral Home — they were the best, he said — and left me to make the call.

My hand trembled as I dialed the number.

"I need a casket delivered to Parkland Hospital's emergency entrance. Right away. The best one you have."

"What's your name, sir?"

"My name? My name is Clint Hill. Put it in my name. I need the best damn casket you have. Do you understand?"

Oh, God. Oh, God.

"It's for the president . . . the casket is for President Kennedy."

I hung up the phone and went back into the hallway. Paul Landis was still standing outside the door to the trauma room. Stoic and strong, he was holding it together. Somehow, we were all holding it together.

Mrs. Kennedy walked out of the trauma room, followed by the two priests.

"Thank you," she said to them, looking

each of them in the eyes. "Thank you so very much."

I started walking toward her.

Down the hall, I heard Emory Roberts's voice telling some of the agents to get to Love Field. He wanted everything secured, all the buildings cleared.

"Only our people and local law enforcement. That's it. And call Colonel Swindal and tell him we're heading back to Washington."

I looked at my watch and realized the casket should be here any minute.

We were going back to Washington — with the president in a casket. Oh God.

I went back to the room with the phone and dialed the Dallas White House Switchboard.

"This is Clint Hill. I need to speak to Bob Foster, immediately."

As I waited for Bob Foster, the lead agent on the children's detail, to get on the phone, I nearly lost it.

The president's words as he said goodbye to his almost three-year-old son played over and over in my mind.

Take care of John for me, won't you, Mr. Foster?

John would be waiting for the helicopter.

When he heard the helicopter, he'd run to the window, knowing his daddy was in the helicopter. But this time, his daddy was coming home in a casket.

Take care of John for me, won't you, Mr. Foster?

Agent Foster and I decided that John and Caroline should be taken to Mrs. Kennedy's mother's home in Georgetown. They'd be safe there.

And John would be spared the sound of the helicopter.

I swallowed hard and walked back into the hallway.

I looked at Mrs. Kennedy, now sitting in the ordinary portable straight-backed chair that had been drug into the hallway. She looked so all alone. Paul was with her, there were people all around, and yet she was alone in her sorrow. Oh how I wished I could relieve her pain.

Emory Roberts came to me and said, "Clint, we need to get Vice President Johnson to Air Force One and go back to Washington. We don't know how big this situation is and we need to remove him from the area."

"That makes sense," I replied.

"He wants Mrs. Kennedy to come with him — tell her that."

"I'm sure she will not leave the president. But I'll ask."

I walked over to her. She looked so fragile.

"Mrs. Kennedy, Vice President Johnson is going to go back to Washington and he would like you to go with him."

She looked up at me. Her eyes told me before she said it.

"Tell the vice president I'm not going anywhere without the president."

There was no mistaking the determination in her voice.

"Thank you, Mrs. Kennedy."

I went back to Roberts with the answer to his question.

Soon the answer came back from Roberts. Vice President and Mrs. Johnson were going to Love Field and would board Air Force One, but would not leave until Mrs. Kennedy went with them.

The casket arrived and I signed the receipt. We were wheeling it in and I could see Paul, Ken O'Donnell, and Dave Powers trying to shield Mrs. Kennedy from seeing it. The sight of the casket made everything so final. I could see the anguish on her face, I could feel it in my heart, and there was nothing I could do.

We still had no idea who was behind the assassination. Was it one person? A conspiracy? Were they after the vice president or others?

What we did know was the sooner we got out of Dallas, onto Air Force One, and back to the White House, the better. But Vice President Johnson wouldn't leave on the presidential plane without Mrs. Kennedy, and Mrs. Kennedy wasn't leaving without the body of the president.

And now there was another problem. The Dallas County medical examiner had arrived and informed us that we could not remove the president's body from the hospital until an autopsy had been performed. Texas state law required that, in the case of a homicide, the victim's body could not be released until an autopsy was performed in the jurisdiction in which the homicide was committed.

A homicide? The president has just been assassinated. This is no ordinary homicide.

It could be hours or perhaps a day or more before the procedure would be complete. This was completely unacceptable.

Roy Kellerman, Ken O'Donnell, and Dave Powers tried to convince the authorities that since this involved the President of the United States, we should be able to take his body back to the nation's capital for an autopsy.

The Texas authorities said no.

The discussion continued and became somewhat heated. Very heated. This was all happening in a very small area — a hallway, really. Paul Landis and I looked at each other. We knew what was going to happen. Texas law or not, we were taking the president's body back to Washington.

Inside the trauma room, the president's body was being placed in the casket. The hearse from Oneal Funeral Home was waiting at the emergency room entrance. Andy Berger, one of the agents from the President's Detail, was sitting in the driver's seat. Paul stayed close to Mrs. Kennedy as I made sure the corridor between Trauma Room No. 1 and the hearse was secure.

Finally, the Texas authorities conceded — with one stipulation. We could take the president's body and return to Washington, as long as there was a medical professional that stayed with the body and would return to Dallas to testify.

"We have the right man for the job," I said. "Admiral George Burkley, the president's physician." The discussion was over.

Mrs. Kennedy walked silently with us, as we wheeled the casket down the hall. She watched as we strained to lift the casket, with her husband's body inside, into the back of the hearse, and then as Admiral Burkley got in there with it.

I turned to Mrs. Kennedy and gently touched her arm. "We can ride in this car right behind the hearse, Mrs. Kennedy."

She looked at me, her eyes pooled with pain. "No, Mr. Hill, I'm riding with the president."

So I opened the door of the hearse and Mrs. Kennedy climbed in. I climbed in right behind her, and we scrunched together, sitting on our knees, still in our bloodstained clothes. There we were, in the back of the hearse — a casket containing the President of the United States, Admiral Burkley, Mrs. Kennedy, and me.

Love Field had been completely sealed off from the public. Agent Andy Berger drove the hearse to the rear steps of Air Force One, and I helped Mrs. Kennedy out. Paul Landis had ridden in the car behind us, and rushed to Mrs. Kennedy's side.

The crew of Air Force One had removed some seats in the rear of the aircraft to make room for the casket. Now we had to get the casket up the steps into the back of the plane.

Paul stayed with Mrs. Kennedy, while I

helped my fellow agents lift the casket out
of the hearse. Silently, and with as much
dignity as possible, we heaved the heavy
bronze casket up the narrow steps of the
portable staircase. Everybody was emotionally shattered. You couldn't stop to think
about what it was you were actually doing.
Step by step, we finally made it to the top,
only to discover that the casket was too wide
to go through the door.

We had to get it in. There was no choice.
We had to get the casket onto Air Force
One. So we broke off the handles, and
jammed the casket through the door, as
Mrs. Kennedy watched from the bottom of
the steps.

Once the casket was in place, Mrs. Kennedy walked up the stairs and sat in the seat next to the casket. She was joined by O'Donnell, Powers, and Admiral Burkley. For all intents and purposes, Lyndon Johnson was now the president, so the agents on the 4:00–midnight shift were guarding him, guarding the new president. I was concerned about how that might make Mrs. Kennedy feel. Also, having witnessed the tense scene at Parkland Hospital regarding removal of the body, I thought it best that an agent stay with the casket to verify that Admiral Burkley had remained with the casket as well.

I needed to confer with ASAIC Kellerman about plans for our arrival, so I went to Agent Stewart Stout, the shift leader, and said, "Stew, I think, out of respect for President Kennedy, an agent should stay with the casket." He agreed and Agent Dick Johnsen went back to sit with Mrs. Kennedy and the others.

Everyone was eager to get wheels up and get out of Dallas, but now we had another problem. We learned that Vice President Johnson needed to be sworn in while still on the ground in Dallas. That required a federal judge. Calls were made, and federal judge Sarah Hughes arrived and boarded Air Force One.

Before the swearing-in ceremony began, I was notified that Mrs. Kennedy wanted to see me, in the presidential cabin. I walked through the aircraft, past Vice President Johnson and his staff, and into the compartment.

She was standing there, still in her pink suit. Less than six hours earlier, I had seen her in Room 850 at the Hotel Texas, putting on the finishing touches — the hat, the gloves — and now, the accessories were gone, and the beautiful suit was crusted with blood. We had tried to convince her to change her clothes, but she refused. "Let them see what they have done," she said.

"Yes, Mrs. Kennedy, what do you need?"

She walked toward me, extended her hands, and grasped mine.

Looking into my eyes, she asked, "What's going to happen to you now, Mr. Hill?"

Tears welled in my eyes and my lips trembled. "I'll be okay, Mrs. Kennedy. I'll be okay."

With all her sorrow and heartbreak, I thought, *to have concern for me at this time. She really is a remarkable lady.*

I returned to my seat in the forward section of the aircraft as Mrs. Kennedy joined Vice President and Mrs. Johnson for the swearing-in ceremony. I stood behind

Kellerman with Colonel James Swindal, the pilot of Air Force One, at my side, and we watched Lyndon Johnson become the thirty-sixth president of the United States.

Colonel Swindal went back to the cockpit, I took my seat, and Air Force One lifted off the runway from Love Field in Dallas. It was 2:47 P.M.

The flight to Andrews Air Force Base was marked with a solemn, sad, quiet atmosphere. And yet, there was work to be done and plans to be made. The Johnson administration people were calling and planning for their future. The Kennedy people were subdued but making plans as to what to do on arrival in Washington. It was decided to have the autopsy conducted at Bethesda Naval Hospital since President Kennedy was a former naval officer. We would go there by motorcade. President Johnson would go by helicopter to the White House.

There was a large crowd waiting when we arrived at Andrews, at 5:58 P.M. Air Force personnel and their families, members of the cabinet, the House and Senate, the diplomatic corps, the media — they were all there to pay their respects to the assassinated president, and his young widow.

As soon as Colonel Swindal brought the

plane to a stop, the front steps were put in place and the Air Force moved in a hydraulic lift at the rear door of the plane, to lower the casket down to ground level.

I had moved to the rear of the aircraft to be near Mrs. Kennedy. There was a flurry of activity in the front section, and bursting down the aisle, not paying attention to anyone, came Attorney General Robert Kennedy. He embraced Mrs. Kennedy and touched the casket, his eyes filled with tears.

Several of us moved the casket onto the lift, and then Mrs. Kennedy, the attorney general, and members of the fallen president's staff surrounded the casket as it was lowered to the ground. Agents, staff members, and Air Force personnel helped place the casket in the waiting Navy ambulance.

Mrs. Kennedy once again insisted on riding in the back with the president. This time the attorney general joined her. On the plane, Mrs. Kennedy had requested Bill Greer drive the ambulance.

He was the president's driver. He should have the honor of driving him one last time.

Roy Kellerman, Dr. Burkley, and Paul Landis joined him in the front seat. I rode in the car immediately behind the ambulance with Dr. John Walsh and members of President Kennedy's "Irish Mafia" — Ken

Bobby Kennedy, Mary Gallagher, Mrs. Kennedy, and Clint Hill watch as casket is loaded into Navy ambulance

O'Donnell, Dave Powers, and Larry O'Brien.

The forty-five minute drive to Bethesda Naval Hospital seemed endless. Sitting in the front seat, staring at the taillights of the ambulance. The events of the day playing over and over in my head. The sounds of grown men weeping in the backseat. Tears would well up in my eyes, and I'd blink them back. Swallow hard.

When we arrived at Bethesda, the body was taken to the autopsy room accompanied by Dr. Burkley, and Agents Roy Kellerman and

Bill Greer. Paul and I escorted Mrs. Kennedy to the presidential suite on the seventeenth floor. We set up a security post as friends and family began to arrive to see Mrs. Kennedy. Paul and I were the only ones that could identify these people, so we became the gatekeepers. Phones were ringing, people were coming and going, and yet the night was going by very slowly. We were waiting for the autopsy procedure to be completed and it was nerve-racking.

At about 2:45 A.M., the phone rang. It was Roy Kellerman.

"Clint, we need you to come down to the autopsy room."

"Yes, sir. I'll be right down."

I left the seventeenth floor with Paul in charge and went to the autopsy room. As I approached the door Kellerman stepped out and said "Clint, before the autopsy is closed, I need you to come in and view the president's body."

I had a good idea as to why I had been selected to do this. I knew I had to do it, but I dreaded it. I simply nodded to Kellerman that I understood.

"I know this isn't going to be easy," he said, "but we decided that since you are the closest to Mrs. Kennedy, it's important for you to see the body, in case she has any questions."

I took a deep breath, as Kellerman opened the door.

Lying on a table, covered with a white sheet, was the body of President Kennedy. Only his face was exposed, and it looked like he was sleeping.

Bill Greer was there, and Dr. Burkley, and General Godfrey McHugh, President Kennedy's Air Force aide. There were additional people I did not recognize. A man in a white coat stood beside the table. I'm sure they told me his name, but it didn't register.

The man gently lowered the sheet just enough to expose the president's neck, and he began describing the wounds to me. A wound in the front neck area where a tracheotomy had been performed at Parkland Hospital in an effort to revive the president. He said it covered an exit wound. Then, rolling the president gently over to one side, he pointed out a wound in the upper back, at the neckline, quite small. This, he said, was the entry wound that corresponded to the exit wound at the throat.

Moving the body back and slightly to the left he pointed out the wound in the upper-right rear of the head.

I swallowed hard, listening closely, as the

doctor explained what had happened. It appeared that the impact of the bullet hitting the president's head was so severe, it caused an explosive reaction within the makeup of the skull and brain, so portions of the brain erupted outward, and a portion of the skull with skin and hair attached became like a flap.

The image of what I saw when I was wedged up above the backseat came flashing back into my mind. The head wound was exposed to me and I could see into his brain, part of which had exploded outward. It looked like somebody had flipped open the back of his head, stuck in an ice-cream scoop and removed a portion of the brain, then scattered it all over Mrs. Kennedy, the car, and myself. It was a horrific sight. And I couldn't get it out of my mind.

"Yes, Doctor," I said. "That is exactly what happened. I know. I saw it. I was five feet from the president when the impact occurred."

If only I had run faster, reacted a little quicker . . .

The explanation by the doctor and my observation of the body was concluded. I thanked the doctor and returned to the seventeenth floor.

"What did they want?" Paul asked.

I told him what had just transpired. "They assume Mrs. Kennedy will at some point want to know the details of the president's wounds. I am quite sure that will never happen."

Paul shook his head. "No, that will never happen."

Dave Powers and Kenny O'Donnell had gone to a nearby mortuary and purchased a mahogany casket to replace the one from Dallas that we had damaged. Sometime after 3:00 A.M. we were notified that the procedures had all concluded and everything was ready to leave for the White House.

Family members were still present so a small motorcade was set up. The casket bearing the body of President Kennedy was placed in the Navy ambulance. Once again, Mrs. Kennedy and the attorney general got in the back with the casket. Agent Greer drove with Mr. Kellerman in the front seat. I followed in White House car No. 1 with the president's sister Mrs. Jean Smith, Mrs. Robert Kennedy, Secretary of Defense McNamara, and Dr. Walsh. Paul rode in car No. 2 with O'Donnell, O'Brien, Powers, and Dr. Burkley.

We arrived at the White House at 4:24 A.M. A U.S. Marines honor guard met us at the Northwest Gate and marched in formation in front of the ambulance as we drove up to the North Portico entrance to the White House. The sight of those young Marines, their chins held high, paying respect to our fallen president, in the black of night, was almost more than I could bear.

We left here two days ago with a young, vibrant, active man as President of the United States, and now we are bringing him home in a casket.

Military body bearers removed the casket from the ambulance and carried the president into the White House to the East Room. There the casket was placed on a catafalque identical to one used for Abraham Lincoln in 1865. The family gathered around and an honor guard was formed and placed on duty around the casket.

As I watched this sad ceremony unfold, Agent Paul Rundle, a close personal friend, approached me.

"Clint, is there anything I can do?"

I simply shook my head no; there was nothing anyone could do. There was nothing anyone could do to relieve the pain, the anguish, the sense of failure and guilt I felt.

Mrs. Kennedy, along with her friends and family, went up to the second-floor living quarters. I went to my office in the Map

Room and wrote some notes about what had happened. After being reassured Mrs. Kennedy was in her quarters with no immediate plans, I got in my car and drove across Memorial Bridge to my apartment in Arlington. It was 6:00 A.M.

I arrived home to find my seven-year-old son, Chris, and two-year-old son, Corey, still asleep. My wife, Gwen, was there to greet and console me. I managed to shave, shower, and eat a little something before I was back in the car on the way to the White House. There was no time to grieve. No time to rest.

When I got to the White House, I went straight to my office. Paul Landis had arrived at the same time. I shut the door, and we talked about the events of the past twenty-four hours. It was tough. We were both exhausted — mentally, physically, and emotionally shattered.

Nobody would ever be able to understand what we had been through. Nobody. Not our families, our friends, not even the other agents. To know the president and Mrs. Kennedy like we did, and to see him assassinated before our very eyes, was the tragic bond that Paul and I shared.

But there was no time for mourning — we still had Mrs. Kennedy to protect.

25
THE FUNERAL

It had rained overnight, and now the rain was coming down steadily, but gently. It was as if the heavens were shedding tears, mourning right along with the rest of the world. I hadn't seen a television, didn't know it at the time, but word of the assassination had spread from Dallas to New York to England, France, and Ireland; to

Germany, Greece, Italy, India, Pakistan, Ethiopia, and the Soviet Union; down to Mexico and South America. President John F. Kennedy had touched the world, and now the world was in mourning.

The agents on the President's Detail were rotating shifts for President and Mrs. Johnson, and their daughters. Setting up additional security at the Elms — the vice president's private residence — doing all the advance work for the venues planned for the state funeral. They were short of manpower and working double shifts. Paul Landis and I were the only agents with Mrs. Kennedy. There was nobody to relieve us.

A private Mass was scheduled in the East Room at 10:00 A.M. Paul and I watched as Mrs. Kennedy gathered with members of the Kennedy family and close friends, as they cried and prayed together, near the casket of the slain president.

When it concluded, Mrs. Kennedy came up to me and said, "I want to go to the president's office. Will you please get Mr. West?"

We called J. B. West, the chief usher, and he met us in the Oval Office. She wanted to make note of the president's personal things. Things she wanted to bring with her. The packing had already begun. As we walked around the room, everything was a reminder of a special memory. There was his rocking chair, the glass-encased coconut shell from his PT-109 rescue, family photos, the scrimshaw carved into a whale's tooth she had given to him as a gift the previous Christmas.

She took one last look at President John F. Kennedy's office, and we walked out the door.

I returned to my office and began to add to my notes about the past two days. I knew sooner or later the word would come down: *Write a report on all activities of the first lady and yourself and have it ready tomorrow.* I wanted to be prepared.

Early that afternoon Mrs. Kennedy called and said, "Mr. Hill, I need to go to Arlington National Cemetery in a little while. Can you have the car ready?"

Arlington Cemetery. She had to choose a burial plot for her husband.

"Of course, Mrs. Kennedy. I'll be waiting for you in the Diplomatic Reception Room when you are ready to go."

I called Sergeant Watkins, the driver assigned to Mrs. Kennedy, and he brought her Chrysler limousine to the south grounds, along with a follow-up car. It was almost 2:00 P.M. when Mrs. Kennedy, Robert Kennedy, Mrs. Jean Smith, and Mrs. Pat Lawford came down in the elevator.

Paul Landis and I accompanied them on the short drive from the White House, over Memorial Bridge to the National Cemetery. Secretary of Defense Robert McNamara was there to meet us. The five of them walked around a portion of the cemetery, comparing the views across the river, and finally settled on a certain spot. Looking across the Potomac at the Lincoln Memorial, and beyond that to the Washington Monument and U.S. Capitol. It was a beautiful location — so peaceful and serene — a place where the public could come and pay their respects. This would be the final resting place for President John Fitzgerald Kennedy.

Throughout the rest of the day, Mrs. Kennedy remained mostly in the second-floor living quarters, where she was conferring with her brother-in-law, Sargent Shriver, and others about the funeral, and all activities leading up to it. She was actively engaged in each and every detail of the planning.

I knew that she wanted it to be perfect, and I marveled at her strength. She had seen her husband brutally assassinated right next to her, the day before, and now she was directing the biggest state funeral our country had ever had. Not only would it be the final event she planned at the White House, but it would also be the most important and the most complicated. On top of everything, though, she wanted it to be personal.

She remembered how the president had so enjoyed the Scottish Black Watch performance on the South Lawn just prior to the trip to Texas, with their bagpipes and drums and dances. She asked someone to track them down, and ask if they would so honor the president by marching in his funeral procession.

At midnight, Paul and I were assured Mrs. Kennedy had retired for the night and we discontinued for the day. The next day was going to be busy — a private Mass in the morning for members of the family, friends, and White House staff, followed by a formal procession to the U.S. Capitol, where the president's body would be taken to lie in state. We both went home, and tried to get some sleep.

I came in early on Sunday, November 24, knowing there would be endless details to coordinate, and I was thankful for that. As long as I had something to plan, something to arrange, I didn't have to think about the events of November 22.

I had been summoned to SAIC Jerry Behn's office in the East Wing. He knew I was having a difficult time emotionally and wanted to thank me and try to lift my spirits. We were engaged in conversation when Eve Dempsher, Behn's trusted secretary, interrupted.

"I'm sorry to disturb you, Mr. Behn, but General McHugh is on the line for Mr. Hill."

"Put him through," Behn said as he handed the phone to me.

"This is Clint Hill."

"Clint, I'm in the mansion and we have a problem," Godfrey said with urgency in his voice. "You better get over here to the East Room fast. Mrs. Kennedy wants to view the president."

"I'll be right there."

I excused myself from Mr. Behn and ran from the East Wing to the mansion. General Godfrey McHugh, President Kennedy's Air Force aide, led me to the East Room, where Mrs. Kennedy was standing by the door with Attorney General Robert Kennedy.

She was dressed in a black suit, with a knee-length skirt, and had a black veil over her hair. I could tell she hadn't eaten, hadn't slept. She looked so fragile.

"What can I do for you, Mrs. Kennedy?"

She looked at me with hollow eyes and said, "Bobby and I want to see the president."

The image of the white-coated doctor pointing out the wounds in the autopsy room flashed into my mind. She had not seen the president since the body was placed in the casket at Parkland Hospital, and I had no idea what her reaction might be. The last time Bobby had seen the president, his brother was alive.

"All right, Mrs. Kennedy. Let me make sure everything is okay."

I motioned to General McHugh and we entered the East Room. He went to the officer in charge of the honor guard and said, "Please have your men do an about-face and leave the room so Mrs. Kennedy can have some privacy."

Before the officer could respond, Mrs. Kennedy said softly, "No, just have the men turn around, they can stay where they are. Just have them move away a little."

The officer gave the honor guard an about-face and had them take three steps away from the casket. General McHugh and I walked up to the casket, moved the flag down about midway, and opened the casket.

The mortician had done a great job. The president looked so peaceful. I closed my eyes, swallowed hard, and stepped aside.

Mrs. Kennedy and the attorney general walked up and looked into the casket. A few seconds went by and Mrs. Kennedy turned to me and said, "Mr. Hill, will you get me a scissor."

"Yes, of course, Mrs. Kennedy."

I walked briskly to the usher's office and got a pair of scissors and brought them to Mrs. Kennedy. I turned around, and took a few steps away to give her and the president's brother some privacy.

As I stood there, I could hear the sound of the scissors. I knew what she was doing.

Bobby lowered the lid of the casket, and as they turned and began to walk away, the sight and sound of their agony is something I will never forget. Mrs. Kennedy handed me the scissors and they walked to the elevator and went to the living quarters.

General McHugh and I checked the casket to make sure it was closed securely. I looked at my watch and noted the time: 12:46 P.M. That was the last time the casket was opened.

I returned the scissors to the usher's office, and as I placed them in the drawer, I noticed, at the very tip, a strand of chestnut-colored hair.

As I was walking back to my office, there were several White House staff people standing together and I heard one of them say, "That bastard deserved to die."

What? I assumed they were talking about the president. I walked over to them and angrily said, "What the hell did you say?"

They told me Lee Harvey Oswald, the person charged with killing the president, had just been shot. I was stunned.

I didn't have time to dwell on it. The procession to the U.S. Capitol was about to begin.

The military honor guard carried the casket from the East Room of the White House out the North Portico and placed it on a caisson pulled by six white horses. Mrs. Kennedy followed behind, clutching John's and Caroline's hands — one child on each side. Members of the family walked behind the three of them, and Paul and I followed. Mrs. Kennedy got into the waiting limousine with her children and the attorney general, as President and Mrs. Johnson slid in with them.

There was a long procession of cars, family members, members of Congress, and Secret Service agents. Pennsylvania Avenue had been closed off, and as we departed the

White House, I was shocked by what I saw. As far as the eye could see, there were people. Standing in the cold, along Pennsylvania Avenue all the way to the Capitol, it was a mass of people. Hundreds of thousands. But as we slowly proceeded, following the horse-drawn carriage, the only sound you could hear was the clop-clop of the horses' hooves hitting the pavement, and the steady beating of the military drums.

I scanned the crowd, as I always did, but I'd never seen a crowd like this before. There were no screams, no shrieks, no requests to stop and shake hands. There was just dead silence, somber faces, and tears.

When we got to the Capitol, Paul and I stayed in position on either side of Mrs. Kennedy. With the American flag high atop the Capitol at half-mast, the military band played the most moving version of "Hail to the Chief" I had ever heard.

Mrs. Kennedy, wearing a sheer black veil over her face, tried to hold in the tears. But it was impossible. Standing next to her, with John and Caroline by her side, I too was struggling to keep my emotions in check.

Nine military pallbearers removed the flag-draped casket from the caisson and began to carry it up the thirty-six steps at the east side of the Capitol. I could see the strain on the faces of the men, and I felt for them. I knew how heavy it was, and the pressure they felt to carry the president with dignity. We walked behind them — Robert Kennedy, Caroline and John, Paul Landis, Mrs. Kennedy, and me.

The casket was placed in the center of the Rotunda, and as members of the Congress, family, and friends observed, the moving ceremony began.

During one of the eulogies, John became rambunctious. He didn't understand what was going on, why he wasn't allowed to talk. He had been told, of course, that his father was gone, and not coming back, but he really didn't understand at all. So two of the children's detail agents took him to a nearby office to try to keep him occupied.

Senate Majority Leader Mike Mansfield stepped up to the podium, just a few feet away from Mrs. Kennedy and Caroline, and began to speak.

"There was a sound of laughter," he began. "In a moment, it was no more. And so she took a ring from her finger and placed it in his hands.

"There was a wit in a man neither young nor old," Mansfield continued, "but a wit full of an old man's wisdom and of a child's wisdom, and then, in a moment it was no more. And so she took a ring from her finger and placed it in his hands."

His voice started to break, but he continued.

"There was a husband who asked much and gave much, and out of the giving and the asking wove with a woman what could not be broken in life, and in a moment it was no more. And so she took a ring from her finger and placed it in his hands, and kissed him and closed the lid of a coffin.

"A piece of each of us died at that moment."

Mansfield went on to speak of the things President Kennedy gave to all of us, the things he stood for. It was incredibly moving and emotional for all who were there.

A large presidential wreath was brought out, and President Johnson, with his head bowed, placed it at the end of the casket.

The room was silent as Mrs. Kennedy, holding hands with Caroline, walked up to the casket. Mrs. Kennedy touched the casket with her black-gloved hand and knelt, as Caroline, watching her mother, did the same with her own little white-gloved hand. They knelt together and kissed the flag that covered the casket, and there wasn't a dry eye in the room.

The ceremony concluded, and we re-

turned to the White House. Now the president's body would lie in state, allowing the public to file past and pay their respects. The funeral and burial would take place the next day, Monday, November 25.

I knew Mrs. Kennedy wanted to walk some of the way in the funeral procession but I did not know the details. SAIC Behn called me and said, "Clint, are you aware of what Mrs. Kennedy intends to do during the funeral procession?"

"Well, yes, she has mentioned that she intends to walk part of the way."

"That is really going to create a problem," he said. "We have I don't know how many heads of state coming from all over the

601

world, not to mention every high-ranking official in the U.S. government, including President Johnson. And if she walks, they will feel compelled to walk."

"Believe me, I understand, Jerry. But, if that is her intent, rest assured that is what she will do."

"Listen, we really need your help. This funeral is going to stretch our security capabilities to the max as it is. Will you please try to talk her out of it? You are the only one who even has a chance."

"I'll try Jerry, but when she makes up her mind to do something, there's little chance of talking her out of it."

She was upstairs in the residence, so I called and told her I needed to speak with her.

"Come on up. I'll be in the Treaty Room," she said.

I took the elevator to the second floor and walked down the hall to the Treaty Room. She was waiting in there for me.

"Hello, Mr. Hill. Come in," she said. She was pale and drawn; her face looked incredibly sad. It was like she was there, but she wasn't. She was cordial, and in control, and clearly capable of making decisions, but her spirit was gone.

I suppose some people may have said the

same thing about me.

"Mrs. Kennedy, I've been told you intend to walk in the funeral procession tomorrow and I wanted to clarify what exactly it is that you intend to do."

"Oh Mr. Hill, you are always looking for the little details in everything. Are you concerned?"

"Yes, ma'am, I am."

"Well, don't worry, I've decided not to walk all the way, only from the White House to St. Matthew's."

"Mrs. Kennedy, there is a lot of concern about other people who might decide to walk, if you walk. Heads of state, for example."

"Well, Mr. Hill, they can ride or do whatever they want to. I'm walking behind the president to St. Matthew's."

I knew that determination in her voice. Oh how well I knew it. She had made up her mind, and nobody was going to be able to talk her out of it.

"Okay, Mrs. Kennedy. Thank you for telling me your plans."

I left, returned to my office, and called SAIC Behn.

"Jerry, I've talked to Mrs. Kennedy and she does intend to walk during the funeral procession tomorrow, but only from the

White House to St. Matthew's."

"No chance to talk her out of it, Clint?" he asked.

"Believe me, Jerry. Nothing is going to change her mind. She is walking."

Later that day, Prince Radziwill, Mrs. Kennedy's brother-in-law, arrived from Europe. I was in my office the evening of Sunday, November 24, when the phone rang.

"Clint Hill," I answered.

"Oh, Mr. Hill," the familiar voice began — which meant to me, I was about to be asked to do something not in my job description — "Stash has just arrived from Europe and really wants to pay his respects to the president. Do you think you can arrange it?"

"I'll do what I can, Mrs. Kennedy," I replied. "What exactly does he want to do?"

"He wants to go to the Capitol and I've heard you can't get in for hours. Can you help him?"

"When does he want to go?"

"He is ready now."

"Tell him to come down to the Diplomatic Reception Room and I'll take him to the Capitol."

"Thank you, Mr. Hill."

I called for a White House car, Stash came down, and we were driven to the Capitol. He and the president had been close. I too had gotten to know Stash well over the past three years, and we had shared some memorable experiences. Tonight we were sharing a deep and profound loss.

Mrs. Kennedy had been right. The wait to get in to view the casket in the Rotunda was hours. Hundreds of thousands of people had lined up for the opportunity to circle around President Kennedy's casket. People eight abreast in a line that stretched forty blocks.

I escorted the prince past all the people, and took him right into the Rotunda where the president lay in state. I identified myself and explained to the officer in charge of the honor guard who Stash was, and he was permitted to approach the casket, pray, and pay his respects.

On the way back to the White House, he said, "Thank you, Clint. I'll never forget what you did for me." He was very emotional, and it tore me apart.

The next day, November 25, was John's third birthday. Both President and Mrs. Kennedy had been planning on making it a special day for him. They had each mentioned it to John as we left for Texas four days earlier. Instead we were taking John, along with his mother and sister, to his father's funeral.

How sad, I thought. *John will go through life remembering November twenty-fifth more for the day his father was buried than for it being his birthday.*

The number of people wanting to pay their respects to the president at the Capitol was so vast that the hours had been extended through the night. The doors finally closed at 9:00 A.M. There would barely be enough time to get everything ready for the ceremony, remove the president's body from the Capitol, place it back on the caisson, and return to the White House, where the world leaders were gathering. The schedule called for Mrs. Kennedy and the children to leave the White House at 9:45 A.M. and drive to the Capitol. The ceremony would be brief, and by 10:00 A.M. the procession from the Capitol to the White House would begin.

Mrs. Kennedy decided it would be best if Caroline and John did not go to the Capitol this morning for the short ceremony. She and the president's brothers, Bobby and Ted, would go alone and the children would remain at the White House. Sergeant Watkins brought Mrs. Kennedy's Chrysler limousine to the North Portico. I got in the front passenger seat, with the three of them in the back, and we drove out the Northeast Gate onto Pennsylvania Avenue and down to the Capitol.

The avenue was lined with people the entire way. More than 250,000 of them had gone through the Rotunda since the president lay in state, and more would have, if time had permitted.

We arrived at the Capitol, marched up the steps, and entered the Rotunda. I stood back as Mrs. Kennedy and the two brothers went directly to the casket, knelt, and prayed. They rose, and we all walked back out the same door, down the steps, and waited at the ground level as the casket was lifted off the bier and brought down the steps. Once again my thoughts were with the honor guard, carrying this very heavy casket down that long set of stairs. It was obviously very difficult, but they made it, and placed it back onto the caisson. The cortege was formed and the procession began to move from the Capitol to the White House.

As we progressed slowly up Pennsylvania Avenue, the size of the crowd increased and the silence emanating from the teary-eyed people was deafening. We arrived at the White House to find a sea of people comprised of the diplomatic corps and two hundred foreign dignitaries from nearly one hundred countries around the world. They had traveled from Europe and Asia, from Africa and Australia, as well as North and South America. There were princes and princesses, kings and queens, presidents and vice presidents, prime ministers and foreign ministers. But the names really told the story. Charles de Gaulle, Haile Selassie, Prince Philip, Queen Frederika, King Baudouin of Belgium, Berlin mayor Willy Brandt, and Ireland's president, Éamon de Valera to name a few. Included in this mass of humanity was Lyndon Johnson, the new president, and his wife, Lady Bird.

All of these people had gathered to accompany Mrs. Kennedy as she walked behind the caisson that carried the president's body, from the White House to St. Matthew's Cathedral.

The security was complex, to say the least. Many of the leaders had come with their own security personnel, and they were mixed in with people who had been brought in from all areas of the U.S. government to assist the State Department, which was responsible for protecting visiting heads of state. Nearly every Secret Service agent from around the country — more than 250 of them — had flown in to help.

The procession left the White House led by a company of U.S. Marines. Next came nine pipers from the Scottish Black Watch, their bagpipes belting out the songs of Ireland the president so loved, as they marched ahead of the six gray-and-white horses pulling the caisson bearing the president's body. Next came the presidential flag, followed by Black Jack, the riderless horse.

The walking procession came next, led by Mrs. Kennedy, Bobby and Ted Kennedy, flanked by Paul Landis on the left and me on the right. The various heads of state were to follow, but at the last minute Mrs. Kennedy decided she wanted Caroline and John, who were riding in the Chrysler limousine, to be close to her. They had been behind President Johnson and the mass of world leaders, so Agents Tom Wells and Bob Foster worked their way through the dignitaries to get the car up front. Now the procession could begin.

The haunting bagpipes started to play, and we walked.

Lining the one-and-a-quarter-mile route to the cathedral were thousands upon

Clint Hill (left) walks with Mrs. Kennedy and family during funeral procession. President Lyndon Johnson in background.

thousands of people, weeping. Step by step we walked, Mrs. Kennedy with her black-veiled head held high, as the people — black and white, children with parents, and elderly folks with canes — openly grieved.

The Requiem Mass at St. Matthew's was extremely emotional. Mrs. Kennedy sat with Caroline and John on either side of her, and I sat directly behind Mrs. Kennedy. Luigi Vena, a tenor from Boston, sang "Ave Maria," just as he had at the Kennedys' wedding in 1953. Cardinal Cushing, who officiated, was a friend of the Kennedy family and had performed the services for Patrick's funeral, just three and a half months earlier. During the service, at one point he referred to the president as "Dear Jack." When he said that, it was just too much for Mrs. Kennedy, and the stoic demeanor she had displayed to this point briefly faded.

I had anticipated the need for handkerchiefs and had a couple handy. I reached from directly behind her and placed one in her hand. She used it the rest of the service.

At one point, as had happened on Saturday in the Rotunda, John got fidgety. With Mrs. Kennedy's nod of approval, Agent Foster picked him up and took him to an anteroom. In an effort to keep him occupied, Bob had him practice his salute.

He wasn't doing too well, still insisting once again on saluting with his left hand. It had been two weeks since his visit to Arlington Cemetery with his father on Veteran's Day. But a Marine colonel happened to be watching, and he walked in and said, "John, you are doing it all wrong, this is the way you salute." He demonstrated using the right hand with an emphatic gesture. Sure enough, John caught on. Six weeks of instruction by his agents with only minimal results, and just three minutes with the Marine colonel and he got it right.

When the service concluded, Mrs. Kennedy with Caroline and John, one in each hand, led the mourners from the cathedral and stood on the outside steps while the casket was removed and placed on the caisson. I was standing just behind and to the right of Senator Ted Kennedy, who was next to Mrs. Kennedy, and the children. When the casket was secured, directly in front of us, the military rendered a salute to their fallen commander in chief. I saw Mrs. Kennedy lean down to John and whisper something into his ear.

He thrust his tiny shoulders back, raised his right hand to his brow, and in an emphatic gesture never to be forgotten by anyone who saw it, just as the Marine colonel had instructed, three-year-old John Fitzgerald Kennedy Jr. saluted his father.

It was almost more than I could bear. I looked around and saw colonels and generals and colleagues — some of the toughest men I knew — and they too were fighting to hold back tears.

The plan had been for Caroline and John to accompany their mother to Arlington National Cemetery and ride with her. But at the last minute, Mrs. Kennedy decided to have them return to the White House. We

had run out of cars, so Agents Foster and
Wells located one being used by the Joint
Chiefs of Staff, and confiscated it for their
use. Needless to say, the relationship between the Secret Service and the Joint
Chiefs of Staff was rather strained for a
while.

While Caroline and John went back to the
White House, Mrs. Kennedy rode behind
the caisson, the presidential flag, and Black
Jack to Arlington National Cemetery. It was
now midafternoon as we approached the
cemetery. People lined the streets the entire
way, and you could see their faces filled with
grief, tears rolling down their cheeks. As we
inched our way across Memorial Bridge,

leading the mile-long procession of limousines filled with dignitaries, I looked up, straight ahead on the hill to the spot Mrs. Kennedy had chosen for the grave site. A sudden realization hit me like a punch.

I travel across this bridge two times every day, and from now on, I will be looking at President Kennedy's grave as I cross into Virginia from Washington.

If only I had reacted quicker, run faster . . .

We arrived at the grave site and watched as the honor guard removed the president's casket and carried it to the burial site. As we walked slowly to the burial site, I heard a sound, a slight roar, that got louder and louder as fifty Air Force and Navy jets flew over in tribute. Then, another roar, but this time the sound seemed familiar to me, that high-pitched whine of a perfectly tuned set of jet engines. It was Air Force One flying very low with Colonel Jim Swindal at the controls and the crew on board that knew and served President Kennedy so well. As Swindal dipped the wings of Air Force One in salute, I clenched my jaw. Swallowed hard.

As the service progressed, I knew there was a moment approaching and I was concerned as to how Mrs. Kennedy would react. It was the twenty-one-gun salute, three volleys by each of seven riflemen. How would she react to gunfire only three days after that sound cracked through the air in Dallas? She was standing next to Robert Kennedy near the end of the casket. I was about to walk to her when the cemetery superintendent leaned over and warned her what was about to happen.

She trembled with each and every shot, but managed to maintain her composure.

It was time to light the Eternal Flame. From the moment she started planning this heartrending day, she had the idea of an eternal flame — just like the one at the Tomb of the Unknown Soldier in Paris. She overcame the objections and negative attitudes of everyone who said it was too complicated a job to be done in time. I was proud of her intestinal fortitude and positive attitude, which enabled her to do it. The Eternal Flame was her triumph.

She was handed a lighted torch and bent forward to ignite the flame. The fire danced as she passed the lighted torch to Bobby Kennedy, who in turn handed it to Ted, each symbolically igniting the flame. The United States flag that had draped the casket was folded and presented to Mrs. Kennedy. It was time for Taps, the final ending to a military funeral.

The bugler, standing off to the side, started playing and the sound rolled through the hills surrounding Arlington National Cemetery. He was feeling the pressure of performing before thousands in person and millions on TV. He flubbed a note and recovered quickly. I felt sorry for him, knowing he would never forget it, and the world had it recorded for posterity.

Mrs. Kennedy thanked the military commander and we entered the waiting limousine and drove back to the White House.

The day was far from over. First there was a small reception in the upstairs Yellow Oval Room, in the residence quarters, for a few special people: Charles de Gaulle; Prince Philip; Emperor Haile Selassie; Ireland's president, Eamon de Valera. After offering her sincere thanks to these men, she went to the Red Room, where a larger reception was held for the scores of other foreign dignitaries. This involved a lot of people and I was concerned about her being able to stand the strain. If she felt it, she didn't show it.

I thought this would certainly be the end for the day and she would go to the second-floor living quarters and retire for the night. Instead, as the reception was winding down, she motioned to me.

"Yes, Mrs. Kennedy, what can I do for you?"

"I may want to go back to Arlington later," she whispered. "I'll call and let you know."

I was exhausted, and she hadn't slept any more than I had. How she could keep this up I didn't know. I notified Paul that we needed to make arrangements with the superintendent's office at Arlington. This was to be completely private, and kept absolutely confidential.

When Mrs. Kennedy finally went to the second floor, I went to the Map Room and more or less collapsed in my chair. Shortly before midnight, she called.

"Yes, Mrs. Kennedy," I answered.

"Mr. Hill, Bobby and I want to go to Arlington now. We want to see the flame."

"Certainly, Mrs. Kennedy. I'll get the car."

I called Sergeant Watkins and he brought the car around. We took Mrs. Kennedy and Bobby to the cemetery as Paul followed in another car. As we drove across Memorial Bridge, there straight ahead of us flickering on the hillside was the Eternal Flame. It was a moving, very emotional sight.

We drove up to the site and walked to the grave. Mrs. Kennedy had brought a small bouquet of flowers, and she placed them on the fresh earth. Mrs. Kennedy and Bobby knelt and prayed, then stood and looked back across the Potomac at the lights of the memorials. We all got back in the car, and returned to the White House.

No press, no public, complete privacy. Just the way Mrs. Kennedy wanted it.

■ ■ ■ ■

Part Five:
After the
White House

■ ■ ■ ■

26
OUR FINAL YEAR

Clint Hill watches as Mrs. Kennedy visits her husband's gravesite

The days following the funeral are somewhat of a blur. I was physically exhausted and emotionally drained. I had kept my emotions buried. I could not let Mrs. Kennedy, the other agents, or anyone else, for that matter, be aware of exactly how I felt. I had to be strong and hold up the tradition of the Service. Mrs. Kennedy had been traumatized and she was being so strong. I couldn't break down. But the truth was, I was overcome with guilt, a feeling of failure, and a sense of responsibility for not being able to prevent the assassination.

There was no time to grieve, no counseling, no time off. Keeping busy was the only thing that was keeping me going. It was the best medicine I had.

Mrs. Kennedy was staying busy, too. She knew she had to move out of the White House — the Johnsons had told her to take her time, but she said she would leave after Thanksgiving, on December 6. There were so many decisions that had to be made, so much for her to think about. Even though she had the help of Mary Gallagher, and Provi, as well as her staff and the president's staff, the final decisions were all hers to make. Where to live? What to do with the dogs, the horses? But first, she had to go see the president's father in Hyannis Port.

On Thursday, November 28, Agent Bob Foster and I took Mrs. Kennedy, Caroline, and John to Arlington to visit the grave site. Mrs. Kennedy's sister Lee, Provi, and Miss Shaw came along. To see the children at the grave of their father — hollow eyes, a three-year-old's questions, no more rides on the helicopter. It was gut-wrenching. It was Thanksgiving Day.

Agents Landis, Meredith, and Wells had flown ahead to the Cape, and after our brief visit to Arlington, we boarded an Air Force aircraft at Andrews to Hyannis Port. It was an extremely emotional time. Mrs. Kennedy was so close to the ambassador and always before, her visits had been a shining light in his days. Now there was no light in anyone's eyes. This was the third child Ambassador and Rose Kennedy had lost in violent death. Son Joe in World War II, daughter Kathleen, known as "Kick," in an airplane crash, and now the president to an assassin's bullet. What was there to be thankful for?

Paul and I and the children's agents had assumed we would stay with Mrs. Kennedy and the children until she left the White House. After that, we didn't know what was going to happen. None of us could bear the thought of leaving them.

Sunday, December 1, we headed back to Washington. Earlier in November, my wife, Gwen, had found a new apartment in Alexandria — one with more space, for just a few dollars more a month. Unbeknownst to me, George Dalton and Jim Bartlett, two

Navy men that handled the boats at Hyannis Port — Jim had been the one who had valiantly tried to teach me to water-ski — had shown up on the doorstep and helped Gwen move. I arrived home to the new apartment, piled high with boxes, and beyond grateful for the kindness of two friends.

The next morning, back at the White House, I received a call from Chief Jim Rowley.

"Clint," Mr. Rowley said, "there is going to be a ceremony tomorrow morning at eleven o'clock in the fourth-floor conference room in the Treasury Building. You are going to receive the Treasury Department's highest award for bravery. Secretary Douglas Dillon wants you there at ten-thirty. Your wife and children are invited to attend as well."

"Okay," I said.

"Mrs. Kennedy plans to be there," Rowley added. "Congratulations, Clint."

I didn't know what to say. *Why am I getting an award?* I had heard that Rufus Youngblood, the agent who was with Lyndon Johnson in Dallas, was getting an award. He had jumped on top of the vice president and shielded him from the sniper. He was successful.

I don't deserve an award. The president is dead.

I didn't know what to say.

"Thank you," I finally said.

I hung up the phone and told Paul what the chief had said. Paul congratulated me, but he knew how I felt.

I called home to tell Gwen.

"It looks like you are finally going to meet Mrs. Kennedy," I said.

The next day, I arranged for Gwen to park on West Executive Avenue — the driveway of the White House. When she and the boys arrived, I walked out to meet them, and together we walked next door to the Treasury Building.

There was a small room next to the fourth-floor conference room. Paul Landis had brought Mrs. Kennedy, her sister, Lee, and the president's sisters Jean Smith and Pat Lawford. I was surprised to see them there — the president's sisters.

I introduced them to my family and Mrs. Kennedy said, "You have such fine-looking young sons, Mr. Hill."

I looked into her eyes, still so filled with pain. *Did mine look the same?*

"Thank you, Mrs. Kennedy. They are good boys."

At eleven o'clock, we went into the conference room for the ceremony. Some of the press were there. They snapped pictures and took notes as Treasury secretary Douglas Dillon made a speech and presented me with the award. I was embarrassed by all this undeserved and unwanted attention, but I accepted the award and thanked Secretary Dillon, as Mrs. Kennedy stood and watched.

My family went home, and I went back to my office, glad it was over.

Friday, December 6, was moving-out day. Two good friends of President and Mrs. Kennedy, Mr. and Mrs. Averell Harriman, had graciously offered their home in Georgetown as a temporary residence to Mrs. Kennedy and the children. Everything had been packed and sorted, with most of the belongings being sent into storage until Mrs. Kennedy decided where she and the children would live on a permanent basis.

President Johnson had also decided to award the Medal of Freedom, posthumously, to John F. Kennedy, at a ceremony in the State Dining Room, on this day. As Attorney General Robert Kennedy accepted the award on behalf of his brother, Mrs. Kennedy watched, sitting in a small adjacent room, behind a folding screen, her presence unannounced until the ceremony was over.

Everything had been packed and loaded into trucks. Now it was time to say good-bye. Mrs. Kennedy said good-bye to Chief Usher J. B. West and the household staff — staff that had grown to love John and Caroline. It had been such a joy to have children in the White House. Throughout the entire house, from the upstairs maids to the stewards in the Navy Mess, tears were flowing.

A few days earlier, Secret Service Chief Jim Rowley had called me into his office.

"Clint," he said, "President Johnson has requested the Secret Service provide protection for Mrs. Kennedy and the children for at least one more year. We have agreed to do so."

"I'm glad to hear that, Mr. Rowley. I think it's a good decision."

"The president told Mrs. Kennedy, and said she could have any agents she wanted. Take her pick."

I nodded. A lump filled my throat. I would do whatever Rowley requested — he was my boss. I would understand completely if she didn't want me. Every time she sees me, it must bring back the horrible memories of that day, that dreadful day in Dallas. But I couldn't imagine not being with her.

"Clint, Mrs. Kennedy didn't hesitate. She wants Bob Foster, Lynn Meredith, and Tom Wells to stay with the children."

I nodded. Held my breath.

"And for herself, she said there was no choice to be made at all. She wants Paul Landis and Clint Hill."

Tears welled in my eyes.

"Thank you, Mr. Rowley. Thank you."

So on December 6, as Mrs. Kennedy and the children moved out of the White House, so did I. I would no longer have my office in the Map Room. Jerry Behn said Paul and I could share a desk in his office temporarily, but we'd have to figure something else out. We were no longer on the White House Detail.

Mrs. Kennedy, Miss Shaw, Caroline, and John got into the limousine at the South Portico and we drove from the White House together for the last time. It was quiet. Nothing was said. There was just a heavy sadness inside all of us.

The Harriman house was at 3038 N Street Northwest — just three blocks down from the house where Mrs. Kennedy and I first met. As we drove through the narrow streets with the historic redbrick homes on each side, the memories came flooding

Clint Hill, Mrs. Kennedy, and Caroline arrive at Harriman residence, 12/6/63

back. Three years earlier, she was eight months' pregnant, and I was so disappointed to have been given this assignment.

John was carrying an American flag as he jumped out of the car and went inside. A few neighbors and a handful of curious onlookers were standing nearby, watching us, but far fewer people than I had imagined would be gawking.

This looks pretty good. Maybe the people will leave her and the children alone, out of respect.

The Harrimans had left some of their household staff to assist Mrs. Kennedy, and that first night, it almost felt like they were staying in a hotel with personal servants there to help in every way.

The next weekend Mrs. Kennedy wanted to go to Atoka. "I guess we will have to drive," she said. No longer did we have helicopters at our beck and call. She told me that from now on she was going to call the house at Atoka "Wexford," after President Kennedy's ancestral home in County Wexford, Ireland. It was nice to get back to the country again, to be around the horses she loved so. But still the smile did not return. The laughter was gone.

When we returned to the Harriman house in Georgetown, she informed me that she and the children would be spending Christmas and New Year's in Palm Beach, staying at the C. Michael Paul residence again. We would leave the following Wednesday.

"I wanted to give you something, Mr. Hill," she said as she handed me a typewritten letter. "I sent this letter to Secretary Dillon, and I thought you should know. I'd like you to pass it along to the other agents on our little detail, too. Go ahead, read it now."

I began to read the letter — it was two-and-a-half pages long, single-spaced, so it took me a while.

Dear Douglas:

I would like to ask you one thing that was so close to Jack's heart — he often spoke about it —

It is about our Secret Service detail — the children's and mine. They are such exceptional men. He always said that, before he left office, he was going to see that the highest possible recommendation was left in each of their files — with the suggestion that each of them be really given a chance to advance, as they normally would, in the Secret Service.

She wrote that this in no way was speaking against the president's detail — he was devoted to them all.

They were perfect and the President loved them.

But, my detail and the children's were younger men. They all had children just the ages of Caroline and John . . .

You cannot imagine the difference they made in our lives. Before we came to the White House, the thing I dreaded most was the Secret Service. How wrong I was; it turned out that they were the ones who made it possible for us to have the happy close life that we did.

She wrote about how she had requested us to be firm with the children so they would not get spoiled, yet at the same time be unobtrusive so they weren't viewed as special by their friends.

It seems to me now that the qualities they had to have to do this job so beautifully — so that I have two unspoiled children — and, so that I always felt free and unhindered myself, are really the most exceptional qualities . . . they needed tact, adaptability, kindness, toughness, quick wittedness, more than any other members of the Secret Service. And every one of them had it.

She wrote about how she and the president often discussed how sad it was that these "devoted and clever men" were taking John to the park and missing out on all the exciting work like state visits, and advance trips — the things that would help them advance their careers. They were afraid that because we had been so good with the children, that we would be forever "left in the backwater with no chance to advance" and that would be terribly unfair to men so devoted to their profession.

The point of the letter was to request that all the men on the First Lady and Children's Detail be given special consideration to advance, at the end of this assignment, because Chief James Rowley "couldn't find better men if he combed the earth."

She listed the five men of whom she was speaking: Clinton Hill, Paul Landis, Lynn Meredith, Robert Foster, and Thomas Wells. Next to my name she wrote:

No need to tell you about him. He was a brilliant advance man before he was assigned to me. He was so much better than the rather dense USIA men the embassies sent when I went abroad, that I ended up by having him handle all press and official details . . . he could do everything.

I couldn't help but smile at that part. Oh, Mrs. Kennedy . . . She concluded the letter with an apology for going on so long and finally:

They served the President as well as any one in his government, by protecting his wife and children with such tact, devotion and unobtrusiveness that it made our White House years the happy ones they were.

Tears welled in my eyes. I looked at her, looked into her brown eyes, those beautiful eyes the color of espresso that melted powerful men and created envy in women the world over. There were no secrets from me in those eyes.

I put down the letter, and wrapped my arms around her and held her for a moment.

"Thank you, Mrs. Kennedy, those are very kind words."

We had been through so much together, Mrs. Kennedy and me. And now it was time to move to a new chapter in our lives. It wasn't going to be easy, but we had to go on.

We had made it through the first Thanksgiving, but Christmas in Palm Beach was exceptionally difficult. Ambassador Kennedy and much of the rest of the family were there, as well as Lee and Stash and their children, but there was no *Honey Fitz* to take out for a lunchtime cruise, no anticipation of high-level meetings, far fewer Secret Service agents around.

There were times when I wondered if I myself could go on. It was just so damn painful.

After the holidays, we returned to Washington. Mrs. Kennedy had bought a house across the street from the Harriman's, at 3017 N Street — a large brick colonial that had lots of room and two beautiful magnolia trees out front. We moved in and at first, it seemed perfect. The private backyard was paved with a big tree in the center, and John would ride his little tricycle around and around. But almost immediately, the crowds started to come. People would stand on the sidewalk with cameras, trying to peer in the windows, and as soon as we walked out the front door, they'd snap photos, one right after the other. It really got bad when a tour company started bringing buses by the house. The buses would squeeze down the narrow street and stop, allowing the people to get out and take pictures. We tried to have the operation ceased, but the city allowed the buses to carry on.

Mrs. Kennedy and the children started spending more and more time away from Washington. They went skiing in Stowe, Vermont, she took a trip to Antigua, and a lot of trips to New York City, where we stayed at the Carlyle Hotel.

We were all trying to keep busy, planning the next trip, making arrangements. But everywhere we turned, there was something to remind us of what had happened. You couldn't look at a newspaper, you couldn't watch television. The Warren Commission was investigating the assassination, and both Paul and I were required to write sworn statements and memorandums about what had happened. I was called to testify, at length. We were forced to relive those six seconds in Dallas over and over and over.

But by far the most difficult thing to deal with was what was right there in front of us every day. Being with Mrs. Kennedy and John and Caroline, seeing their sadness, the hollowness in their eyes, and feeling that we were the cause of their anguish. When Mrs. Kennedy had asked me, *What's going to happen to you now, Mr. Hill?* I had told her, *I'll be okay.* But as the time went on, I wondered if any of us would ever be okay.

On June 12, 1964, Paul handed in his resignation. He had given himself six months to see if he would feel better. But nothing got better. It got worse and worse. It was just too damn painful.

I was disappointed that he was leaving, but I understood. I understood completely.

That summer, the summer of 1964, Mrs. Kennedy decided to move to New York City. There, among the crowds, she thought perhaps she and her children might be able to somehow blend in, and have some privacy. All she ever wanted was a little privacy.

I took her house hunting, and she finally settled on a large apartment across from

Central Park at 1040 Fifth Avenue. It was close to the Metropolitan Museum of Art, just a few blocks from Stephen and Jean Kennedy Smith's place, and within walking distance of the Carlyle Hotel. She knew the neighborhood well, and it was exactly what she wanted. While the apartment was being furnished and decorated, I lived at the Carlyle, in a small room on the same floor as Mrs. Kennedy's suite, and stayed there for a few months after she moved in to the apartment.

Mrs. Kennedy had an office on Park Avenue, and Nancy Tuckerman had stayed on as her assistant. She was working on plans for the Kennedy Library, and continued to answer the thousands of letters that continued to pour in.

It was coming up on a year since the assassination, and both of us realized it was time to move on. On my last day in New York, she threw a surprise farewell party for me in her office. There weren't many people there — just her small staff, and the other agents. They tried to make it upbeat and we shared memories of the fun times we had had together. Mrs. Kennedy brought out a large cardboard poster that they had all signed. The poster had a cutout picture of an anonymous Secret Service agent, complete with sunglasses. Above the agent, in big letters it said: MUDDY GAP WYOMING WELCOMES ITS NEWEST CITIZEN. Not knowing what my next assignment was, it was a joke insinuating I was being sent to some remote town out in the middle of nowhere. We all laughed — it was typical of Mrs. Kennedy's humor.

Then she handed me a black three-ring binder filled with photos that chronicled our four years together. The title page said: THE TRAVELS OF CLINTON J. HILL.

Under each photo were typewritten captions like: *GREECE: At first he stayed unob-*

trusively in the background (only recognized by his dark glasses). There were photos of me carrying her bags in various places and the caption read: ANY PLACE: Our able agents are always eager to serve. There was the photo in the rowboat near Paestum, Italy, in which I'm screaming at the top of my lungs and she was laughing like crazy: ITALY — Musical accompaniment to the pull of the oars. There were pictures from Ravello — the ones the press had taken of her in her bathing suit, and swimming, and one in which she's on a sailboat giving me instructions. Morocco — a photo of us walking and laughing, on which she had handwritten: Mr. Hill — Are you happy in your *work? — JBK.*

It was priceless.

We had been through so much together, Mrs. Kennedy and me. More than anyone can imagine.

More than anyone can ever know.

EPILOGUE

May 1994

She is one of the most iconic and recognizable women in the world. Elegant, dignified, the epitome of class, a lady in every sense of the word. Now Jacqueline Bouvier Kennedy Onassis lay dying of cancer, in the New York City apartment she had called home for thirty years, and I couldn't control my tears.

I knew she was ill, of course. I had read in the *Washington Post* in February that she had been diagnosed with non-Hodgkin's lymphoma and was undergoing treatment. The reports had been convincing that the disease was in its early stages and treatable. For the briefest of moments, I had thought about calling her. But when I rehearsed in my mind what I might say, I couldn't seem to find the right words. We had been to hell and back, Mrs. Kennedy and me, and while we had both gone on with our lives — if you could call it that — I knew that the mere sound of my voice would take her back to that one day that changed everything, and the sound of her voice would do the same to me. It was just too damn painful. I couldn't bring myself to dial the number.

I hadn't heard much about her condition again in the media, but I found myself thinking of her more frequently, and wondering how she was doing.

A few days earlier, I had received a call from Dave Carpenter, the Secret Service Special Agent in Charge of presidential protection.

"Mr. Hill," he said, "President Clinton and I were talking about the Kennedy administration, and your name came up. We were talking about the terrible tragedies the family has endured, and now, the sad news that Mrs. Kennedy is so terribly ill."

"Yes," I answered. "I was aware that she is undergoing treatment for cancer."

"Well, we were talking about how much she meant to the people of the United States — and the entire world — and the president asked me if I knew whatever happened to the agent who had been with Mrs. Kennedy. I told him that you had retired, and you still lived in Northern Virginia. He then asked me if I could arrange for him to meet you.

Would you be agreeable to that?"

I was completely taken by surprise. I couldn't understand why President Clinton would want to meet me, but I knew from past experience, when the President of the United States wants to meet you, you go. Most people never have that opportunity.

"Of course," I said. "I'd be delighted to meet the president. Just tell me when and where."

The appointment was arranged for Thursday, May 19, at the White House, in the Oval Office.

Ever since I retired from the Secret Service in 1975, there wasn't much that got me excited about getting up each day, but I have to admit, having the president ask to meet me was a pretty big deal. This morning, I woke up at 5:00 A.M., as I always do, but today was different. Today I had something to look forward to.

After showering and shaving, I dressed in my best dark blue suit, with a starched white shirt and a burgundy tie, and made sure I left the house with plenty of time to get into the District. From the moment I backed out of my driveway in Alexandria, Virginia, it was almost as if the car were on autopilot, straight to the White House. The instant I turned onto West Executive Avenue and pulled up to the guard gate, a feeling of pride and fond memories swept over me in a sudden wave.

Dave Carpenter met me and escorted me through the west entrance. We passed the uniformed security post, still in the same place on the ground floor of the West Wing as it had been all those years ago, past the hallway leading to the staff mess and the Situation Room. Past the room where barber Steve Martini at one time cut my hair every two weeks, past W-16, the Secret Service ready room, up the steps to the Cabinet Room and down the hall to the Roosevelt Room to await the appointed time.

Soon the door opened and we were escorted across the hall and into the Oval Office.

President Clinton strode toward me as Agent Carpenter said, "Mr. President, allow me to introduce you to Mr. Clint Hill."

Smiling genuinely, President Clinton reached out his hand.

"Mr. Hill, it is an honor to meet you. Welcome back to the White House."

An honor? To meet *me?*

As I shook his hand, I said, "Mr. President, trust me, the honor is all mine."

He was extremely gracious and made me

feel as if I were the most important person on his agenda that day.

"Mr. Hill," President Clinton said, "we have learned that Mrs. Onassis's condition is extremely critical and deteriorating. I wanted to personally thank you for your service to her and for your distinguished career with the Secret Service."

We talked briefly about Mrs. "Onassis" — I still can't bear to call her that — to me she will forever be Mrs. Kennedy. We discussed her terrible disease, the various tragedies she had endured, and what a great lady she was.

As I looked around the room, I realized the desk being used was the same one young John Jr. had been photographed peering out from those many years ago. Memories of times past came flooding back through my mind. Both good and bad. How I met Mrs. Kennedy back in 1960 shortly after the election. Going through the last stages of her pregnancy before John was born. That joyous event. Her first visit to the White House as a future first lady. Time spent in Palm Beach before the Inauguration. The adjustment to White House life. The first trips to Glen Ora in Middleburg — the estate she rented to get away from the confines of the White House. Summers in Hyannis Port and cruises on various yachts in the Mediterranean. Christmases and Easters in Palm Beach. Adventurous visits to New York City and the wonderful experience of staying at the Carlyle Hotel. The trips to India, Pakistan, Italy, Greece, Morocco, Paris, London, San Juan, Mexico City, Bogota, and Caracas. Such wonderful, memorable times. Yes, the sad and tragic times, too. The joyous birth and then tragic death of Patrick Bouvier Kennedy. The horrible memory of that dreadful day in Dallas as the president was assassinated in her presence. The grief and sorrow that followed as I struggled with my own emotions and tried my best to provide strength and support to her, Caroline, and John. The going-away party she and her staff arranged for me. The memories came flooding back like a fast-moving motion picture swirling inside my head as I stood there with President Clinton in the Oval Office.

Having served five presidents, I knew how valuable the president's time was, and after about ten minutes, I could tell he was leading the conversation to a close.

We shook hands, and again the president thanked me for my service and reiterated what an honor it was to meet me. Agent Carpenter escorted me back to my car, and

I drove home.

All afternoon and into the evening, I couldn't get the memories out of my mind. I went into the dark basement of my home where I've kept my emotions buried for all these years, and flipped on the old television that sits next to my desk. It wasn't all that long ago that I'd have sat here all alone on the tattered sofa with a bottle of scotch and a carton of cigarettes, trying to forget the painful past. So many years wasted. Now I just sit here, alone with my memories, thinking about Mrs. Kennedy, and wishing I could speak to her again, wishing I could hear her say, one more time, "Oh, Mr. Hill . . ."

I knew I should just go to bed, but I had become a man with a routine. I always watched *Nightline* before calling it a night. Promptly at 11:35 P.M. Ted Koppel appeared on the screen and made the announcement I was dreading: *Jacqueline Kennedy Onassis died only a few moments ago, this evening at 10:15 Eastern time at the age of sixty-four.*

I couldn't believe she was gone. I always expected I'd be dead long before her. God knows I should have been. I never imagined what it would feel like to no longer have her in the world. Hardly a week has gone by without a photo of her in some magazine, some tabloid — the kinds she always used to have me buy so she could see what was being said about her. And every time I saw a paparazzi-snapped picture, I knew exactly what she was thinking in every shot. I could see it in her eyes. There were no secrets from me in those eyes.

We had gone through so much together, Mrs. Kennedy and me.

I sat there, staring at the television set, the images of her playing over and over, my memories right there on the screen. I was overcome with a deep sense of loss. The tears streamed down my face, and I was not ashamed.

ACKNOWLEDGMENTS

We would not have been able to write this book without the assistance and encouragement of many people. First and foremost, we must acknowledge former Secret Service agent Paul Landis. Your willingness to share and relive the good and bad times of those four unforgettable years made the writing of this tribute possible. You opened your home and your notes to us without question, and supported us every step of the way. Our friendship with you and Mary Jo is priceless.

Louise Burke, Jen Bergstrom, and Mitchell Ivers at Gallery/Simon and Schuster — your suggestion to write and bring to life the close relationship between Mrs. Kennedy and Clint Hill was the impetus for this project, and we are grateful you convinced us to do it. We truly appreciate your sincere interest and support throughout the process. Mitchell — we are so fortunate to have you in our corner.

To our publicists, Mary McCue and Jen Robinson, we hope you know how much we appreciate your tireless efforts, creativity, and enthusiasm. Thank you also to Natasha Simons, Sally Franklin, Larry Pekarek, Jaime Putorti, Lisa Litwack, and Alexandre Su for your behind-the-scenes efforts to help make this book one of which we are very proud.

To our literary manager, Ken Atchity, thanks for believing we could do it and for your ongoing efforts to bring this story to life.

To former Secret Service agents Tom Wells, Ron Pontius, and Ken Giannoules — your memories and retained notes and reports were of immeasurable assistance, and we can't thank you enough.

To our editor-in-chief extraordinaire, Wyman Harris, and his wife, Gay, your assistance, guidance, and encouragement were invaluable. We are grateful for your limitless gift of time and keen eye for detail. You kept us on track. A special thank-you to Connor McCubbin, our intern for the summer of 2011, for your research skills and proofreading.

One of the most enjoyable yet arduous tasks was sorting through the thousands of photos of the Kennedy White House years, and choosing which ones to include in the book. Thank you to Mindy Parsons for your tenacious research and liberal gift of time to help source the photographs. To David Shaw and Juliet Cuming, thank you for allowing us to use those wonderful images from the Fifty Mile Hike taken by David's father, Mark Shaw. And to Tom Putnam and the staff at the John F. Kennedy Library, including Laurie Austin, Maryrose Grossman, Amy MacDonald, and many others — your pride in what you do is evident, and we are so grateful for your support, enthusiasm, and generous assistance.

To Gary Silversmith, you are to be commended for your care and restoration of the USS *Sequoia*. Our special thanks to you and the crew for allowing us to experience a memorable evening on that famous yacht.

To Managing Director Erich Steinbock and the incomparable staff of the Carlyle Hotel in New York City, thank you for helping us remember those glorious days in the 1960s when the Kennedys were in residence by experiencing it ourselves. It is wonderful to know that the Carlyle's unparalleled service and timeless elegance is the same as it always has been.

Finally, to all the men and women we

encountered in our travels who told us, "I can't wait to read it!" — your enthusiasm gave us the much-needed push to keep moving forward.

LISA McCUBBIN: Thank you to my sons, Connor and Cooper — you are the lights of my life — and I am grateful to you for your strength and support during this difficult year. To Clint, well, I think you know how I feel about you. It has been an honor and a privilege to work with you on this story. Your trust in me, and your willingness to open your heart to relive this part of your life, made this a rewarding experience I will never forget. You are extraordinary — a gentleman in every sense of the word.

CLINT HILL: To my sons, Chris and Corey, thank you for giving me the time and space to pursue this project. Your assistance with personal family issues has been above and beyond the norm. You continue to be my pride and joy. Thank you, Gerald Blaine, for introducing me to Lisa McCubbin, your coauthor of the book *The Kennedy Detail*. I vowed I would never write or contribute to a book about my life in the Secret Service, but through my participation in that project, I realized that the information I had was of historical interest and should be available to the general public. It was also emotionally beneficial and therapeutic for me.

Thank you, Lisa McCubbin, for bringing me out of my dungeon, where I languished for years in my emotional prison. You got me to slowly release some of that emotional baggage by providing a trustworthy outlet. You were someone in whom I could trust and have confidence. You listened and were interested. You cared. You helped me find a reason to live, not just exist. I will never forget when my friends told me I never looked better; I was getting back to my old self. A friend of my oldest son said, "Mr. Hill, it is so nice to see you smile again." Those words were said because you helped me revive my life. This book has been written because you made it possible. Yes, you are a great writer, but more important, you are a great person. I am forever in your debt. Thank you.

PHOTOGRAPH CREDITS

Associated Press: 11, 61, 174, 177 (bottom), 189, 225, 333, 339, 344, 473, 486, 560, 589, 601, 610, 629, 638

Clint Hill personal collection: 29, 31, 322, 328, 335, 356, 426, 640

Abbie Rowe, National Park Service/John F. Kennedy Presidential Library and Museum, Boston: 33, 91, 95

Bettman/Corbis: 64, 116, 262, 407, 613, 621

Cecil Stoughton, White House/John F. Kennedy Presidential Library and Museum, Boston: 68, 97, 177 (top), 229, 249, 310, 314, 374, 384, 425, 449, 455, 471, 543, 577

John F. Kennedy Presidential Library and Museum, Boston: 122, 144, 147, 172, 201, 268, 276, 290, 295, 316, 394, 441, 635

Robert Knudsen, White House/John F. Kennedy Presidential Library and Museum,

ABOUT THE AUTHORS

Clint Hill is a former United States Secret Service agent who was in the presidential motorcade during the John F. Kennedy assassination. Hill remained assigned to Mrs. Kennedy and the children until after the 1964 presidential election. He was then assigned to President Lyndon B. Johnson at the White House. In 1967, when Johnson was still in office, he became the Special Agent in Charge (SAIC) of presidential protection. When Richard Nixon came into office, he moved over to be the SAIC of the vice presidential protective division. In 1972, Hill was promoted to the position of assistant director of the Secret Service, responsible for all protective forces. He retired in 1975.

Lisa McCubbin is an award-winning journalist who has been a television news anchor and reporters, hosted her own radio show, and spent more than five years in the Middle East as a freelance writer. She is the coauthor of the *New York Times* bestseller *The Kennedy Detail*. Visit her at www.lisamccubbin.com.

The employees of Thorndike Press hope you have enjoyed this Large Print book. All our Thorndike, Wheeler, and Kennebec Large Print titles are designed for easy reading, and all our books are made to last. Other Thorndike Press Large Print books are available at your library, through selected bookstores, or directly from us.

For information about titles, please call:
  (800) 223-1244

or visit our Web site at:
  http://gale.cengage.com/thorndike

To share your comments, please write:
  Publisher
  Thorndike Press
  10 Water St., Suite 310
  Waterville, ME 04901